BASTARD FEUDALISM

THE MEDIEVAL WORLD

Editor: David Bates

Already published

CHARLES THE BALD

Janet Nelson

CNUT

The Danes in England in the early eleventh century

M.K. Lawson

WILLIAM MARSHAL

Court, Career and Chivalry in the Angevin Empire 1147–1219

David Crouch

KING JOHN

Ralph V. Turner

INNOCENT III

Leader of Europe 1198–1216

Jane Sayers

THE FRIARS

The Impact of the Early Mendicant Movement on Western Society

C.H. Lawrence

ENGLISH NOBLEWOMEN IN THE LATER MIDDLE AGES

Jennifer C. Ward

JUSTINIAN

John Moorhead

BASTARD FEUDALISM

Michael Hicks

BASTARD FEUDALISM

Michael Hicks

LONGMAN
London and New York

Longman Group Limited,
Longman House, Burnt Mill,
Harlow, Essex CM20 2JE, England
and Associated Companies throughout the world.

*Published in the United States of America
by Longman Publishing, New York*

© Longman Group Limited 1995

First published 1995

ISBN 0 582 06091 5 CSD
ISBN 0 582 06092 3 PPR

British Library Cataloguing-in-Publication Data

A catalogue record for this book is
available from the British Library

Library of Congress Cataloging-in-Publication Data

Hicks, M. A. (Michael A.)
    Bastard feudalism/Michael Hicks.
        p. cm.— (The Medieval world)
    Includes bibliographical references and index.
    ISBN 0–582–06091–5. — ISBN 0–582–06092–3 (pbk.)
    1. Great Britain—History—Medieval period. 1066–1485. 2. Power
(Social sciences)—England—History. 3. Land tenure—England—
History. 4. Feudalism—England—History. I. Title. II. Series.
DA176.H53   1995
942.03—dc20
                                                                94–34281
                                                                CIP

Set by The Midlands Book Typesetting Company
Produced by Longman Singapore Publishers (Pte) Ltd.
Printed in Singapore

CONTENTS

PREFACE

The subject of this book has been dominated for over a century by two great historians, Bishop Stubbs and K.B. McFarlane, whose influence has shaped and constrained all others in the field. Recently, however, an explosion of interest and high quality publications has necessitated a more fundamental reassessment. This book considers the topic as broadly as possible. Inevitably, therefore, it depends heavily on the work of others, even as it imposes over-riding interpretations on their own conclusions. Much of my own research also has proved too parochial to be used or was founded on perspectives that were too limited, chronologically or thematically. I have learnt enormously from the work of others and the book is therefore very different from that envisaged in the early and late 1970s or even in 1989. This author, therefore, has more debts than most: to my editor David Bates and Longman who encouraged me to write it; to the shade of McFarlane, the past influence of Charles Ross and T.B. Pugh; to those many historians acknowledged in the footnotes (above all, M.E. James); to George Bernard, Christine Carpenter, Peter Coss, David Crouch, Anne Curry, Barrie Dobson, Ralph Griffiths, Gerald Harriss, Michael 'Beaufort' Jones, Michael 'Brittany' Jones, Tony Pollard, Simon Payling, Carole Rawcliffe, Colin Richmond, Nigel Saul, and Roger Virgoe. All of whom, however, will agree that what is written here is my interpretation and my responsibility. My wife Cynthia and children have heard it in its many recensions and the former corrected the whole text. But it is to my parents to whom I dedicate this book.

All quotations have been modernised. The term 'connection' applies to all a lord's followers; retinue, to those used for a specific purpose, e.g. war; and affinity in the specialised sense in chapter 3.

Throughout this book, place of publication is London unless otherwise stated.

Winchester, September 1993

EDITOR'S PREFACE

'Bastard Feudalism' is one of those constructs historians have thrust on to past ages, and which was entirely unknown to those contemporary men and women who lived through the time when it was supposed to have been in existence. As Michael Hicks explains in a thorough historiographical introduction, the term is a Victorian invention, given its classic nineteenth-century exposition in Bishop Stubbs' renowned *Constitutional History*. There was created a society which was in many ways an evil one, in which the hierarchical structures of the feudalism introduced after the Norman Conquest were perverted by contracts made between the great nobles and lesser men in which money payments were involved and in which the greater agreed to protect the weaker and the latter to serve his lord. The effect was to subvert the administration of the law and to give the aristocracy large retinues with which they could pursue private feuds and – ultimately – destabilise the kingdom during the period of the Wars of the Roses. Power was upheld by the twin evils of livery and maintenance. England was only rescued from this miserable state by the Tudors.

There has been a significant reinterpretation of this gloomy picture in the course of the past one hundred years. It was above all the great Oxford historian of the later Middle Ages in England, K.B. McFarlane, who drew attention to the constructive features of Bastard Feudalism and saw its features as integral to and supportive of the social structures of fourteenth- and fifteenth-century England. McFarlane did not sanitise Bastard Feudalism, but he did succeed in creating a plausible view of society in which elements which could be termed Bastard Feudal took their place in the context of a wider and more diverse society. It is no exaggeration to say that McFarlane set the agenda from which later scholars have worked. But it must also be said that in the course of the last five years, the subject has been redefined and reassessed in ways which differ dramatically from the approaches of both Stubbs and McFarlane. A series of scholars have convincingly recognised social formations which can legitimately be termed bastard feudal in the two centuries which precede the classic bastard feudal period of the fourteenth and fifteenth centuries, while others have identified the continuance of the same formations into the Tudor and Stuart periods. And within the classic period, many of the premises of McFarlane's exposition have been questioned.

Michael Hicks' book ranges over a period of five centuries and puts Bastard Feudalism into a broader perspective than any previous writer. Most importantly of all, he puts the structures of a bastard feudal society into the context of aristocratic power and domination as it was exercised over a period of five centuries and more. Numerous specialist studies are brought into focus and their general significance is evaluated, with results that are striking and original. Michael Hicks is an author who brings extensive experience of research and writing on late medieval England to the task of compiling this latest contribution to the Medieval World series. Equally importantly, however, is the fact that he has digested and reflected on the large mass of literature produced in recent times by historians working on the medieval and early modern aristocracies. The result is a book which is an original contribution to English Medieval and Early Modern History.

David Bates

ABBREVIATIONS

Bean	J.M.W. Bean, *From Lord to Patron* (Manchester, 1989)
Bellamy	J.G. Bellamy, *Bastard Feudalism and the Law* (1989)
Bellamy *Crime*	J.G. Bellamy, *Crime and Public Order in the Later Middle Ages* (1973)
Bernard, *Nobility*	*The Tudor Nobility*, ed. G. Bernard (Manchester, 1992)
Bernard, *Power*	G. Bernard, *The Power of the Early Tudor Nobility* (Brighton 1985)
BA	British Academy Records of Economic and Social History new series
BIHR	Bulletin of the Institute of Historical Research
Cameron	A. Cameron, 'The Giving of Livery and Retaining in Henry VII's Reign', *Renaissance and Modern Studies* xviii (1974)
Cooper	J.P. Cooper, *Land, Men and Beliefs* (1983)
Coss	P.R. Coss, 'Bastard Feudalism Revised', *Past and Present* 125 (1989)
Coward	B. Coward, *The Stanleys, Lords Stanley and Earls of Derby 1385–1672* (Chetham Soc. 3rd ser. xxx, 1983)
'Debate'	'Debate: Bastard Feudalism Revised', *Past and Present* 131 (1991)
Dunham	W.H. Dunham, *Lord Hastings' Indentured Retainers 1461–83* (Transactions of the Connecticut Academy

	of Arts and Sciences xxxix, New Haven Conn. 1955)
EHR	*English Historical Review*
EcHR	*Economic History Review*
HMC	Historical Manuscripts Commission
Hicks	M.A. Hicks, *Richard III and his Rivals* (1991)
Hicks, *Clarence*	M.A. Hicks, *False, Fleeting, Perjur'd Clarence* (rev. edn, Bangor 1992)
Holmes	G.A. Holmes, *The Estates of the Higher Nobility in 14th Century England* (Cambridge 1957)
James	M.E. James, *Society, Politics and Culture* (1986)
McFarlane, *England*	K.B. McFarlane, *England in the 15th Century* (1981)
McFarlane, *Nobility*	K.B. McFarlane, *The Nobility of Later Medieval England* (Oxford, 1973)
Mertes	K. Mertes, *The English Noble Household 1250–1600* (Oxford, 1988)
Moreton	C.E. Moreton, *The Townshends and their World* (Oxford, 1992)
Myers, *EHD*	*English Historical Documents 1327–1485*, ed. A.R. Myers (1969)
P&P	*Past and Present*
Prestwich	M. Prestwich, *English Politics in the Thirteenth Century* (Basingstoke 1990)
PRO	Public Record Office
Pugh	T.B. Pugh, 'The Magnates, Knights and Gentry', *Fifteenth-century England, 1399–1509*, ed. S.B. Chrimes, C.D. Ross and R.A. Griffiths (Manchester 1972)
Stenton	F.M. Stenton, *First Century of English Feudalism* (2nd edn Oxford 1961)
Stone	L. Stone, *Crisis of the Aristocracy 1558–1642* (Oxford 1965)
TRHS	*Transactions of the Royal Historical Society*
Walker	S.K. Walker, *The Lancastrian Affinity 1361–99* (Oxford 1990)

Chapter 1

WHAT IS BASTARD FEUDALISM?

. . .

DEFINITIONS AND PARAMETERS

Bastard Feudalism is a label devised by historians to make sense of the past. There are many more familiar labels of this type such as the Wars of the Roses, the Reformation, and Feudalism itself. None were current at the time and all are modern inventions. Historians find it convenient to ascribe *this* label to *this* theory, *that* one to *that* hypothesis, to a collection of related features, to that group of events, or to those relationships. For most historians, Bastard Feudalism has a precise meaning and signifies a particular set of relationships, a specific period in history, and a special type of society. Unfortunately which particular, specific or special phenomenon is seldom agreed. Other historians are much less confident and less combative. They protest that they do not know what Bastard Feudalism is or doubt that it existed at all. A definition to which all subscribe is not attainable, but a working criterion is essential.

This book defines Bastard Feudalism as the set of relationships with their social inferiors that provided the English aristocracy with the manpower they required. The nature of this manpower and these relationships is explored in chapters 2, 3 and 4. Among the various carrots and sticks that bound men together, periodic payment with money features prominently, whereas grants of land from greater to lesser aristocrats are relatively unimportant. The uses made of those relationships are examined in chapters 5, 6, and 7. Bastard Feudalism is traced from its inception to its demise in chapter 8 and will be viewed from the contrasting points of view of lords and retainers, kings and victims.

Bastard Feudalism is a large topic with many ramifications. It mattered to people at the time and it matters to historians now. It has a habit of intruding into subjects that at first appear quite distinct. At one level Bastard Feudalism is just a mechanism: a way of achieving a range of results as opposed to other ways practised at other times. But Bastard Feudalism was a *central* mechanism for the waging of war, the conduct of local government, the operations and consultations of national government, and for the administration of justice. Paradoxically it was also the means whereby civil war was waged, local government obstructed or subverted, that national government was rendered ineffectual, parliament packed, and justice was thwarted or perverted to suit private ends. Then as now, Bastard Feudalism was a highly controversial topic, that was silently accepted when all was well or volubly blamed for the political and social maladies of the time. For modern historians, the nature of Bastard Feudalism, whether it was integral or parasitical, and its perceived effects are fundamental to our whole understanding of English society. Was England a society based on conflict or co-operation, on arbitrary threats of force or the rule of law, on values that were military or civilian? The topics and issues interlink and are not readily disconnected. Bastard Feudalism is at the heart of them all.

What is the period under scrutiny? Taking the broadest possible view, Bastard Feudalism falls into that phase of English history characterised by the rule of a monarchy supported, assisted and/or partnered by an aristocracy. This phase occupies the thousand years from King Alfred to Queen Victoria. All this time our aristocracy was an aristocracy of birth rather than of merit and was hereditary. Aristocrats dominated society through the variety of roles that they took on: as lords, superiors in class and rank, masters, employers, householders, patrons, purveyors of justice, and holders of royal or public office. They commanded in war, took the lead in national politics, and directed local government through the power that they derived from their control of men. Manpower was secured through a range of different mechanisms or relationships: through service in their households, through tenancy of their estates, and through employment and payment for services. Only in the twentieth century did the English aristocracy lose its sway.

These ten centuries witnessed enormous changes in government and society. My generalisations about aristocratic power apply to varying extents at different dates. Whilst they are defined so broadly as to be hardly deniable, few historians could accept that the resemblances over a thousand years outweighed the changes that occurred over the same timespan. If Professor Crouch sees the shifts between 1100 and 1300 as cosmetic,[1] we all know how different was the society of King Alfred from that of Victoria and how much that was different again lies in between. This book crosses the normal chronological boundaries separating the specialisms of half a dozen different groups of historians, all engaged in studying their chosen era for its own sake and frequently from sources unique to their period. This book depends on their work on their material and imposes an overarching interpretation.

Yet this study is not imperialist. It has not defined Bastard Feudalism so as to take over the era traditionally regarded as feudal or to make that society into a subset of Bastard Feudalism. Nor does it find it meaningful to imitate Professor Coss in categorising Bastard Feudalism merely as a subset of Feudalism:[2] this is a case where the significance lies in the differences rather than the similarities. It deliberately excludes Anglo-Saxon and eleventh-century England and their attendant debates on Anglo-Saxon and Norman overlap and the existence of Feudalism before the Norman Conquest. Elements of Bastard Feudalism found before 1100 are treated as antecedents. The period covered begins when what is traditionally called Feudalism was up and running in mid-twelfth-century England. What is unique and central to Feudalism is defined as the bond between lord and

1.   'Debate', 168.
2.   Ibid., 197.

vassal based on the hereditary tenure of land and its use for military service. What is unique and central to Bastard Feudalism is periodic payment for service. It must be emphasised that these features are unique and central, not exclusive: both Feudalism and Bastard Feudalism involved other types of service, in other venues, and from non-aristocrats. Often these others are more numerous and more frequent than either payment with land or by annual fees. Roughly from 1150 to 1300, as we shall see, this feudal bond co-existed and interacted with other types of bastard feudal relationship.

This book also excludes events after about 1650. Some historians, perhaps most, will consider this cutting off point too late. Yet Bastard Feudalism was very much alive in Tudor and Early Stuart England up to and beyond the English Civil War. It is actually harder to justify breaking off in the mid-seventeenth century, which does not really mark the death of Bastard Feudalism. Major changes did occur then. It was then that feudal tenures and feudal incidents were abolished and that the professional army and civil service were created. The aristocracy was ceasing to be primarily a military caste and had almost shed their military ethos. But the English aristocracy did survive the English Revolution, perhaps more powerful nationally and in local government than before. Historians as different as Dr Mertes and Professor Stone have found it easier to draw a contrast with the early eighteenth century. Beyond 1660 lies the rise of alternate sources of capitalist wealth, the emergence of the middle class and the class system, the relative and absolute decline of the aristocracy, and the constitutional monarchy and the parliamentary democracy with which we are all familiar today and with which our medieval forebears certainly were not. Beyond the English Revolution, moreover, lies yet another cohort of historians, for whom Bastard Feudalism is an unfamiliar tool and an unhelpful hypothesis. That some bastard feudal relationships and results persisted, persist today, and may indeed have been significant or even important, does not justifying protracting the study beyond the point where it is convenient and illuminating. After all, Bastard Feudalism is a label that we historians have devised and defined for our own convenience.

4

Chapter 1 reviews current historical understandings of Bastard Feudalism. Chapter 2 examines the categories of service which together made up a connection, chapter 3 discusses the quantity and quality of such ties, and chapter 4 considers the legality of Bastard Feudalism and its ramifications. These chapters are the basis for the next three chapters, which examine the uses of bastard feudal connections in peace and war. Chapter 8 considers what befell Bastard Feudalism up to 1650 and chapter 9 briefly assesses its overall contribution to the bastard feudal centuries.

. . .

THE BASTARD FEUDAL ARISTOCRACY

If Bastard Feudalism embraced the whole of society, it affected those at the top most of all. All lords and most retainers were members of the landed élite or aristocracy, who constituted a single class. Throughout the five hundred years under discussion the aristocracy lived principally off the revenues of their estates, which were cultivated for them by their tenants or salaried staff. The aristocracy were a hereditary military caste who did not undertake manual labour. Within their ranks there were two main divisions, the nobility and the gentry. The nobility commanded and the gentry served. Thus far, so good. But such generalisations conceal enormous shifts within these groups that need outlining if the discussions that follow are to make sense.

Between 1150 and 1350 the nobility were tenants-in-chief of the crown: either earls, never much more than a dozen in total, or the barons (or leading men), who numbered two hundred or more and varied greatly in wealth. This state of affairs was of course a continuation of conditions which had existed since 1066. Not very different were the leading mesne tenants or honorial barons. After 1350 the nobility became ever more select and stratified. Some particularly well-endowed barons were grouped with the earls rather than the rest even in the late twelfth century. Whilst all the barons were noble and eligible to attend parliament as peers under Edward I (1272–1307), in practice many were seldom or never summoned and only a hundred at any one time. By 1388 a mere 48 barons had become parliamentary peers, who had established a hereditary right to a summons, and the rest were shut out. Such lesser aristocrats became known as the gentry. A few non-parliamentary barons, like Hylton or Camoys, continued to use their title. The barons, moreover, became the lowest rank of a more differentiated peerage: above them emerged viscounts in 1440, marquises (1443) and dukes (1337) as well as the existing earls. Such ranks came to be granted only to those capable of living at the appropriate style and by the fourteenth century promotion to the higher ranks of the peerage presupposed the attainment of the qualifying income. By 1337, for example, earls needed 1,000 marks a year (£666 13s. 4d.). Surviving figures for noble incomes can easily mislead, not least because those from different periods are not strictly comparable, but as a rough guide around 1450 two noblemen had incomes over £6,000 and the poorest a mere £200. Noblemen were expected to live up to their income. Their superior status was recognised by the sumptuary laws, which allowed them to dress in extravagant ways forbidden to the gentry and other social inferiors. Generally it was these higher ranks that contemporaries and modern historians alike have called *magnates* or great men. Their landed estates, income, and power far exceeded those of lesser peers and gentry.

The gentry were those aristocrats who were not noblemen. The term did not exist in 1150, when what this book calls the gentry were the lesser barons and those aristocrats below the barons, but it has been convenient for this book to use it throughout. Most twelfth-century gentry were knights. Historians have dubbed as honorial barons those who owed the service of several knights to their lord or stood particularly high in his esteem: 'an honorial baron was, like his master the magnate, a nobleman, though a dependent one'.[3] Such men were aristocratic both in origin and outlook and entrusted with important governmental functions by Henry II. Their numbers diminished sharply from the late twelfth century. This was Professor Coss' 'crisis of the knightly class'. Recognising this development, but nevertheless needing knights, Henry III required those wealthy enough to

---

3.   D. Crouch, *The Beaumont Twins* (Cambridge 1986), p. 115; *Image of the Aristocracy in Britain* (1992), pp. 22–6.

support knightly status to take up knighthood or suffer financial penalties (distraint of knighthood). The level of income that qualified non-knights for knighthood was set at £20 in 1241. Some who were this rich nevertheless preferred not to take on the expense and responsibilities of knighthood. Knights henceforth were of genuinely high status, able to afford considerable luxury, and their ranks were swelled in the fourteenth century by those barons who failed to become parliamentary peers. In the fourteenth century the most important knights were promoted to the rank of banneret. Those who were not knights but were nevertheless aristocrats were called esquires and shared in their martial training and outlook. There were always other, inferior, aristocrats or *gentilz*, the gentlemen, who were recognised from 1413 and ultimately became the most numerous. None of these grades worked with their hands: many of the gentlemen were lawyers or bureaucrats.

Traditionally the nobility went through a bad patch during the Tudor era. Once this was thought to be due to the hostility of the crown towards them as a class, a conclusion no longer credible. More recently they have been portrayed as the victims of a 'crisis of the aristocracy 1558–1642', in which they lost their lands, their standing and their power. That conclusion also is now untenable. Although the very greatest houses had all disappeared by 1521, the peerage changed very little before the early seventeenth century, when peerages were sold for cash: the number increased to 126 in 1628. Such creations increased the wealth of the nobility as a whole, but reduced the average level of resources. Most of the lands of dissolved monasteries passed through the hands of the crown to those of the gentry, who enlarged their share of England's wealth in the sixteenth and seventeenth centuries and greatly increased their numbers as well. In the process, moreover, many church estates that had been controlled in practice by the peerage passed to those of the gentry.[4]

Thus far the aristocracy have been viewed in retrospect and categorised in the light of their later division into

4. Cooper, pp. 17–37, esp. 19, 36; F.M.L. Thompson, 'Social Distribution of Landed Property in England since the 16th century', *EcHR* 2nd ser. xix (1966), 505–17, esp. 514.

peers with hereditary seats in the House of Lords and gentry, who were eligible only for election to the House of Commons. We thus exalt their role in parliament and their hereditary title far above the significance that such issues enjoyed for much of their history. For contemporaries, whether disinterested observers or social inferiors, such distinctions may have been cosmetic when nobility and gentry alike were heads of households, heirs to large estates, and lords of manors. 'Every lord', lamented one fourteenth century preacher,

> every lord beholdeth [an]other, how he is arrayed, how he is horsed, how he is manned; and so envieth [the] other . . . The squire is not satisfied unless he lives like a knight; the knight wants to be a baron; the baron an earl; the earl, a king . . . .[5]

For this study, the gentry feature not just as retainers, but as lords of men themselves. Even peers could serve those greater than themselves. For too long historians have made too much of this distinction between peers and gentry for periods when the differences were largely artificial. This book will try to bridge the gap. Nobility and gentry were members of the English aristocracy: they shared the same lifestyle, education, outlook, and aspirations. If the titled nobility erected such Elizabethan prodigy houses as Hardwick, it was gentry who erected those at Longleat and Montacute, just as the builders of those last medieval castles at Bodiam, Nunney and Caister lacked seats in the House of Lords.

The Norman nobility was a military caste made up entirely of knights. They received the physical training necessary to become knights, indulged in such knightly exercises as jousting and hunting for pleasure, read from choice – if they could read – romances about chivalric heroes of the past, and greeted war as an opportunity rather than a disaster. To peruse most traditional histories of England from 1066–1640 is to learn how the nobility progressively changed from professional soldiers

---

5. G.R. Owst, *Literature and the Pulpit in Medieval England* (2nd edn Oxford 1961), pp. 311, 313. In the same vein, see P.J.C. Field, *Life and Times of Sir Thomas Malory* (Cambridge 1993), p. 124.

into sedentary civilian administrators. That, however, is a mistaken interpretation. Not just the nobility of the middle ages, but that of the Tudors and Stuarts was a military caste. Aristocrats were still trained in arms and were constantly preparing for war. 'Command of men in foreign wars or against rebels', Mr Cooper reminded us and Dr Bernard repeated, 'was an essential function of the Tudor nobility, whether old or new' and, indeed, of their Early Stuart counterparts too.[6] Castiglione's *Book of the Courtier*, that vehicle for the education of the aristocracy in the classics, nevertheless envisaged that the Renaissance courtier should be primarily a soldier. We should not forget that his most distinguished English pupil, the author of the *Apologie for Poetrie*, was that same Sir Philip Sidney that fell in battle at Zutphen (1586). It was the nobility and gentry who became the Lords Lieutenants and militia officers of the Stuarts, the generals and subordinate commanders of the English Civil War. 'War, then, was not an aberration', Dr Bernard writes. 'For the nobility it was usually welcome. In the early Tudor period, as in the age of Edward III, "war was the supreme expression of the social purposes for which the military aristocracy existed" '. Even that most plebeian and sedentary of ministers, Henry VIII's Thomas Cromwell, was anxious to establish his military credentials. 'There was no sharp division between a noblesse d'epée and a noblesse de robe', concluded Helen Miller. But only a few noblemen devoted their whole lives to arms: from William Marshal under the Angevins to the Lords Mountjoy in the fifteenth and sixteenth centuries there were always some who made war into an all-encompassing profession.

Administration was always expected of the nobility. 'Most . . . of the court aristocracy of the later twelfth century', writes Crouch, 'were administrators first and soldiers second, sometimes a long way second'.[7] Military prowess alone, McFarlane observed, was not enough to

6. Cooper, p. 79; Bernard, *Nobility*, pp. 9–10; J.S.A. Adamson, 'The Baronial Context of the English Civil War', *TRHS* 5th ser. xl (1990), 101–2. For what follows, see H. Miller, *Henry VIII and the English Nobility* (Oxford 1986), p. 35; Bernard, *Power*, ch. 4.
7. D. Crouch, *William Marshal* (Harlow 1990), p. 3.

secure promotion to the late medieval nobility: administrative service was necessary too. And so it goes on. Many
late medieval and early modern noblemen were ministers
of the crown. So, too, in the localities: from the twelfth
century knights were required for many administrative
purposes and the nobility and gentry filled ever more local
offices for the crown as the centuries passed. Nobility and
gentry were alike an aristocracy of service. England was
never a country made up of the self-contained principal-
ities of absolutist noblemen exempt from outside interference; rather it was a unitary state in which many powers,
central or local, indeed ever more powers, were reserved
to the crown. Such service was the means of promotion to
and within the nobility by that greatest of English patrons,
the king. Every generation from William the Conqueror
witnessed the raising of trusted royal servants from the
dust by royal favour. In every generation there were
parvenus exciting contempt, envy and fear, from the
'new men' of Henry I to Piers Gaveston under Edward II,
from Thomas Cromwell under Henry VIII to James I's
favourite the Duke of Buckingham. The ancient nobility
that ruffled its feathers and stood on its dignity was
seldom very old: such Tudor grandees as the Earls of
Shrewsbury and Derby acquired their titles only in 1443
and 1485 respectively and new ones, such as the Russells
and Seymours, were still being added. And despite all
their emphasis on birth, lineage and hereditary renown,
such earls were as vital a part of the Tudor nobility of
service as Thomas Cromwell or William Cecil.

For Chaucer, as Coss has shown, lordship or seigniory
over other men was an essential attribute of the aristocracy. Such lordship could mean feudal lordship or the
lordship of the manor; all heads of those households
whose accounts were recently edited were called lords,
whether feudal lords or not, because they had command
of men. It was also the language of deference: to address
barons or knights as 'dominus' or 'messire' in the twelfth
century or as 'my lord' or 'sir' somewhat later often be-
tokened respect rather than service. Seventeenth-century
men dressed, ate, and worshipped in rank order, cringed
to superiors and condescended to inferiors, and doffed
their hats accordingly. Though lords and masters in their

own houses, they also served, for throughout our period service was both honourable and necessary. It did not disparage the server: an earldom, for example, was compatible with custody of James I's personal privy. 'Service', in Coss's words, 'is one strong element of continuity across the period we have been discussing': a comment agreeable to such diverse historians as Sir Frank Stenton, Allen Brown, David Crouch, Scott Waugh, Chris Given-Wilson, G.L. Harriss, Rosemary Horrox, Penry Williams, and M.E. James. By service of greater men they were able to exercise authority delegated to them by their lords and thus partook of their lords' worship and power. What the Anglo-Saxon cniht and the Norman knight had in common was that both depended on greater men. 'It was difficult to be just a knight', wrote Professor Allen Brown, 'as a single isolated figure, *tout court* and by yourself. In reality you had to be a knight to someone else, to owe service or to take service with a lord' . . . So, too, as we have seen, the high nobility; so, too, the squires, who were originally attendants on knights; so, too, the mere gentlemen. One's status in one's society originally depended on the status of one's lord and how one depended on him. It was consequently difficult, if not impossible, to stand aside from lords – which was almost tantamount to standing outside society – or from involuntary involvement in local government, and from warfare. This concept of service enabled lords at all levels to delegate their affairs to those with sufficient local standing to enforce their wishes without hazarding their own control. 'The administration of a great honour', wrote Stenton, 'of the kingdom of England itself, depended on officers who must themselves be powerful if they were to uphold their lord's authority'.[8] That service was honourable even for aristocrats and that authority was delegated to those strong enough themselves to enforce

8. Stenton, p. 83; R.A. Brown, 'Status of the Norman Knight', *War and Government in the Middle Ages*, ed. J. Gillingham and J.C. Holt (Woodbridge 1984), p. 23; P.R. Coss, *The Knight in Medieval England 1000–1400* (Stroud 1993), pp. 9, 12; P.R. Coss, *Lordship, Knighthood and Locality* (Cambridge 1991), p. 325; *Household Accounts from Medieval England*, ed. C.M. Woolgar (2 vols BA xvii, xviii, 1992).

it are two themes that recur throughout our five centuries of Bastard Feudalism.

. . .

BASTARD FEUDAL ORTHODOXY

Bastard Feudalism was a term of abuse coined in 1885 by Revd Charles Plummer, for whom it was a degeneration from Feudalism itself and behind all that he most deplored about late medieval England.[9] Plummer's objections cannot be fully understood without appreciating what Feudalism meant to him, even though his notions have been updated and refined in many ways by subsequent historians.

For Plummer, Feudalism was a social system based on the ownership of land. Occupiers of the land did not own it absolutely, but held it in tenancy for service from landlords, who exercised rights of jurisdiction over it. Feudal society was like a pyramid, with the monarch at the top, successive levels of tenants below, and a host of peasants at the bottom. The latter, many of them unfree, were an exploited class. Their labour supported their feudal superiors, who siphoned off their surplus. Kings and villeins were separated by many intermediaries.

English Feudalism, so Plummer and his contemporaries believed, was the creation of William the Conqueror after the Norman Conquest. After taking possession of all the land in England, William had parcelled it out among his leading supporters as tenancies (fiefs) to be held in return for clearly defined services. Most of the recipients of such grants, his tenants-in-chief, held their land in return for the military service of specific numbers of knights: some 60, some 20, some five and so on. The tenants-in-chief in turn granted (or enfeoffed) much of their land on their own tenants for the service of enough knights between them to meet their own obligations to the king. Sometimes these mesne tenants, as they were called, also enfeoffed subtenants owing knight service through a process called subinfeudation. The service of a knight was a knights fee,

9. J. Fortescue, *Governance of England*, ed. C. Plummer (Oxford 1885), pp. 15–16. For the rest of this section, see ibid. pp. 15–29; Hicks, pp. 3–8.

a term applied also to the land (such as a manor) that a knight held for such service. All fiefs owed certain feudal incidents as additional services, notably aids, and such others as relief, wardship and marriage if hereditary, as almost all were by the mid-twelfth century. The military service that tenants-in-chief owed to the king was called the service due (*servitium debitum*) and was itemised in 1166 in the *Carte Baronum* (charters of the barons), in which tenants-in-chief declared how many knights they had enfeoffed on their estates. The king was never restricted to direct relations only with his tenants-in-chief: *ultimately* everybody owed their service and an overriding obligation of allegiance to the king himself. Moreover, the Norman kings had inherited a local government system, based on counties and hundreds with their own courts and officers, independent of feudal landholding.

The estates of the tenants-in-chief were called honours or baronies and consisted both of lands that were kept in hand (or demesne, as they were called) and those that were subinfeudated. Every honour or barony had its own court to which tenants by knight service owed suit and which they were obliged to attend. Such courts advised the lord and judged cases involving the tenants. Whether kept in hand or enfeoffed, a lord's lands were divided into manors, within which some land was customarily kept in hand by the lord (again, called the demesne) and the rest was let out to peasants, who rendered services in the form of rent and unpaid labour on their lord's demesne. This labour supported those above them. Whether tenant-in-chief, mesne tenant or subtenant, baron or knight, the holder of the manor was the manorial lord and exercised authority over the manor and its tenants through his manorial court. A landlord was no mere farmer or rentier, but a lord exercising jurisdiction over others. All tenants by knight service were lords. Often feudal lords enjoyed additional jurisdiction – franchises or liberties – over their tenants and neighbours. The most fully articulated study of this definition of Feudalism was set out in Sir Frank Stenton's classic Ford Lectures of 1929 that were published in 1932 as *The First Century of English Feudalism*.

This image of Feudalism, recently condemned as fief-centred, had considerable attractions to Victorian scholars. First of all, because it existed primarily for the public good – the defence of the realm – and because allegiance was reserved to the monarch. Private war was banned. Secondly, because the lord and vassal owed reciprocal obligations and their relations were clearly defined and above board. Thirdly, relationships were stable and enduring: how could they be otherwise, when the reward was as concrete and permanent as a hereditary grant of land? Lords took responsibility for the conduct of their vassals. Admirable though such features were, they could not last for ever, and anybody committed to constitutional progress could not wish that they had. Decline set in in the twelfth century and was almost complete in the thirteenth. The integrity of fiefs, honours, baronies and knights fees was broken by the partitions and amalgamations that inevitably accompany any hereditary system. Henry II (1154–89) habitually demanded only a quota of the *servitium debitum* – five knights instead of 60, for example – and exacted payment (scutage) instead. The quota and scutage were still exacted by Edward I (1272–1307), but the last two summons of the feudal host, in 1327 and 1385, were of minimal military significance. Most important of all, Henry II's law reforms – most notably the assize of novel disseisin and the jury system – attracted litigants to the royal courts and expedited the decline of honorial and baronial courts, which seems to date between 1180 and 1230. This latter development was particularly desirable, since it signalled the victory of public justice and held out hope both for the rule of law and equality before the law without fear or favour. Feudal tenure as a system of land law and feudal incidents long survived the society that created it.

Imagine, then, the outrage of Plummer and his contemporaries when feudal military service and feudal justice were succeeded by a military and judicial system more selfish, arbitrary and partial than anything that had proceeded them. Where Feudalism reserved service and allegiance to the king, Bastard Feudalism need not. Where feudal ties were clear, public and honourable, bastard feudal ones were ill-defined and morally uncertain. Instead of stable hereditary tenancies, Bastard

Feudalism consisted of payments of cash for short-terms that were easily terminated. Rather than controlling and disciplining errant tenants, the late medieval lord was commonly his retainer's accessory in crime. In all these ways, Bastard Feudalism was a degeneration from Feudalism and was its illegitimately begotten offspring. The results were anti-social. Bastard feudal armies of liveried retainers supplied lords with the manpower to indulge in violent crime, private war, rebellion, and civil war. Bastard Feudalism enabled lords to bribe and coerce judges, jurors and sheriffs, to maintain criminals in their crimes, to thwart and subvert royal justice and administration, and to establish with impunity their arbitrary and self-interested rule in their own localities. Livery and Maintenance was an alternative, and equally pejorative, label for Bastard Feudalism.

Whilst it was Plummer who coined the phrase Bastard Feudalism, he was far from alone in his views. In the 1870s and 1880s a whole succession of high-minded liberal Victorians were investigating the late medieval contribution to English constitutional progress. They all subscribed to what has been called the Whig Interpretation of History: the natural and inevitable progress towards the parliamentary democracy and rule of law that existed in their own Victorian era. Between them, they blamed Bastard Feudalism for much that was wrong in late medieval England, from the Wars of the Roses to Livery and Maintenance. It was natural for them to identify the crown with progress and the magnates with reaction. It was Stubbs, author of a classic three-volume *Constitutional History*, who determined the curriculum for late medieval English history for the first half of this present century and who ensured that no other point of view was seriously entertained. What academic research took place during these years – and much of it was excellent – occurred within the framework of Stubbs' orthodoxy. Thus Professor Prince identified Bastard Feudalism as the basis of the Indenture System used by Edward III to recruit his armies in the Hundred Years War, H.G. Richardson analysed its role in determining parliamentary elections, and Helen Cam denounced it yet more cogently for its malign effects on the judicial system.

15

Thus Bastard Feudalism remained essentially as the Victorians had left it until K.B. McFarlane re-assessed it in the 1940s. He was certainly interested in the role of Bastard Feudalism in waging civil war, in Livery and Maintenance, and in rigging parliamentary elections, but he considered these not to be essential features but byproducts, the result of abuses and failures of political control. There was nothing illegitimate about Bastard Feudalism as a system, but it could be employed for illegitimate purposes. It was the business of government to ensure that it was not, to maintain order and the integrity of justice, to curb private war, and to impose obedience on offending magnates. Strong kings, like Henry V, did; weak ones, like Henry VI, could not. What was at fault was the weakness of the crown, not the inherent wickedness of Bastard Feudalism.

McFarlane had already broken with the constitutional history that still dominated the Oxford school of history to which he belonged. McFarlane did not see late medieval politics as an abstract and anachronistic battle between those for and against long-term constitutional development. Politics was conducted by real people, both kings and magnates. No mere stereotypes or villains, noblemen had valid interests and points of view and were the genuine participants in politics that the chroniclers depicted. The nobility mattered at the time, and therefore to later historians, because of their rank, their wealth, and the men that they controlled. McFarlane's interest in the nobility led him to the study of their estates, their estate administration, their retinues, and thus to the Bastard Feudalism that provided their manpower. Bastard Feudalism originated, so McFarlane thought, in the crown's demand for military service late in the thirteenth century, which prompted Edward I to contract for troops with the nobility and for the latter to contract with retainers for the balance. The chosen instruments were indentures of retainer and indentures of war.

Indentures were a common type of legal contract in which several copies of an agreement were written on a single sheet of parchment. This was then cut into two or more separate copies along a jagged or *indented* line and sealed by all parties. Each party received an identical copy

16

of the contract sealed by the other party and difficult to forge. Indentures of retainer and war were merely indentures used for the specific purpose of retaining for life or for particular campaigns. Indentured retainers were usually gentry who bound themselves personally to serve their lord for life in peace and war; in return for service done and to be done. Their lord normally offered an annual fee or annuity and his good lordship in the retainer's just quarrels. Very often – particularly in earlier indentures – the retainer was granted subsistence from the lord's household (bouche of court) when on his service and was guaranteed compensation for loss of horses in time of war. Since both parties freely entered into the contract, both could freely end it: many did; many moreover contracted their services to more than one lord. What held them together, in short, was not a binding contract, but their mutual advantage. McFarlane considered that it was those who entered into such a solemn contract – the *indentured retainers* – who were at the centre of a nobleman's retinue and that they were the most significant members of it. Such was the case with the retinue of John of Gaunt, Duke of Lancaster (d. 1399), the greatest of noblemen, which McFarlane treated as the model of all late medieval retinues. The spirit of Bastard Feudalism was that set out in the indenture of retainer. What such retainers contracted to do, so McFarlane argued, was what was understood by all those other annuitants, feed men, officers and well-wishers, who also belonged to retinues and for whom no indentures survived or perhaps ever existed.

McFarlane's magisterial articles of 1944–45 were a watershed. What was written earlier on Bastard Feudalism is now scarcely read and his work is the departure point for what has followed. McFarlane himself was not to die for another twenty years and his relevant writings, collected in two volumes in 1973 and 1981, have provided the framework for subsequent work. His influence was felt also through those many postgraduate students who researched under his direction and taught, wrote, published and supervised their own research students. Prominent here are Professor Charles Ross, founding father of the Bristol Connection, and the Carpenter Affinity of Dr Christine Carpenter. McFarlane left a school of historians committed, like him, to a view of Bastard Feudalism based on a retinue comprised principally of gentry who were non-resident and retained by indenture and/or fee: what are often called extraordinary retainers. The starting point was usually the noble family – the Percies, Beauchamps, Staffords, Mowbrays, Hollands, Courtenays, Talbots, Hungerfords, or Greys of Ruthin; sometimes the group, such as the Yorkshire Baronage or the Lords Appellant; less frequently the individual nobleman, like successive earls or dukes of Lancaster, dukes of York, Bedford, Norfolk or Clarence. Detailed analysis of estate records produced a long list of 'retainers': leading officials, such as the lord's chancellor or chamberlain; occasionally lesser members of the household; estate officials, from receivers and auditors to stewards, bailiffs and reeves; annuitants and indentured retainers, some of them lawyers; and a large number of miscellaneous individuals described as 'servants' or encountered in the act of service. Whilst many such individuals were retained by several lords, it was generally felt that one lord took precedence and could be confidently identified by the modern historian. Exceptions were made of feoffees and lawyers, whose loyalties could not safely be deduced from their actions on behalf of a particular client. The list of retainers was then related to particular localities and local government office to build up a picture of territorial power; their operation in concert, in riots or elections or warfare, was accepted as evidence of the operation of the retinue; and it was assumed, barring evidence to the contrary, that such concentrations of power could be deployed on the national scene.

Research into the records of the central courts has provided ever more evidence for this kind of study. Local politics were now about the clashes, co-operation and general interaction of nobility; national politics merely translated such relationships on to the national stage. Much valuable work resulted, but major problems remained unresolved. Never were lists of retainers complete: estate accounts were patchy and the composition of the household was generally obscure. Those who were retained were assumed to matter more than those who were not, and it was assumed that all gentry were retained by some nobleman. Researchers had great faith in their capacity to identify prime allegiances, to prioritise lawsuits and various kinds of ties, and to deduce motives for action. Ironically, relatively little attention was paid to surviving collections of letters, which McFarlane himself had used to identify motives, whether to explore the shades of commitment between the partisan retainer and the mere well-willer, or to place retainers in the context of such other ties as kinship and neighbourhood. The gentry, as McFarlane demonstrated right at the start, had their own range of concerns and lords had to manage them rather than dictate.

McFarlane, therefore, provided starting points for a range of the other approaches which have been explored by his pupils; probably, indeed, there is nothing to be said that McFarlane has not anticipated somewhere in his writings! Individually and collectively, the McFarlane school has done much to extend and amplify his legacy and devoted a whole conference to re-assessing it at Durham in 1993. Research has now diverged to a point where disagreements among them are fundamental and wide-ranging and where McFarlane's work is the departure point rather than the framework for future research. In 1989–91 no less than five late medievalists attempted their own interpretations of Bastard Feudalism. Recent contributions may be divided between those writing on the period before 1300, those concerned with the fourteenth and fifteenth centuries, and those working on England under the Tudors and Early Stuarts. There has been surprisingly little cross-fertilisation between them. Regrettably little: historians have worked at cross purposes and recurring patterns have been overlooked.

· · ·

THE FIRST CENTURIES OF BASTARD FEUDALISM

McFarlane traced the origins of Bastard Feudalism back to the indenture system used to fight the Hundred Years War. The essential features were the indenture of retainer for life and paid military service. These developments have since been pushed back in time. The earliest indentures of retainer of the classic type date from the reign of Edward I, who as early as 1270 raised a crusading army by very similar contracts. These, too, were preceded by a range of other contracts, some of them indentured. Many had continental parallels: thus the *fief-rentes* or hereditary annuities, which were granted for homage or service in lieu of land by English kings and occasionally by English lords, were commonplace in the Low Countries from 1107. The particular types of contract may have varied with circumstance, but the existence, objectives and results of such contracts remained the same. 'The phenomenon was widespread', writes Professor Scott Waugh.

> I have found more than seventy cases involving agreements for annual, lifetime payments based on a written agreement between 1220 and 1230, in addition to the more than thirty-two pensions uncovered by Dr Maddicott and others. ... Although the surviving baronial archives do not preserve any systematic record of retaining or retainers, nonetheless evidence culled from a wide variety of sources, especially from legal cases involving disputed contracts, clearly demonstrates that contractual retaining was well-established by the mid-thirteenth century. ... By the early fourteenth century even relatively small estates had been burdened with annuities and pensions.[10]

Crouch pushes this process back to about 1140. The Norman kings were paying foreign mercenaries from 1070, in 1101 on terms akin to later indentures of retainer, who played crucial roles in most of their battles. As early as the late tenth century troops were being paid by west Frankish territorial princes.[11] Perhaps our notion of Feudalism is at fault, as suggested by Professor Allen Brown:

10. S. Waugh, 'Tenure to Contract: Lordship and Clientage in Thirteenth-Century England', *EHR* ci (1986), 819–20; K.J. Stringer, *Earl David of Huntingdon 1152–1219* (Edinburgh 1985), pp. 166–7; G.G. Simpson, '*Familia* of Roger de Quincy, Earl of Winchester and Constable of Scotland', *Essays in the Nobility of Medieval Scotland*, ed. K.J. Stringer (Edinburgh 1985), pp. 117–18. For the next sentence, see Crouch, *Image*, pp. 135–6 for Osbert of Arden's endowment of Thurkil Fundu on terms akin to later indentures.
11. I am indebted to Professor David Bates for this observation. For what follows, see Crouch, *William Marshal*, p. ix; R.A. Brown, *The Normans and the Norman Conquest* (1985), p. 201.

These things happened in the feudal age without incongruity and (to express oneself with something less than clarity) there is nothing necessarily 'unfeudal' about the 'non-feudal' elements in 'feudal armies'.

Instead of the rigidity traditionally ascribed to Feudalism, there was considerable flexibility in how lords secured and rewarded service. 'We perceive through them a society which was scarcely one of lords and vassals at all', writes Crouch, 'where conditions approximated to what is conventionally called "Bastard Feudalism" '. A new consensus has thus driven the origins of Bastard Feudalism – at least when it is defined in terms of retaining by contract – back to 1220 and even to 1140.

Feudal military service last made a significant contribution to the wars of Edward I. He contented himself with the quota rather than the full *servitium debitum* for his first Welsh war of 1276–77, substituting 375 knights for the 7,000 due, extracted scutage from the rest, and raised other troops by other means. The *feudal* retinues of the greatest magnates were insignificant: the Earl of Warwick was liable for 15 knights, the Earl of Gloucester for 10, and the Earl of Oxford for three. Such magnates did not content themselves with such contingents, however, but voluntarily brought many other men whom they may have paid under indentures of retainer, but for whom they themselves received no royal wages. Whatever method of recruitment was used, the identity of those who served was the same. Moreover, the king's household not only organised and financed the war, but supplied the largest single component. The knights of the king's household numbered 700 at their peak and sometimes constituted a third of the cavalry or one division of the army. Granted annual fees and robes, supplemented in war by wages, keep and compensation for dead horses, the king's 'household-in-arms' was always available for immediate use and could be expanded or contracted according to need.

The military household was not an innovation of Edward I. It was no less important to Henry III, Henry II, or Henry I and perhaps as far back as William I. It was to pay them that Norman England developed its precocious financial system. Comprising a 'hard core of élite fighting troops', they played a crucial role at the battle of Tinchebrai in 1106, constituted one-third of the victorious army at Brémule in 1118–19, and won the battle of Bourgthéroulde by themselves in 1124. Increased to several hundred knights when needed, they were cut back when no longer required. Of course earlier monarchs had military households which fall chronologically outside this study: the huscarles of Cnut and his successors and before them the household warriors of Alfred and Beowulf. Household knights were particularly committed to the Norman kings, who employed them on all kinds of military, administrative and diplomatic business, and were the reservoir of talent for royal favourites. Serving in hope of advancement, many received grants of land or were married to heiresses, and Henry I promoted three to earldoms. Paid service, military or otherwise, was normal throughout the twelfth and thirteenth centuries, and kings turned first for military support not to their feudal tenants, but to their paid household knights.[12]

Traditionally historians have measured the power of the Norman baronage in terms of the knights they had enfeoffed with estates supplemented by those living in their households. Before enfeoffment began, immediately after the Conquest, all knights must have been remunerated in other ways and probably most lived in their lords' households. 'From the very commencement of knight-service', wrote Round in 1895, 'the baron who had not enfeoffed knights to discharge his *servitium debitum* must always have hired substitutes to the amount of the balance'.[13] It was the inconvenience of this arrangement that impelled the bishop of Worcester and abbots of Ely and Abingdon to enfeoff their knights. Most enfeoffment had occurred by 1135, but some continued thereafter, particularly in the North. As late as the *Carte Baronum* of 1166, Walter de Aincourt had enfeoffed only 11 knights

---

12. J.E. Morris, *The Welsh Wars of Edward I* (Oxford 1901); M. Prestwich, *War, Politics and Finance under Edward I* (Oxford 1972); J.O. Prestwich, 'War and Finance in the Anglo-Norman State', *TRHS* 5th ser. iv (1955); 'Military Household of the Anglo-Norman Kings', *EHR* xcvi (1981); M. Chibnall, 'Mercenaries and the *Familia Regis* under Henry I', *History* lxii (1977). These papers are reprinted in *Anglo-Norman Warfare*, ed. M. Strickland (Woodbridge 1992).
13. J.H. Round, *Feudal England* (1909), p. 270.

of the 40 he owed and Hugh de Lacy listed nine household knights after those who were enfeoffed.[14] Household knights were universal. Actually, of course, there were always knights in addition to those enfeoffed, baronial households always had a military dimension, and every lord needed to attract new men to his service to counteract natural wastage. It was always possible for newcomers like William Marshal to build up an affinity of unattached knights quite independently of any landed base.

Historians of English Feudalism have overstressed the *servitium debitum*, service due to the crown, and neglected the service due to lords about which charters of enfeoffment are less explicit. Lords additionally expected military service to themselves, castleguard, escort duty, hospitality, suit of court, scutage and other financial dues.[15] Peace was more common than the war that was the knight's métier and peacetime service was essential from the start. Those who were enfeoffed were perhaps already household knights serving for keep, pay, and in the hope of land. That the lord gave them land shows how much they were valued; to receive a large grant for the service of several knights, to become an honorial baron, was a mark of even higher esteem. As time passed, however, the pattern of enfeoffment increasingly represented the valuations of past generations. Those settled on the land ceased to be the lord's closest and most valued servants and the services they offered depreciated as military service and castleguard were commuted in the twelfth century and finally abandoned around 1300. Honorial barons and feudal tenants were replaced in their lord's esteem by household knights constantly attendant on him and available for a range of miscellaneous services. The lord's court and council consisted of his leading officials and knights attendant on him, sometimes also tenants, rather than honorial barons, lesser feudal tenants, and townsmen who occur principally when the lord arrived in their locality.[16]

14. Stenton, p. 139; H.M. Chew, *Ecclesiastical Tenants-in-Chief and Knight Service* (Oxford 1932), pp. 114–16; W.E. Wightman, *Lacy Family in England and Normandy 1066–1194* (1966), pp. 198–9.
15. Round, *Feudal England*, p. 270; Stenton, esp. pp. 170–7; B. English, *The Lords of Holderness 1086–1250* (Oxford 1979), p. 167.
16. Implied by Simpson, '*Familia* of Roger de Quincy', pp. 105–18.

By the mid-twelfth century lords could no longer re-allocate subinfeudated estates to the new men. Spare land for subinfeudation was available only in outlying areas, such as Ireland, Scotland and northern England. 'Soldiers were raised by a mixture of means', writes Crouch, 'and enfeoffment was a temporary, passing expedient, con-venient only while there was a surplus of land for redis-tribution'.[17] To secure the service he needed – military, administrative, domestic and ecclesiastical – a lord had increasingly to finance appropriate rewards from lands held in demesne: hence the range of devices identified by Waugh, now characteristically for life rather than for ever. Recipients were, above all, the professional administrators needed to run their estates, now managed directly, and the professional lawyers representing them in the royal courts now supplanting the barons' own honorial courts. Edward I adapted such contracts for military purposes and it was by further adaptations that his earls raised non-feudal retinues several hundred men stronger than the trivial feudal quotas that they were obliged to contribute.

There is now a consensus that Bastard Feudalism started earlier than McFarlane supposed and that it had important functions in peacetime. In the broadest sense, however, as Professor Coss has remarked, this is an adap-tation of McFarlane's interpretation rather than a return to the hostility towards Livery and Maintenance of Plum-mer etcetera, which McFarlane had supplanted rather than openly refuted. In 1989, however, Coss produced a radically revised model, which had much in common with the earlier version and reveals a neo-Marxist hos-tility to Bastard Feudalism as a phase in the 'feudal mode of production'. Neither contractual retaining, which emerged from the new pressures on magnates as estate managers under Henry III, nor the new-found role of the household, were the main issue: corruption of the judicial system was. It was in the middle years of Henry III's reign that the most notorious bastard feudal abuses proliferated, resulting – in Dr David Carpenter's words – in 'the emergence of a pattern of magnate rule in the shires similar to that which was to dominate England in

17. 'Debate', 170.

the later middle ages'. None of this resulted from the contractual indenture, military considerations, or the operation of the noble household. Other explanations must
therefore be sought. Coss finds them in the reaction of
magnates to the success of Angevin legal reforms, the
victory of royal over private justice, and the forging of
ever more direct links between crown and subjects. 'Bastard feudalism was a response to the resurrection of public authority within feudal society and within the feudal
state'. Threatened with the dissolution of their power by
the success of the new royal judicial system, the magnates
infiltrated and corrupted the new system at every level,
drawing lesser men in ever greater numbers into their retinues. Far from leading to greater cohesion, such activities
caused greater instability. 'First, the territorial dimensions
of the affinity sometimes gave rise to conflicts between
magnates and their dependents'. The good attribute often
claimed for Bastard Feudalism – the role of arbitration
– could only be a pale 'substitute for the efficient and
relatively impartial rule of law' and was only necessary
because of the conflicts generated by Bastard Feudalism
itself. Such comments could have been written (from their
very different standpoints!) by Charles Plummer a century or Helen Cam half a century ago.

> A third area of instability similarly arises from the magnates'
> quest to be allowed to maintain their traditional role as
> dispensers of patronage. . . . Notwithstanding the tendency,
> seemingly, for more and more to be sucked into retinues
> and affinities as the bastard feudal system deepened, and
> notwithstanding too the impressive appearance of aristocratic
> might, the real suitors were the patrons not the clients; it
> was they whose survival depended upon the continuance of
> the system.

Contemporaries recognised not only the abuses, but that
there was 'something deeply wrong with the way society is
functioning and the sense that there are means of making
it function better'. Hence, argues Coss, the attempts of
the Commons to curb retaining that were defeated under
Richard II. Bastard Feudalism was about aristocratic control of the provinces and that 'depends upon negating the
capacity of the public courts to transcend the old order'.

Its demise is thus the story of 'the decline in the capacity of the feudal mode of production and its attendant thought-processes to constrain and contain the evolving role of the state'.[18] In Marxist parlance, the next stage was a capitalist mode of production.

Coss's article generated two responses from historians of his own period. Whilst in general agreement and clear that earlier examples of retaining and abuses were mere antecedents – 'the scale on which this took place was transformed by the Angevin legal reforms' – Dr David Carpenter saw the appointment of local gentry to shire office as offering 'the magnates the opportunity to pervert the whole system'. For Crouch, on the other hand, McFarlane's Bastard Feudalism was already there in the twelfth century.

> It is not being merely reductionist to see the political ground-rules of later medieval society in place in England in the twelfth century: what changes there were between 1100 and 1300 were matters of degree and cosmetic.

Enfeoffment was never more than one, shortlived, means of recruiting men. Noble domination of the shires through bastard feudal retinues dates back to at least Roger Earl of Hereford in the 1140s and the notorious abuses existed before the Angevin legal reforms were even conceived.

Not surprisingly, it was Crouch at whom Coss directed his reply, accusing him of a 'narrow fief-centred definition of feudalism' much like 'McFarlane's consequent retinue-centred model'. Bastard Feudalism is not about retaining, but rather about

> the invasion and subversion of law courts and offices of administration. It is this latter which in my view lies at the heart of bastard feudalism. . . . For me this penetration of institutions is not a secondary, but a primary matter. I rejected, and still reject, the McFarlane view which sees bastard feudalism as flowing simply from the replacement of the tenurial bond with the cash nexus.

Different types of retaining are mere mechanisms and the differences that Crouch identifies more often a matter of emphasis. What is at issue is 'a total social formation'

18. Coss, 27–63.

called Feudalism, says Coss, returning more overtly to his Marxist vein:

> It is dominated by a seigneurial class, or classes, whose power is territorial, is based ultimately upon physical force, and involves the direct subordination of man to man. . . . Within this social order the greater feudatory needs to dominate the lesser, and he must continue to do so if he is to remain on a superior plane. . . . The second point which needs stressing is that the heart of magnate power, at least *qua* magnate rather than a simple seigneur, lay in dominating local society.

Coss expressed surprise at the absence of any response from late medieval historians.[19] That, however, is understandable on several grounds. Coss's arguments demand time for assimilation. Understandably they fit best into the period for which they were devised – the twelfth and thirteenth centuries – and sometimes he seeks to explain developments that late medievalists find difficult to recognise. Moreover, his paper coincided with a mass of new work on later medieval Bastard Feudalism, including at least three major re-interpretations – by Professor Bean, Professor Bellamy and the present author. All three agreed with Coss that the time has come to move on from McFarlane and to frame a new synthesis. However original they were – and each had much that was new to say – none was as radical as Coss himself. All three, by his definition, were mere adaptations of McFarlane's orthodoxy and all were as limited as McFarlane himself in their chronological scope. This book takes account of all this new work, by Coss and the others, treats the whole chronological span from 1150 to 1650, and sets out a new synthesis. It is thus the response that Coss expected.

. . .

THE CENTRAL CENTURIES, *c.* 1300–1500

It is historians of McFarlane's own chosen period, the fourteenth and fifteenth centuries, who have followed his guidelines most closely. Accepting his judgement that tenure by knight service was obsolete and prevented by inadequate sources from study of the household, they focused

19. 'Debate', 165–203, esp. 168, 180, 191, 193, 198–200.

their attention on retainer of the gentry by indentures and, failing them, by the annuities recorded in their estate accounts. One neglected fruit was our much improved understanding of that host of professional estate administrators and lawyers whose service was not to the estate of a single lord but to a whole constellation. It was in terms of indentured retainers and annuitants without offices – *extraordinary* retainers, in short – that a host of theses and publications discussed noble retinues. Such retinues were revealed to be very similar throughout the fourteenth and fifteenth centuries. John of Gaunt's retinue, on which McFarlane relied, proved to be even more exceptional than he had supposed; the only other of comparable size, that of William Lord Hastings (d. 1483), contrasted sharply with Gaunt's and was used by Professor Dunham to explore the theme of 'good lordship' and to construct a chronology of retaining. Unfortunately, both of Dunham's principal achievements have foundered on the realisation just how exceptional Hastings's retinue was.[20] As late as 1989 Professor Bean considered that there had been little progress since McFarlane's own work in this area:

> It is difficult to avoid the conclusion that there has never been a thorough analysis of the relationship between the contract system and 'bastard feudalism', despite the importance given it in the classic interpretation.

That was the daunting task he undertook himself.[21] Professor Michael Jones and Dr Simon Walker are undertaking a complete edition of surviving indentures of retainer.

Like McFarlane, Bean identified several types of tie – indentures of retainer, annuities, and liveries – and ranged recipients in concentric circles depending on their function. All wore livery, whether resident in his household, estate officers, or extraordinary retainers; only a minority made indentures or received annuities. He too saw the life-indenture as the objective both of lord and man, thus the most appropriate yardstick to measure other relationships, and one, moreover, that varied from

20. Hicks, ch. 12.
21. Bean, p 7. For the next 3 paras, see Bean, esp. pp. 30, 46, 48, 115, 129, 173, 175.

lord to lord and from time to time according to circumstance. Retaining originated, in Bean's view, 'from relationships that over a century before had been located within the household'. *Bachelor* was a synonym for the household knight of the thirteenth century and many of the earliest indentured retainers were bachelors, who enjoyed 'special trust within the immediate entourage of his lord' and brought their own valets and grooms with them when they visited their lord.

> There thus emerges a picture of a great household composed, in part at least, of some smaller households, absorbed within the greater one when their lords attended their lords. ... At any one time the household was no more nor less than the body of those in attendance on their lord, whether in peace or war.

Service in the household carried with it a particularly intimate tie of lordship and loyalty. Indentured retainers were not permanent residents of the household – had they been, no indentures would have been needed – and in the fifteenth century they were normally non-resident. 'The history of the relationship of lord and man in late medieval England is one of the decline in the importance of the household'.

Bean concluded, as early historians had done, that all the nobility recruited gentry in these ways, but never apparently very many of them. This tentative impression was confirmed as the rule by Mr T.B. Pugh's analysis of the nobility's income tax returns of 1436. Only at times of crisis did great lords like Richard Duke of York (d. 1460) significantly expand their retinues at great personal cost.[22] 'For the so-called "overmighty subject" civil war was an exorbitantly expensive business'. Responses to crises could explain the exceptional burden of fees encumbering the northern estates of the Percies and Nevilles from the 1440s; alternatively, however actually deployed, these retainers were financed indirectly from their salaries as wardens of the marches towards Scotland, for which no accounts survived or perhaps ever existed.

22. Ibid., p. 172; Pugh, pp. 101–5; McFarlane, *England*, pp. 236n, 237; *Nobility*, pp. 103–4.

Extraordinary retaining was on too small a scale, writes Bean, 'to explain the power of certain magnates in the politics and society of late medieval England'. Even John of Gaunt could not retain all the gentry anywhere. Extraordinary retaining cannot even account for the escorts several hundred strong that accompanied great magnates in the turbulent 1450s.

> Even if he brought out all his household men and all his knights and squires retained by indenture, a leading duke or earl would still have to raise additional men, at least for the needs of civil war.

The tenants from his estates were the most likely source.

If Bean tested McFarlane's theories across the whole range of surviving indentures, many other historians, as indicated, have tested them against particular retinues. Generally the results have been disappointing, providing detailed exemplification of old ideas rather than new insights. No other retinue is as well-documented as that of John of Gaunt and none has been as thoroughly reassessed. Dr Simon Walker was able to draw not merely on the indentures and estate accounts used by McFarlane so long ago, but also on household accounts newly discovered and on the legal records that came into common use since McFarlane's day. He too identified several categories of follower, McFarlane's concentric rings, and found that even Gaunt could not meet all his manpower requirements from those permanently in his service. The duke's household was 'the centre of the duke's activities' in time of peace and grew in numbers throughout his life. The growth may reflect in part the transfer of recipients of casual livery, now illegal, into legal employment in the household. Members of the household were a quarter of the duke's men. In war time it was the indentured retinue that mattered most. Since Gaunt was primarily interested in war, the indentured retinue commonly held centre stage, and Walker himself often equates retainers with indentured retainers. There were 173 such indentures in 1382. They did not change how people lived, but 'merely formalised and recorded, for a specific occasion, the unwritten rules by which they always lived'. For Walker, like McFarlane, indentures encapsulated the spirit

30

of Bastard Feudalism, which mingled loyalty, honour, service, and the élitism of a professional cadre. If the specific occasion was generally military, the retinue could operate territorially or in local politics, although this was not its prime objective and it was not organised or recruited with that end in mind. 'This did not mean that Gaunt could neglect the local standing of his affinity, only that it was not his over-riding concern'. Its composition could reflect traditional or even tenurial connections, but varied from time to time:

> Consequently, the changing social composition of the Lancastrian affinity can best be explained as a positive response to a change in the duke's needs and expectations of service, marked by a conscious decision to concentrate on quantity rather than quality.

That is to view it from the lord's point of view. From that of the retainer, Gaunt was a generous employer who paid high fees, whose service offered prestige and scope for personal enrichment, and he was the greatest of all good lords. Retainers did not abandon earlier associations on recruitment and their quarrels could embroil their lord. Despite his vast resources, Gaunt was not always effective in such circumstances and was on occasion defied with impunity. Walker's conclusion here casts doubt on 'the role of the great magnates and their retainers in creating the violence and disorder undoubtedly endemic in late medieval England', which he attributes to the growing assertiveness of the gentry. If even Gaunt was powerless, must not all others have been? It was not that Bastard Feudalism was 'an abusive form of social organisation', but that practitioners of abuses needed to be curbed.[23] McFarlane's point.

Outside Gaunt's vast connection, indentured retainers and annuitants were relatively rare. Simple arithmetic indicates that not all gentry could be retained and thus that some were free of bastard feudal commitments. Historians were therefore encouraged to make the nobility *members* rather than *masters* of county communities. Dr Saul in 1979 and Professor Richmond in

23. Walker, esp. pp. 9–10, 36, 249, 257, 260.

1980–81 explored the political independence of the gentry and their capacity to decide for themselves, whilst theses on the nobility gave way to the study of county communities.

Many late medieval counties lacked a dominant peer and rarely if ever did one hold more than a fraction of the land. The natural processes of life and death united and broke up estates, placed them in the hands of heirs, and transferred large portions for long periods to widowed ladies even without the mortgages and forfeitures that befell so many. Far from the calm suggested by descent in the same family for centuries, even the most longlived estates were constantly changing and many a peer had to eke out long years on a portion of his inheritance waiting for ancestresses to die. The misfortunes of the Mowbrays, most of whose lands were encumbered by dowagers for most of the fourteenth and fifteenth centuries, were exceptional only in degree. So, too, with the lesser nobility and the gentry: Professor Richmond has traced the kaleidoscopic changes of gentry landholding in mid-fifteenth-century Norfolk.[24] Far from instruments of political direction, stability and social cohesion, noble estates could become power vacuums, themselves at risk to predatory marauders, and disorder was unleashed.

Even for McFarlane, the study of retaining and noble estates was never more than a means to an end, that end being to understand local and national politics. Inevitably this involves focusing on events thought worthy of record, which McFarlane found predominantly in the *Paston Letters* and others discovered in the records of the central courts. Such cases, mainly dealing with violent and criminal feuds, sprouted a crop of case studies in the learned journals. Peace and concord, inevitably, passed unrecorded and unpublished. Whereas McFarlane had argued that it was not Bastard Feudalism that was corrupt, but merely its abuse, studies using such records and

24. C. Richmond, 'Landlord and Tenant', *Enterprise and Individuals in Fifteenth-Century England*, ed. J. Kermode (Stroud 1991); *Paston Family in the Fifteenth Century: The First Phase* (Cambridge 1991). For the next two paras, see Hicks, pp. 10–34.

informed by such perspectives have tended to magnify the level of disorder and to land the nobility with the responsibility for it.

This is the line taken by three groups of historians for very different reasons. Professors Storey and Bellamy stress Bastard Feudalism's role in the perversion of justice in the tradition of Plummer, Stubbs and Cam. For Professor Richmond and Dr Rowney, the nobility had lost control of their retainers, who habitually flouted their authority. Thirdly, Dr Christine Carpenter presents the ties of retaining as binding and exclusive, yet constantly shifting as retinues suffered continuous erosion and threats. At the root of both Bellamy's and Carpenter's interpretations are disputes over the tenure of land – issues too central to the aristocracy's essential interests to ignore. Such disputes dominated local politics, which consisted of a struggle to control local government interspersed with outbreaks of violence. Bellamy calls these 'land wars' or 'gentleman's wars'. Even the positive side of Bastard Feudalism, the arbitration of disputes, often failed to settle them. Bastard feudal anarchy, it thus appears, reflects the weakness rather than the strength of the nobility.

To fully understand the nature of bastard feudal society thus depends on the nature of the bastard feudal tie itself and on that there is evidently no longer a consensus. For too long late medievalists have been content to stress the distinctive features of their era and to quote McFarlane, whilst historians of surrounding centuries have been advancing their knowledge and uncovering ever more continuities. The time has now passed when McFarlane's exposition can be accepted uncritically or when it provides satisfactory answers to all or any of the questions that historians want answered. What is necessary, first, is the re-assessment of the personnel and quality of Bastard Feudalism undertaken in chapters 2, 3 and 4, which then permits, secondly, the more confident exploration of bastard feudal politics and society that follows in chapters 5, 6 and 7.

. . .

THE LAST CENTURIES OF BASTARD FEUDALISM

Victorian and early twentieth-century students of Bastard
Feudalism were content to accept that Bastard Feudalism
had been curbed by Henry VII, who had legislated against
retaining, imposed punitive fines on offenders, and had
used his court of Star Chamber to suppress both Livery and Maintenance. This interpretation held sway in
academic circles into the 1960s and even later in school
textbooks, some doubtless still used. Yet it flew in the face
of the facts for – as J.P. Cooper observed – retaining, liveries and maintenance persisted throughout the sixteenth
century. McFarlane knew this, as he pursued his sources
across the barrier of 1485, but he did not attempt to
write of Bastard Feudalism under the Tudors. Whilst such
leading late medievalists as Professors Dunham, Holmes
and Lander took it for granted that Bastard Feudalism
continued under the Tudors and such Tudor historians
as Professor Loades, Dr Williams, Dr Davies, and Cooper
himself applied medieval insights to the Tudor period,[25]
it was still possible as late as 1985 for Dr Bernard to
lament that so many did not.

> Another cause of the misconceptions about [the importance
> of] the nobility is the failure of many historians of the Tudor
> period to apply to the sixteenth century the insights of his-
> torians working on earlier periods. It is fruitful to examine
> the early Tudor nobility in the light of the reinterpretation
> of the nobility of the fourteenth and fifteenth centuries by
> K.B. McFarlane.[26]

We might have been spared the use of the adjectives 'feudal', 'neo-feudal', and 'quasi-feudal' to describe Bastard
Feudalism and certain historians need have laboured less

25. Dunham, ch. 5; G.A. Holmes, *Later Middle Ages 1272–1485*
(1970), p. 167; J.R. Lander, *Conflict and Stability in Fifteenth
Century England* (1969), p. 180; D.M. Loades, *Politics and the
Nation 1450–1660* (1974), esp. pp. 295–7; P. Williams, *Tudor
Regime* (Oxford 1979), pp. 1–4; C.S.L. Davies, *Peace, Print and
Protestantism 1450–1558* (1977), pp. 53–8, 113–14; Cooper,
pp. 78–96.
26. Bernard, *Power*, pp. 3–4.

hard over 'questions mal posés'. However, it was as an independent scholar working from first principles that Mr M.E. James produced his impressive and wholly independent findings, which medievalists ignore at their peril.

An exception to Henry VII's abolition of retaining of which historians were vaguely conscious were the 'feudal' or 'neo-feudal' survivals to be found in such remote and peripheral backwaters as the far North. It was these that James studied in a series of meticulous, perceptive and classic studies of the great regional nobility and of the major northern risings of 1536–37 and 1569. Far from encountering bastard feudal anarchy, he encountered a highly conservative society respectful of birth, rank, tradition and custom in which bastard feudal connections were a force for stability, order and justice. The values differed from those propogated by the Tudor state, but were no less esteemed and were internalised and sanctioned by long exercise. Great lords were 'natural rulers' of their own 'countries': 'It is most natural and not less honourable that his lordship should have the government and rule under the Prince here in this county of Northumberland', wrote George Clarkson about 1567. What was true of the Percy earls in Northumberland, at Cockermouth in Cumberland, and parts of the East Riding of Yorkshire applied equally to the Cliffords, earls of Cumberland at Skipton-in-Craven (Yorks.) and Brougham (Westmor.), to the Neville Earls of Westmorland in County Durham and Cleveland, and to the Lords Dacre around Naworth in Cumberland. In his 'country' each lord enjoyed unquestioned authority. Power revolved around the great household, 'the organizing centre and ceremonial expression of a magnate connection', where the magnate lived in splendour, eating and worshipping publicly several times a day, surrounded by scores or even hundreds of liveried servants often of gentle birth, and kept open house to all who availed themselves of his hospitality. 'The great households presented an orderly and decorous front, and there was a sense of responsibility to dependants and inferiors that was rare elsewhere'. The household was the nerve centre of a lord's estates and connection, where he and his council received information, conferred patronage, made decisions, and issued directions. The lord showed himself periodically on all his estates, accompanied always by an impressive train of liveried horsemen. His household was drawn from the vicinity where his estates lay and in the Northumberland household those in attendance were rotated three times a year. Household and estate officers were often local gentry with their own properties, which in many cases were held of the lord as feudal lord, and had been so held by their ancestors of their lords' ancestors for many generations. In James's words, this was a 'lineage society' in which gentry dynasties were impelled to serve the noble dynasties by a mixture of family tradition and an 'ethos of service'. Suit of court was still rendered at the baronial courts of Alnwick (Northum.) or Skipton-in-Craven, where their disputes could be resolved. No less than 7 out of 10 servants who accompanied the 5th Earl of Northumberland to London in 1525 came from families of mesne tenants.

> Thus it would be misleading to assume that the men to whom the fifth earl (with complete legality) gave his livery and fee were no more than a body of estate agents and domestic servants, bound to their master by a cash nexus.

Such feudal tenants were already bound to their lords, were predisposed to enter their service and accept their leadership, and turned naturally to them for office or other advancement. Such service was honourable: there was 'an ethos of "service" ' that required them to commit their loyalty to their lord in return for good lordship which entailed protection, reward, and support in their quarrels. Moreover, such gentry did not come alone, but brought their own household and tenants with them; as estate officials, they also commanded their lord's tenants. Here we are thinking not of tenants by knight service, but of ordinary rustics, who kept weapons and horses ready for their lords' summons to arms. There was a strong moral component in their obedience, for they too were deeply devoted to their traditional lords, who, in turn, charged them less than market rents, remedied their grievances, and protected them against oppressive estate and royal officers alike. Here, indeed, was the manpower that made such connections so formidable: thus the 5th Earl of Northumberland (d. 1527) could muster against the Scots 2,280 horsemen and 3,593 footmen from his Yorkshire estates, 1,030 horsemen and 2,011 footmen from Cumberland, and his son 1,967 from the Alnwick estate alone. Another measure is provided by those attending the funeral of Willliam Lord Dacre in 1563, who constituted a 'tight regional connection, bound together by bonds of tenure, kinship and service'. The funeral of the parvenu Lord Wharton, though the king's chosen instrument, was much less impressive, for such connections took generations to develop. Once developed, however, they were remarkably enduring and stable and a force for cohesion and order within the locality where they were to be found.[27]

Drs Coward, Bernard and Smith and Mr Robinson have shown that much the same was true of the Earl of Derby in Lancashire and Cheshire, of the 4th Earl of Shrewsbury in Derbyshire and Hallamshire, and, on a lesser scale, of Lord Darcy in the southern West Riding, and of the Earl of Worcester in South Wales. Derby recruited 7,831 against the Pilgrims of Grace in 1536, when Shrewsbury raised 3,654 men. Shrewsbury's descendant, the 7th Earl, was reminded that 'you are a prince (alone in effect) in two counties in the heart of England'.[28] All these, however, could be also regarded as magnates of the remote highland zone and therefore exceptional. That, however, could not apply to East Anglia, where Thomas Howard, Duke of Norfolk (d. 1572), enjoyed the equally blind devotion of his tenants. Perhaps East Anglia was another 'peripheral region'. 'But', James observed,

> [But] were conditions all that different where the FitzAlans ruled in Sussex, the earl of Leicester from his great castle of Kenilworth, the Berkeleys in Gloucestershire, the earl of Huntingdon in Leicestershire? Was 'feudalism' really a problem of peripheral areas and 'highland zones'?

27. James, chs 1–7, esp. pp. 2, 52, 98, 182. There is much on the ethos of open-housekeeping in F. Heal, *Hospitality in Early Modern England* (Oxford 1990).
28. Coward, pp. 92–3, 97; Bernard, *Power*, pp. 32, 177; R.B. Smith, *Land and Politics in the England of Henry VIII* (Oxford 1970), p. 139; W.R.B. Robinson, 'Patronage and Hospitality in Early Tudor Wales: The Role of Henry, Earl of Worcester, 1526–49', *BIHR* li (1978).

The military role of tenants, he pointed out, 'may be encountered as much in the midlands and south as in the northern and western "highland zones" and "peripheral regions" '. Cooper found leases requiring military service not only in the Welsh borderland, but in Kent, Hampshire, Somerset and Wiltshire.[29] 'I look upon every man possessed of a great landed estate', remarked a contemporary, 'as a kind of petty prince in regard to those that live under him'. 'Extensive areas of [Henry VIII's] England and Wales were dominated by noble families', remarked Helen Miller. 'In some senses early Tudor England was a federation of noble fiefdoms', expands Bernard, who parcels them out: Leicestershire to the Hastings family, Earls of Huntingdon; Lincolnshire to the Duchess of Suffolk; the Earl of Bedford in the South West; and so on. It is a perspective that was shared by contemporaries, such as Thomas Lord Seymour of Sudeley.[30] And, on a lesser scale, there were lesser men – like Vernon, 'King of the Peak' and the Heron masters of Redesdale – of whom the same could be said. Every gentleman had his household and tenants to back him up. Moreover, the Tudor evidence makes it very clear that the office of estate steward conferred command over the tenants and that those who sought stewardships did so with such manpower in mind. Even Henry VIII's minister, Thomas Cromwell, took such a stewardship; the 4th Earl of Shrewsbury was steward to 11 monasteries; and it was as steward of Pontefract that Lord Darcy was such a great man in West Riding.[31] What James found in the far North was actually everywhere commonplace. Yet such authority was never unqualified, Bernard warns us, for there was never a time when 'the north knew no king but a Percy'.[32]

Even extraordinary retaining did not end with Henry VII, but persisted throughout the sixteenth and seventeenth centuries. Indentures of retainer, it is true, became

29. Cooper, pp. 91–3.
30. Bernard, *Power*, pp. 177–80; Bernard, *Nobility*, pp. 221–2; Miller, *Henry VIII*, p. 256.
31. Miller, *Henry VIII*, p. 35; Bernard, *Power*, p. 148; Smith, *Land and Politics*, p. 139.
32. Bernard, *Power*, p. 182.

very rare. Despite diligent searches, neither Dunham, Cameron, Coward, nor Cooper have ever found one.[33] Admittedly annuities persisted and are recorded on the account rolls of the the 2nd Lord Hastings, 2nd Earl of Derby, and 3rd Duke of Norfolk among others. But they are not very numerous and were 'probably not the most significant of the bonds of dependence between great landowners and others'.[34] It was not necessary for great noblemen like the 5th Earl of Northumberland to retain illegally or grant dozens of annuities as his father had done. An inflated household and the multiplication of estate offices could achieve the same result. Lords still feed lawyers and pensioned royal judges and ministers to secure influence where it was most required. Few of the magnates were convicted of illegal retaining and the number of those so retained was also small. But the crown itself periodically issued licences to retain in spite of the statute. Early recipients were Sir Henry Willoughby in 1497 and Sir Thomas Lovell in 1508 and many other licences were issued in batches. In the 1540s 13 men were licensed to recruit 560; under Edward VI, 65 licences for 3900; and up to 1565 Elizabeth had issued 11 licences for 560 men. If, understandably, the recipients were often royal ministers or councillors, the sheer numbers demanded the licensing of many noblemen and leading gentry.[35]

One reason for this was the need of all monarchs for military service from such men against domestic threats, for service against the Scots and on the continent. All the Tudor armies, from 1492 to 1544, were recruited largely from noble retinues and often, indeed, by the well-tried indenture system. Since we have lists of some such companies, we know that even for foreign service they were drawn principally from the households and tenants of the captains. This applied equally to the licensed retinues. Sir Henry Willoughby's company of 200 licensed in 1497 proves in 1511 to be drawn 'from your lands, authorities, realms and offices'; Sir Thomas Lovell's retinue of 1,325

33. Cameron, p. 20; Coward, p. 117; Cooper, p. 80.
34. Coward, p. 117.
35. Cooper, pp. 81, 85.

archers and billmen, first licensed in 1508, comprised principally tenants from the estates of Lord Roos, of which he was custodian, of the abbeys of Waltham and St Albans of which he was steward, of Sherwood Forest of which he was keeper and Nottingham castle of which he was constable. Retainers, household-men and tenants of the great were excluded from the revitalised Tudor militia, depriving it (as was often pointed out) of most of its potential captains, horsemen and its best soldiers:[36] a situation which was tolerated because they were more readily available and organised at greater speed under trusted command whenever crises loomed. What the sixteenth-century evidence makes very clear is that *manred* – the control over numbers of men of military potential – was eagerly sought after by nobility and gentry alike.

Certainly some late medieval magnates stockpiled arms, acquired the most modern weapons, and constructed up-to-date fortresses. Carts of weapons supposedly belonging to the Wydevilles were exhibited in 1483, a great tower keep was constructed at Raglan a generation earlier, and Warwick the Kingmaker had his own artillery. The evidence is much fuller for the Tudor period and has been collected by Professor Stone, ironically to demonstrate that the practice was coming to an end. Queen Elizabeth's Earl of Leicester equipped Kenilworth in Warwickshire to resist a modern siege. There were 100 cannon, 1,500 shot, 450 small arms, and equipment for 200 horse and 500 foot. His father, the Duke of Northumberland, in contrast, had arms for *only* 150 at Syon in 1553; the Duke of Norfolk, similarly, had arms for *only* 100 foot at Framlingham and 70 foot and 20 horse at Kenninghall, both in Norfolk, in 1546. Only the Earl of Pembroke, it seems, could compare with Leicester and Norfolk. It was the crown that required noblemen to equip themselves, reinforcing the requirement by act of parliament in 1557. 'Such evidence as we have', writes Stone,

> suggests that stockpiling of weapons was of modest proportions before 1550, reached its peak between 1550 and 1600,

36. E.g. L. Boynton, *Elizabethan Militia 1558–1638* (Newton Abbot 1967), pp. 32–3.

and thereafter declined. . . . The 1550s and 1560s saw not only a great expansion in the scale of aristocratic armouries but also their modernization.

Perhaps, as he suggests, they were not renewed thereafter, so castle armouries contained only rusting antiquities by the Civil War,[37] but noblemen seem to have kept much larger stocks than in the fifteenth century. They were still useful against an opposition that had nothing better.

Far from seeking to destroy retaining, Tudor governments, it is now agreed, sought to control it and to restrict its benefits to themselves. As Davies wisely put it,

> Suppressing retaining would abolish certain 'artificial' relationships between lords and men, over and beyond the sphere of a lord's 'natural' influence. But that 'natural' influence was a far more important thing; a great man's strength rested partly on his social position, on the general respect for his lordship, partly on the adherence, willing or otherwise, of tenants and other economic dependants. It was these, not indentured retainers, who formed the bulk of most riotous bands . . . .[38]

To forbid the recruitment of servants by the great would have brought the crown in conflict with the hierarchical structure of society itself. 'What, therefore, was really at issue was not the existence of masters and men throughout the social scale but the abuse of power bestowed by these relationships'.[39] Tudor historians accept as crucial the roles of the household, the tenants, and estate officers, who have been largely ignored by late medievalists up to now. Furthermore, James attaches weight to the baronial courts and knights fees that McFarlane and the whole McFarlane school of historians have hitherto ignored. The insights of McFarlane have been applied the Tudor era: it is now time to apply Tudor insights to the later middle ages.

37. Stone, pp. 217–23; Cooper, p. 91. The Wydevilles' arms were also old in 1483, D. Mancini, *Usurpation of Richard III*, ed. C.A.J. Armstrong (Gloucester 1984), p. 82.
38. Davies, *Peace*, p. 55.
39. G.R. Elton, *Tudor Constitution* (Cambridge 1960), p. 31.

. . .

BEYOND McFARLANE

From the vantage point of the 1990s, both Plummer and McFarlane now look parochial and limited. Each confined his discussions to only a fraction of the lifespan of Bastard Feudalism. Plummer saw Bastard Feudalism as something parasitical rather than integral to society. McFarlane concentrated on only one type of bastard feudal tie and probably not the most important. Bastard Feudalism existed before indentured retainers were invented and after they ceased to exist. Indentured retainers, it follows, are not the strand of continuity that links the 1140s and the 1640s. McFarlane spilt little ink on the large-scale aristocratic household and the military service of rustic tenants that bulk so large in the first and last centuries of Bastard Feudalism and now, thanks to Bean and Walker, in the central centuries too. Here are the elements of continuity. However, as Coss made clear, it is not enough merely to bolt on new centuries or new types of retainer on to McFarlane's thesis. A more thoroughgoing assessment is required and is undertaken here.

Yet, as Coss himself indicated, the relationship of lords and retainers remains central. We can now see that there are at least half a dozen different types of retainer bound in at least as many bastard feudal relationships. The first task, undertaken in chapter 2, is therefore to examine the varieties of Bastard Feudalism and then, in chapter 3, to establish their relative importance and assess the quality of the relationships that were involved. Chapter 4, which is pivotal, considers the legality both of Bastard Feudalism and of the abuses with which it is associated. It is these three chapters that then provide the foundation for the analysis of how Bastard Feudalism was employed in peace and war, on the national stage and in the provinces, and which establish whether Bastard Feudalism was indeed the parasitical impediment to constitutional, legal and social progress that Plummer, Cam and Coss have claimed. Chapter 8 traces the demise of Bastard Feudalism.

Chapter 2

VARIETIES OF BASTARD FEUDALISM

Every bastard feudal connection was composed of several different types of men who were bound to their lord by a similar variety of relationships. This chapter looks at each of these categories in turn: household, tenants, officials and counsellors, extraordinary retainers, livery, and finally miscellaneous servants and well-willers. Apart from exploring the nature of each relationship, this chapter considers whether all such categories were to be found in all connections over the five centuries covered by this book and how far their numbers and importance altered.

· · ·

HOUSEHOLD

At the centre of every bastard feudal connection was the household. The household consisted of the lord, his family, and their servants who lived, slept, and dined together in the same house or complex of buildings, whether permanently or on a temporary basis. Relatives and retainers who lived elsewhere are specifically excluded. The essential distinction between those within and outside the household was made by Bishop Grosseteste about 1240.[1] Such households varied considerably in size according to the rank of the head of the household. Between 1574 and 1821, when the mean size of all

---

1. H. Ridgeway, 'William de Valence and his *familiares*', *Historical Research* lxv (1992), 242. For what follows, see *Household and Family in Past Time*, ed. P. Laslett and R. Wall (Cambridge 1972), ch. 5, esp. pp. 126, 135, 154.

households was 4.75 persons and most were smaller, Professor Laslett found the mean size of the households of the nobility and gentry to be 6.6 persons. The difference was made up by additional servants, for 84 per cent of the nobility and gentry groups had servants. Whilst many such households were smaller than 6.6 persons, some were larger, a handful very much larger: for included in Laslett's figures is the household of 50 of the Earl of Lonsdale in 1787, which then comprised merely the earl and 49 servants. The broad outlines can be extended back in time. All noblemen and gentlemen were expected to practise a noble or genteel lifestyle, which entailed attendance by domestic servants. They did not cook, wash up, or serve themselves. For 'mere gentry', with income no greater than two Bridport cantarists in the 1450s, it might be that one attendant might suffice, perhaps a page, or the valet and lady's maid serving William Brent in 1496.[2] The higher the rank of gentleman or nobleman concerned, the larger was his establishment and the more numerous those in attendance. Thus the Duke of Buckingham had 187 servants in 1503–04, the Earl of Essex 50 in 1533, Lord Grey of Ruthin was 'not ostentatious' with 50–60 in 1447–48, and the newly created Lord Marney had 32 in 1523.[3]

Most of the lesser aristocracy probably had less servants than what Dr Mertes has called 'the rather small households of abbots and priors' (large by our standards) which 'only numbered from ten to twenty' or the 'small' establishment of 20–25 servants of the Watertons of Mexborough.[4] Unfortunately, it is only wealthy gentry – the Stonors, Mountfords, Willoughbys, Staffords of Grafton, Fastolf, Brome and Clervaux – for whose finances or households adequate household accounts survive. At the other extreme, the *Black Book of Edward IV*, a king who kept

2. P. Fleming, 'Household Servants of the Yorkist and Early Tudor Gentry', *Early Tudor England* ed. D. Williams (Woodbridge 1989), p. 21.
3. S. Gunn, 'Henry Bourchier, Earl of Essex (1472–1540)', in Bernard, *Nobility*, p. 148; *Grey of Ruthin Valor*, ed. R.I. Jack (Sydney, Australia 1965), p. 53; F. Heal, *Hospitality in Early Modern England* (Oxford 1990), p. 46.
4. Mertes, p. 18.

600 servants, famously assumed that a duke had 240
servants in his household, a marquis 200, an earl 140, a
viscount 80, a baron 40, and a knight 16;[5] only esquires
and gentlemen could manage with less. *The Black Book*
presumed another truth revealed by all other records:
that the aristocratic household was overwhelmingly male,
only the laundress and the damsels of the mistress being
of the female sex. In 1467, for example, Sir John Howard
had only 13 women in a total complement of 106.[6] The
functions that such servants performed did not differ with
the size of the household. Tasks that were undertaken by
single individuals in the residence of a mere knight, like
Sir Thomas LeStrange in the 1530s, or that could be
combined in the single servant of the Bridport cantarists
in the 1450s, became whole offices with their own staff in
the household of a king or duke, where departments more
and more specialised such as the saucery, the buttery of ale
and buttery of wine were to be found. It was a difference
of scale, not of kind. The households of all aristocrats,
whether dukes or mere gentlemen, contained a high
proportion of adult males. Numbers fluctuated daily, as
guests came for meals, retainers stayed overnight, and
servants went on errands.

At the centre of the medieval and early modern household was the hall. The literature of the early medieval period
shows it was there that kings such as Hrothgar and Beowulf
ate and slept. By 1200 the head of the household commonly
slept in his solar or private chamber that he had added at
the upper end and which grew over the centuries into a
chamber suite. At the lower end three doors led to kitchen,
pantry and buttery. These developments mark the division
into upper and lower household, the lower concerning
itself with humble toil – such as the preparation of food
– and the upper providing a congenial environment for the
lord. Though households became ever more elaborate, the
pattern of the twelfth century is recognisable even in the
prodigy houses of Elizabethan and Jacobean England.

5. A.R. Myers, *Household of Edward IV* (Manchester 1959), pp. 96,
   98, 100, 102, 104, 110.
6. *Household Books of John Howard, Duke of Norfolk, 1462–71, 1481–3*,
   ed. A. Crawford (Stroud 1992), xl–xlii.

The upper household or *Domus Magnificencie*, as the *Black Book* called it, has been much studied by historians. Here lived the householder and his family in close proximity to the chamberlain, the chaplain, and the other chamber staff, who attended to their more intimate needs. Prominent among them in the households of the Anglo-Norman nobility were the household knights, not yet enfeoffed or never to be enfeoffed. There were knights chambers at the bishop of Winchester's thirteenth- and fourteenth-century houses at Hambledon and East Meon (Hants). Numbers may have diminished as land was subinfeudated to them, and certainly did when knighthood itself became a rarer distinction. From 1224, when knights required £20 a year from land, they had no need to serve continually in lords' households. Some nevertheless chose to do so. Not surprisingly, as befits men of property, their status rose: bachelors in seigneurial households were often retained by indenture for fees, no longer merely for wages and keep. A lord's demand for genteel attendants was commonly satisfied by valets in the thirteenth century and esquires and gentlemen thereafter.

Members of the upper household were often of the same rank as the head or his near equal; after all, such service was a stage in the education of many aristocratic children. Just as the king had his household knights and esquires, so too had the nobility. Gentry, right down to such mere gentlemen as the Kentishmen John Pympe and John Alfegh, abbots and priors, even the canons of York Minster, had gentlemen in their chambers; others served the city of York.[7] Apart from their designated duties, which in the largest houses can have occupied little time, such men kept their master company, discussing and advising, playing with him at dice and sharing in the chase, fulfilled a multitude of errands inside and out, and

7. Fleming, 'Household Servants', p. 27; R.B. Dobson, *Durham Priory 1400–1450* (Cambridge 1973), p. 119; 'The Residentiary Canons of York in the Fifteenth Century', *Journal of Ecclesiastical History* xxx (1979), 159–60; *Chamberlains Accounts of the City of York*, ed. R.B. Dobson (Surtees Society cxii, 1978–9), p. 72; B.F. Harvey, *Living and Dying in England 1100–1540* (Oxford 1993), pp. 148–9, 160.

contributed to his splendour. They had military functions too: the defence of their lord, to coerce his foes, and as the core of his retinue of war. For the Mowbrays in the twelfth century, their upper household was 'a mobile force of knights and sergeants, who acted as the lord's bodyguard and could be used for any military task'.[8]

At all times the lower household – the *Domus Providencie* – was the larger and employed more staff. In 1467 Sir John Howard probably had 23 people in his upper and 75 in his lower households.[9] Such examples can be multiplied indefinitely. The primary functions of the lower household were menial: staff ran the kitchen, buttery, pantry, stable and other offices. Essential though they were for the successful operation of the household, such lower servants were also humbler in rank: characteristically sergeants, garcons and *pagetti* in the fourteenth century; yeomen, grooms and pages thereafter. As they lived in and were unaccompanied by women, they were apparently unmarried, therefore most probably (but certainly not invariably) young, and by the late fifteenth century often hired by the year. Hence, perhaps, the belief of medieval homilists and Sir Thomas More that they were often dismissed.[10] They too wore livery appropriate to their station, were mounted on horses, and shared in their master's magnificence both in hall and on progress. The *Black Book* was again concerned that they wore their livery and contributed to their master's display.

All this is well known. What is commonly ignored, however, is their military function. Even the lower domestics were able-bodied men, probably young, at a time when all men were expected to bear arms. Their sheer numbers deterred any attack on their master or burglary of his house. Such provision was no mere accident, as Tudor observers appreciated. It was they who were the 'tall fellows' so beloved for ceremonial and military purposes. Sir Thomas More and Thomas Starkey make the point clear: 'in them

8. *Charters of the Honour of Mowbray 1107–1199*, ed. D.E. Greenway (BA i, 1972), pp. lxi-ii.
9. *Howard Household Books*, xl–xlii.
10. T. More, *Utopia*, ed. E. Surtz and J.H. Hexter (Complete Works, iv, New Haven, Conn. 1965), p. 62; G.R. Owst, *Literature and the Pulpit in Medieval England* (2nd edn Oxford 1961), p. 310.

47

standeth the chief defence of England'.[11] This was why 63 of Howard's household in 1484, 64 of Northumberland's in 1523, and 97 of Derby's in 1536 were categorised as combatants.[12] They were even selected for their physical attributes with military objectives in mind. It was often noted how little they had to do in office; practised in arms and quarrelsome, More and Starkey saw them as threats to domestic peace.

> It seems to me by no means profitable to the common weal to keep for the emergency of war a vast multitude of such people as trouble and disturb the peace. You never have war unless you choose it, and you ought to take far more account of peace than war.

Whether military qualities actually determined recruitment earlier is difficult to demonstrate, but such men were certainly able-bodied and arms-bearing like everyone else and did engage in violence from time to time. Perhaps, however, there were proportionately less of them in the households of lesser gentry, which still included damsels, chaplains, and pages in much smaller totals.

. . .

TENANTS

Tenants were those who held land of their lords (including the nobility, religious houses, and the gentry) in town or country by tenures other than knight's service. Most of such tenants were peasants. Tudor landlords took their military service for granted. They all listed those tenants that they could call on for military purposes and included in their calculations tenants of estates that they controlled as stewards. The lists of tenants compiled by Sir Thomas Lovell in 1508 and the Earl of Oxford in 1489 seem to be the earliest Tudor examples.[13]

11. More, *Utopia*, pp. 62–5; T. Starkey, *A Dialogue between Pole and Lupset*, ed. T.F. Mayer (Camden Soc. 4th ser. xxxvii, 1989), p. 53. References to men of short stature sought to reassure, see Mertes, pp. 113–15.
12. *Howard Household Books*, ii.490; PRO E 101/531/34; Coward, p. 98. For what follows, see More, *Utopia*, p. 65; Starkey, *Dialogue*, pp. 53, 86; Stone, p. 212; Heal, *Hospitality*, p. 47.
13. Cameron, 24; *Household Books of John Duke of Norfolk and Thomas Earl of Surrey 1481–90*, ed. J.P. Collier (Roxburghe Club 1844), pp. 493–5.

Oxford, however, kept his records in the later pages of the household book containing the lists of John Howard, Duke of Norfolk (d. 1485), who promised 1,000 men to the king in 1484. He lists over 700 from 44 different places. This was nothing new. Even before his accession to the dukedom in 1483 or even to the peerage in 1468, he had mustered 100 men for service in Cheshire. About 1450 Walter Strickland of Sizergh listed 290 men in his 'book [of] his servants, tenants and inhabitants within the county of Westmorland'.[14]

Strickland's records are the earliest yet identified, but the phenomenon they record was not unique. If the numbers of household men and indentured retainers were always insufficient for the greatest magnates, it is hardly surprising that they recruited more widely as well. As long ago as 1959 Dr Franklin Wright remarked that:

> It is probable that many, if not most, of York's archers and men-at-arms – at any rate in the civil war after 1450 – came either from his own estates or from those of his tenants and 'well-willers'.[15]

A similar point was made about the retinue of George Duke of Clarence (d. 1478) by the present author in 1980 and applied more generally in 1991: 'Second came the lord's tenants. It was these who made up the rank and file – the sheer numbers – when a retinue turned out in force: for example, in civil war'.[16] The most useful accounts are those of Humphrey Duke of Buckingham (d. 1460), who in 1450 had 74 yeomen levied by his estate officers from Staffordshire to London, secured attendance of a further 60 in 1450–51, and brought a further 90 from Kent and Surrey.[17] Besides these, lords sent letters summoning levies of tenants – like those of the Duke of Norfolk in 1453 and the Duke of Clarence

14. *Howard Household Books*, ii.480–92; J. Nicolson and R. Burn, *History and Antiquities of Westmorland and Cumberland* (1777), i, 96n–97n.
15. F.M. Wright, 'The House of York 1415–50' (Johns Hopkins University PhD thesis, 1959), 239.
16. Hicks, pp. 36–7.
17. McFarlane, *England*, p. 235nn; C. Rawcliffe, *The Staffords, Earls of Stafford and Dukes of Buckingham 1394–1521* (Cambridge 1978), p. 47.

in 1471[18] – and we know the actual turnouts. Among the relatively few men on the losing side indicted after the battle of Barnet in 1471 there were several tenants of the Earl of Warwick's manors of Ware and Bushey (Herts) and several natives of properties of the Earl of Oxford in Essex. So, too, with those indicted after riots and private battles, such as those natives of York's lordships of Grantham and Nassington by Fotheringhay (Northants.) implicated in the Dartford debacle in 1452. Seldom however is the underlying reason as explicit as when the bailiff of Pocklington was indicted for mustering the Percy tenants prior to the battle of Stamford Bridge in 1454. Though it is generally obvious why tenants were involved, the reason nevertheless has to be deduced. This type of evidence can be multiplied, for the fifteenth century at least. It demonstrates both that the military use of tenants was widespread in the fifteenth century and that they bulked much larger in noble retinues of war than is normally supposed.

If household and indentures together generated too few men to fight the Wars of the Roses, the same is true of earlier conflicts dating back to the twelfth century and beyond. No tenant-in-chief, however great, owed the service of more than three hundred knights, many had enfeoffed only a handful, but the numbers they turned out were much greater, even allowing for the characteristic exaggeration of chroniclers' figures. Not surprisingly Count Waleran of Meulan found his own knights insufficient for rebellion in 1124. The nine knights expected in 1261 of Henry III's half-brother, William de Valence (d. 1296), could be much enlarged on occasion.[19] Though under-recorded by the chroniclers, archers played a crucial role in the battles and both archers and sergeants in the

18. Hicks, *Clarence*, p. 167; Myers, *EHD*, pp. 272–3. For what follows, see PRO KB 9/41/38; R.L. Storey, *End of the House of Lancaster* (2nd edn Gloucester 1986), pp. 99, 101; R.A. Griffiths, *King and Country* (1991), p. 354. Professor Goodman presumes that 'the constables of the townships played a key role in recruiting and arraying contingents', A. Goodman, *Wars of the Roses* (1980), p. 126.

19. Ridgeway, 'William de Valence', 245; D. Crouch, *The Beaumont Twins* (Cambridge 1986), pp. 20–2.

castle garrisons of the twelfth century.[20] Where did they come from? Often, as commonly stated, they were hired, but that was expensive and implies the ready availability of large numbers of foot-loose mercenaries. Sometimes perhaps they were arrayed. Most probably they were other categories of tenant.

How far back can the evidence be carried? Back to John of Gaunt, who in 1381 directed nine gentry to bring altogether 98 men-at-arms and 460 archers to Berwick, all to be paid by Yorkshire receivers; of these, 10 men-at-arms and 60 archers came from his honour of Knaresborough.[21] Back, too, to 1321, when John Giffard of Brimpsfield's tenants supported him in the Despenser war and when the rebel John Darcy took for granted that his tenants would follow him and guaranteed their good conduct as well as his own.[22] Back, too, to the Barons Wars, for which Dr David Carpenter has recently demonstrated that peasants involved in the fighting often held their lands of lords who had taken the same line: almost certainly *because* of their status as their tenants. Peasants, free and unfree, he points out, comprised much of local garrisons. After the battle of Evesham the Earl of Gloucester used his tenants to seize the lands of rebels. Probably tenants made up most of the armies and most of the casualties, of whom only those of rank are normally recorded.[23] And even in 1215–16, when Professor Painter could not

> discern the feudal connections of the vast majority of the men listed. . . . They were men of little importance in the lower reaches of the feudal hierarchy. Many perhaps were free tenants who did not hold by knight service. . . . The rebel

20. J. Bradbury, *Medieval Archer* (Woodbridge 1985), pp. 40, 57; A.L. Poole, *Obligations of Society in the 12th and 13th Centuries* (Oxford 1946), p. 38; Greenway, *Mowbray Charters*, pp. xxii, lx–lxi; N.J.G. Pounds, *The Medieval Castle in England and Wales* (Cambridge 1990), pp. 47, 122.
21. *Register of John of Gaunt*, ed. E.C. Lodge and R. Somerville (Camden Soc. 3rd ser. lvi, 1937), pp. 560–2.
22. S.L. Waugh, 'The Profits of Violence: The Minor Gentry in the Rebellion of 1321–22 in Gloucestershire and Herefordshire', *Speculum* lii (1977), 855–6.
23. D. Carpenter, 'The English Peasantry in Politics 1258–67', *P&P* 136 (1992), 3–42; M. Altschul, *A Baronial Family in Medieval England* (Baltimore 1965), pp. 111–12.

army that opposed John and the Regent William Marshal was composed of a few great men – barons, honorial barons, and important mesne lords and their hired followers. ... The majority must have been classed as serjeants.[24]

For 1215–16, 1264–65, and 1321–22 it is the wealthier peasants we know about, because they had lands to forfeit: unless they alone were combatants, because they alone could afford weapons, many others probably passed unrecorded. Carpenter's argument from silence is equally applicable to all domestic conflicts from the twelfth to fifteenth centuries, for none of which muster rolls survive.

. . .

OFFICERS AND COUNSELLORS

No lord could manage all his affairs himself. All required administrators to help them. These administrators fell into four main categories: his estate officers; his central administration; his household officers; and his counsellors. These categories changed greatly over time and distinctions between them were often blurred. Moreover, lords could require almost any service of almost any servant.

The first post-Conquest barons did not possess administrations separate from their households, courts and estates. Those with administrative responsibilities or from whom they sought counsel – their officers and counsellors – were members of their household and/or their feudal tenants; some such offices became hereditary. Their manors were run by reeves. Estate and financial management was much simplified by the dual practices of subinfeudation of some estates and the leasing out of the rest. Inflation and rising population from the late twelfth century encouraged direct farming of demesnes, raised baronial incomes, necessitated the employment of professional bureaucrats, and facilitated their payment. The professionalisation of noble bureaucracies had begun. Well before 1300, a recent study has noted, every major

24. S. Painter, *Studies in the History of the English Feudal Barony* (Baltimore 1943), p. 130.

estate had its hierarchy of administrators paid with annuities and liveries.[25] Administrative skills became ever more
specialised over the next three centuries: leasing of the
demesnes reduced the workload, but not apparently the
scale of bureaucracy in the late middle ages; after 1500
commercial opportunities increased once again.

Throughout these five centuries estate officers managed those of the lord's lands that had not been subinfeudated, orchestrated the farming of the demesne,
managed the parks and game, collected rents and other
dues from the tenants, and generally acted as the lord's
agent on the spot. It was these whom the lord commanded
to make purchases, to prepare his chamber for his arrival,
and to muster his tenants. Collectively called his ministers,
they were the reeves, bailiffs, beadles, rent-collectors,
messors, foresters, and parkers, who feature in every
manorial account. Each manor had ministers; on a great
estate there were hundreds of them, each responsible for
his own patch. Often they were of low status, particularly
in the twelfth–fourteenth centuries, when reeves were
commonly unfree tenants elected by their fellows for a
one-year term. This was sometimes long reflected in their
measly emoluments.

Lords withdrew from direct farming of their demesnes
– often by the 1370s, elsewhere in the 1440s, but ultimately
everywhere – and the workload diminished. Emoluments
nevertheless generally increased – often to 2d. a day or
£3 0s. 8d. (£3.03) a year – as service became voluntary,
the status of officials rose, and as more was expected of
them. If mere collection of rents was all that was required,
then indeed 'often the fees paid in connection with these
local offices were far in excess of adequate remunera-
tion for such duties as were performed'.[26] Such officers came to be held indefinitely by men of higher status, yeomen or gentlemen, who often performed their
functions by deputy. The multiplication of such offices
and the appointment to them of non-residents was an
increasingly important means of recruiting retainers from

25. S. Waugh, 'Tenure to Contract: Lordship and Clientage in the
    Thirteenth-Century England', *EHR* ci (1986) 824.
26. Pugh, p. 103.

the gentry in the fifteenth and early sixteenth centuries.

Catering, ceremonial, discipline, accounting, and transport were all concerns of the officers of the household, particularly the heads of departments and the leading accountant, commonly the clerk of the kitchen. Large households aped the development of the crown, adding treasurer, controller and cofferer to steward and chamberlain. Presiding over the household and residing within it, they are best seen as parts of the household, restricted and committed to the service of a specific lord or to one particular lord at a time. The expertise they built up – sometimes one can trace an upward career – could equip them for employment in another household of another lord. Once, however, such men had also been the central administration, the steward of the household commonly collecting receipts from the estate and the estates steward operating from the household. Estate stewardships were sub-divided and localised. From the thirteenth century lords habitually employed a receiver and auditors. Late medieval magnates divided their estates into geographical receiverships, each with its own receivers and auditors, and from the fifteenth century employed surveyors, who a century later were compiling maps and books of reference. Such officers were not resident in the household; they were paid substantial retaining fees and received expenses for the days spent on the job; commonly they served more than one master, sometimes as auditor of one and receiver of another; and they had become professional administrators with a valued expertise that resulted, by the sixteenth century from training.

The first Norman tenants-in-chief granted their highest offices and the largest fiefs to those they trusted most and from whom they preferred to take counsel, often no doubt in the honorial court. Although honorial barons held their fiefs and sometimes their offices by hereditary right, the lord's trust was not hereditary, though his need for counsel was. When later lords made grants, their charters were sealed not necessarily by their greatest tenants, but by their officials, particular tenants and knights – the most favoured and the most trusted, who occurred again and again – and by notables from the immediate locality, who varied from charter to charter. Here in practice we have baronial councils before the name was devised and before councillors were appointed. When such councillors came to be employed, they commonly included household officials, leading estate officers, important retainers, and lawyers. Late medieval baronial councils met regularly as a body, gave advice formally and informally, and undertook administrative tasks both individually and as a body.[27]

Lawyers were a special and growing category of experts whom no bastard feudal lord could do without. From at least the reign of Henry II, lords were liable to become engaged in litigation as plaintiffs or defendants in the royal courts, which did not remain at Westminster, but embarked on judicial progresses (eyres) in the localities. Lords were required to answer for the use of their rights of jurisdiction and even for the very existence of such rights. Title to land, all kinds of trespass and crime were tried in the royal courts. The whole period 1150–1650 witnessed a growth in the extent and complexity of the law, the number of crimes and lawsuits, in litigiousness, in numbers of lawyers and the costs of the law. By the fifteenth century every significant landowner was involved in litigation at least once in his life; many were engaged in many suits simultaneously. Every landowner needed legal knowledge to ensure his settlements were legally watertight and to protect himself as the law became an instrument in local politics. Ramsey Abbey was retaining lawyers from the 1230s, Durham Priory from the 1240s, many religious houses from the 1250s, and many other individuals by the late thirteenth century. Religious houses, towns, magnates and gentry alike employed them: by the 1470s the Yorkshire knightly family of the Plumptons relied heavily on their London agent, Godfrey Greene, to handle all their cases and to consult other experts where appropriate. Initially often churchmen and thus rewarded with livings, from the fourteenth century lawyers were

27. C. Rawcliffe, 'Baronial Councils in the Later Middle Ages', *Patronage, Pedigree and Power in Later Medieval England*, ed. C.D. Ross (Gloucester 1979), pp. 87–106.

commonly laymen who were paid retaining fees, which were supplemented with wages and expenses. Clients retained attornies at the exchequer, king's bench and common pleas, other *legisperiti* or apprentices at law, serjeants at law, and even the royal justices, whose services can readily be imagined; legislation forbidding judges to be retained was only partially effective and did not prevent Chief Justice Fortescue from serving the Hungerfords or Chief Justice Fairfax the Percies.[28] Lords, towns and monasteries often employed several such men, paying them small fees but large expenses when their expertise was called on; further profits could be made from privileged knowledge, e.g. of land sales, or from privileged status, as trustees and executors.[29] Richard Boyle, Earl of Cork, was paying small retainers to eight lawyers in the mid-1630s and feed successive attorneys-general in 1628 and 1637.[30] Lawyers could be feed of counsel by many different employers and indeed needed to be if their fees were to support them, let alone accumulate into the hoards of capital that enabled the successful to establish large landed estates.[31] Thus Edmund Brudenell of Chalfont (Bucks) had fees from 17 different employers in 1435, together worth only £15 6s. 8d., and Sir Roger Townshend (d. 1551) had 13 in 1525: from two peers, a Cambridge college, Pontefract College, and nine priories.[32]

The relationship of the lawyer and his employers, like that of auditor and employers, was comparable to that of a modern solicitor to his clients. Lawyers and professional administrators had many clients and were paid for their professional services. The higher their professional standing, the higher their status and the resulting emoluments. That was all they had to give: they were not committed or exclusively loyal in politics to one lord. Or not necessarily so: John Milewater, receiver of Richard Duke of York, fell at Barnet in 1471 in the service of his son

28. Hicks, p. 147n.
29. Moreton, p. 117.
30. M. Prestwich, *The Three Edwards* (1980), p. 145; G.E. Aylmer, *The King's Servants* (rev. edn 1974), p. 178.
31. E.g. Moreton, pp. 116–30, esp. p. 129.
32. Ibid., p. 28n; McFarlane, *England*, p. 32.

Gloucester.[33] But with the rare exceptions of genuinely redundant posts, e.g. the master of game of the game-less forest of Inglewood (Cumb.), lords expected ministers, administrators and councillors to fulfil the functions attached to their positions. Rents were to be collected, courts held, estates surveyed and rentals compiled, buildings repaired, accounts kept, and litigation conducted. Almost invariably they were.

. . .

EXTRAORDINARY RETAINERS

Extraordinary retainers were usually – but not exclusively – aristocrats. There are aristocrats in almost all connections from the Norman Conquest to the Civil War. In the earlier period they were barons or knights, later members of the peerage and gentry. Even earls sometimes served other magnates, as the 1st Earl of Northumberland served John of Gaunt and his great-great-grandson served Richard Duke of Gloucester. Many aristocrats are included in aspects of the connection that have already been treated. Some served in the upper household; others were officers of the household, estates, or central administrations; yet others were councillors. After 1300 many who entered the law were already gentlemen; almost all attained this status.

Almost all connections included aristocrats who were neither continuously resident nor officials nor councillors. These were what late medievalists call extraordinary retainers. In the eleventh, twelfth and thirteenth centuries such aristocrats were commonly feudal tenants. Most had been granted lands – fiefs or knight's fees – by their lords; a few had been granted money or fief-rentes. Whatever the original intention, by the late twelfth century the fief or fief-rente was held by hereditary right and could not be taken back arbitrarily by the lord. From the late thirteenth to sixteenth centuries it was commonplace for extraordinary retainers to be rewarded by an annuity in cash, usually for life; grants of land still occurred, again for life, for example from Gilbert

---

33. C.D. Ross, 'Some Servants and "Lovers" of Richard III in his Youth', *The Ricardian* 4 (1976), 2–4.

Earl of Gloucester (d. 1295) to Bartholomew Burghersh,[34] but ever less frequently. Such fees were not just granted by the nobility: gentry like the Stonors and Marneys gave them too, though the recipients were humbler and the fees smaller. William de Swinburne of Capheaton (Northum.), who retained two men by indenture in 1278, was a 'country squire who had limited financial means'. So, too, in 1468–70 was Thomas Sandford, who followed up his own retainer by Warwick the Kingmaker in 1462 with three indentures retaining five lesser men and their men to himself.[35]

Here we touch on what so many historians have seen as the watershed between two systems – the transition from Feudalism to Bastard Feudalism. The change matters – life annuities *are* more flexible than hereditary grants of land – but the differences have been exaggerated. There was a long period of overlap: Crouch identifies Bastard Feudalism in the 1140s, life-grants of land persisted in the fourteenth century, and James finds feudal vitality two centuries later. There was much co-existence in between. Large-scale subinfeudation continued on the Celtic fringe around 1200 and feudal levies still mattered to Edward I. For the thirteenth century, Dr Ridgeway observes,

> aspects of this transformation continue to be debated, espe-
> cially . . . the extent of its advance by the middle years of
> Henry III's reign. Most of the retinues studied so far, for
> instance, seem to have been mixed – a third or more of
> the knights of Earl William Marshall and Roger de Quincy
> coming from this source [tenure].[36]

Such an overlap is hardly surprising, since the functions of feudal tenure and bastard feudal contracts were very similar. We know most about the military service due from knight's fees and indentures of retainer, but other services in peacetime – sometimes the same – were normally expected of both. Both kinds of grant enabled a lord to

34. Altschul, *Baronial Family*, p. 209.
35. Bean, pp. 42–3; F.W. Ragg, 'Helton Flechan, Askham and Sand-ford of Askham', *Trans Cumberland and Westmorland Arch. Soc.* xxi (1921), 186–90.
36. Ridgeway, 'William de Valence', 241.

extend his effective authority beyond the bounds of his demesne and to enlist the influence of recipients in his own service, as well perhaps as adding their military resources to his own. Sometimes this might extend a lord's authority into an area where he lacked lands. Certainly it enabled him to tap manpower beyond that normally available to him: thus Humphrey Earl of Stafford, not a significant Cheshire landowner, retained Sir John Maynwaring in 1441.[37]

These military resources should not be seen merely as the service of a single individual. All aristocrats had attendants, even those serving in the upper household. The *Lytell Gest* of Robin Hood sees it as dishonourable for a knight not to be attended by a yeoman; he also had to have a horse. Those who were non-resident or not continually resident – married members of the upper household, estate officials, and extraordinary retainers – had their own households and estates and could call on their own domestic servants and tenants for military purposes. In 1257 the knights of the abbot of St Albans were accompanied by squires when on military service. Several of the knights of William de Valence were themselves accompanied by knights. Late medieval and Tudor lords appreciated this. Sometimes indentures of retainer specified how many attendants to bring: thus when Thomas Earl of Lancaster retained Sir Adam Swillington in 1317, the indenture specified that he would bring three knights and seven men-at-arms with him; Sir Hugh Meinill was merely to bring three knights including himself, and Sir John Eure three knights and seven men-at-arms. The higher the status of the retainer, the more men he was likely to bring: thus in 1319 Lord Latimer promised Lancaster that he would bring 10 other knights and 30 men at arms. After fixing the numbers to be brought by each retainer, eight Stafford retainers added 'or as many persons and horses as the said earl [later duke] list to assigne or command for'; in the ninth case, the number was 'after the degree or power of the said Sir John' Maynwaring.[38] Letters of summons to

37. A.C. Reeves, 'Some of Humphrey Stafford's Military Indentures', *Nottingham Medieval Studies* xvi (1972), 89–90.
38. Ridgeway, 'William de Valence', 247–8; Bean, pp. 49–50; Reeves, 'Stafford's Military Indentures', 88–91.

estate officials asked them to bring their own tenants as well as their lord's or to come 'with all such persons as you may goodly make'.[39] Even where the retainers' own men were not mentioned, their involvement was implied. There is no such clause in the indenture of 1449 between Richard Earl of Salisbury and Walter Strickland, but their presence is implied by a reference to 'all winnings of war to be won or gotten by the said Walter or any of his men that he shall have': perhaps the whole 290 in his list?[40] When Richard Duke of Gloucester retained the Earls of Northumberland and Westmorland, the two Lords Scrope, Lords Dacre, Greystoke and Neville, their men became his men and he became *de facto* 'Lord of the North'. Probably the same applied before 1300, though the published evidence is lacking; clearly no aristocrat, however poor, came unattended.

Military service was important, but fiefs and annuities were not used solely – or, perhaps, even principally – for military service. Extraordinary retainers were those who were retained in no other way and could be genuinely extraordinary or exceptional. Often, indeed, lords used outlying manors as fiefs or the income of outlying estates as fees to enlist the services of those well outside their normal milieu. Norman lords granted land in serjeanty for different types of service to cooks, huntsmen, falconers and minstrels, who were sometimes granted fees by their late medieval counterparts. Grants of both types were made by lords to endow members of their families. Richard de Clare, Earl of Hertford, gave his mistress a fee of £10 a year.[41] Edmund Mortimer (d. 1381) and Roger Mortimer (d. 1398), successive earls of March, 'made contracts of service with a wide variety of people from substantial knights to unimportant servants'.[42] The Staffords' physician and Warwick the Kingmaker's gunner were retained by indenture.[43] John Usher, retainer of Lord Grey of Ruthin, was personally obscure and paid

39. Hicks, *Clarence*, p. 167; *Plumpton Correspondence*, ed. T. Stapleton (Camden Soc. iv, 1839), p. 39.
40. Nicolson and Burn, *History and Antiquities*, i, pp. 96–7.
41. Painter, *English Feudal Barony*, p. 173.
42. Holmes, pp. 60–3.
43. Reeves, 'Stafford's Military Indentures', 91; PRO E 326/6402.

accordingly, like so many other feed men declared by the peerage in 1436.[44] Surely it is dangerous to suppose that such transactions had a military or political significance or significantly extended the influence of the lords? Annuities were a flexible reward or incentive and served a range of different objects, as indeed had grants of knights fees. That many people held fractional knight's fees was because many had been granted fractions: the jargon of military service concealed the financial services required – aids, scutage, etc. – and obscures the fact that military service was often not what was originally required. Just as perilous is the assumption that the initiative lay with the donor. If every indenture of retainer was a contract to the mutual advantage of lord and retainer, so every enfeoffment, it has been argued, was an individual bargain between lord and knight.

Often fees were granted to royal ministers and favourites, who sometimes accrued many such rewards: thus Osbert de Humbria, sheriff of Yorkshire and Lincolnshire, was given two vills in 1100 x 1116 by the Count of Aumale 'because he was of the king's household'; so, too, William de Hastings, a royal dispenser, and the justiciar, Richard de Lucy, were tenants of the honour of Clare in 1166.[45] The Younger Despenser under Edward II, Lords Hastings and Herbert under Edward IV, William Catesby under Richard III and Reynold Bray under Henry VII are well-known examples. This does not mean that these royal favourites were subjected to other employers but rather the reverse. Because of their proximity to the monarch or their standing locally or nationally, such men were able to patronise others, who paid them retaining fees to secure the exercise of that influence in their favour. What was sought was not a transfer of service from king to those paying the fees, but their support in their most influential capacities – as intimates of the crown or of great noblemen; there was no desire to make them dependants, to take priority over the service that made

44. Jack, *Grey of Ruthin Valor*, p. 90.
45. B. English, *The Lords of Holderness 1086–1250* (Hull 1979), p. 146; R. Mortimer, 'Land and Service: Tenants of the Honour of Clare', *Anglo-Norman Studies* viii (1986), 190.

them worth feeing, and such men were careful not to commit themselves in this way. They were the patrons: those paying them were the clients. 'Thus were trusted royal servants courted throughout the later middle ages', observed McFarlane.[46]

There are parallels here in the feeing of the intimates of other great men, such as Sir Robert Holand, chamberlain of Thomas Earl of Lancaster and in the many fees accumulated by estate officials, lawyers and judges. The 4th Earl of Northumberland feed Henry VII's councillor Reynold Bray and Thomas Butler, Earl of Ormonde, chamberlain to the queen;[47] and his son feed Mr Heneage and Mr Page, respectively gentleman usher and chamberlain to Cardinal Wolsey. Fees were not the only forms that such rewards could take. Clerks could be presented to livings, like Edward I's Chief Justice, Ralph Hengham, and his grandson's chancellor William of Wykeham. Somewhat earlier such rewards could take the form of grants of fiefs, like those accrued by the new men of Henry I and other royal intimates, who were certainly not expected to become primarily dependants of such tenants-in-chief. Later in the period leading royal ministers like William Cecil, Lord Burghley, his son Robert Earl of Salisbury, and Henry Howard, Earl of Northampton made fortunes from the payments made for them to exercise their influence with the monarch; so indeed did the Cecils' own secretary, Sir Michael Hickes, for swaying his masters. How ambiguous was this relationship when Cecil and his rival Essex became heads of factions made up of those simultaneously looking to the favourable exercise of their influence and backing them in politics![48] Essex forced people to choose between support or opposition; his earlier counterparts, the Younger Despenser and William Catesby, pressurised others into granting them fees. Such rewards need not, of course, take the

46. McFarlane, *England*, p. 30.
47. J.R. Maddicott, 'Thomas of Lancaster and Sir Robert Holland: A Study in Noble Patronage', *EHR* lxxxvi (1971); Hicks, pp. 379–80.
48. J. Hurstfield, *Freedom, Corruption and Government in Elizabethan England* (1973), pp. 142, 151–2; A.G.R. Smith, *Servant of the Cecils* (1977), pp. 55–80, esp. pp. 68–70; L.L. Peck, *Northampton* (1982), ch. 4.

form of fees; grants of office, such as stewardships, were commonplace. Whilst these may often have been mere sinecures, they could be used by the new-found officer to add the land, tenants and local authority of the donor to himself. Great men like the Yorkist Lords Hastings, Howard and Herbert or Henry VIII's earls of Essex and Shrewsbury accumulated stacks of stewardships, principally from religious houses, and added their authority to their own.

If fiefs came to be held in perpetuity and annuities were commonly for life, both feudal and bastard feudal lords paid for short-term or once only services. Besides indentures of retainer there survive indentured contracts for building bridges, chantries and tombs. Priests, building craftsmen, and labourers were commonly hired by the day, servants in husbandry by the year. Such temporary arrangements applied even to military service: kings and feudal lords hired mercenaries and Edward I laid off some of his military household as surplus to his needs. Indentures of war were used to recruit retainers for particular campaigns. Often, perhaps usually, those concerned were short-term additions to the lord's connection of those not hitherto in his service. Indentures could be used to add to the obligations of the retainer or to define more precisely the military arrangements. Contracts made for a particular purpose for a particular term need not have permanently extended the ranks of any connection.

. . .

LIVERY

Liveried retainers were clad in a distinctive uniform that marked them out as the men of a particular lord. Thus the household of Richard Duke of York wore blue-and-white livery and those of his son Clarence wore green. Livery served to identify retainers individually in peace and war and to make an impressive showing when all were gathered together in a household, as an escort, retinue of war, or on other occasions. To wear a lord's livery implied that lord's support, promised protection against one's enemies, and perhaps also emboldened the wearer to break the law. To have taken a lord's robes 'was a sign that you were one of his men'.[49] Uniform uniform had long reinforced the corporate identity and common purpose of the Black Monks – it was indeed a natural consequence of the bulk purchases of a great institution – and was adopted by religious orders of other colours, the russet-clad Lollards, and London's livery companies. Isolated examples of liveried retainers are recorded in the twelfth century, in 1154 x 1162, and the practice was apparently commonplace by 1218, when a northern bandit was reported to be buying cloth in bulk for his 15 accomplices 'as if he had been a baron or an earl'.[50] Later livery was supplemented or even supplanted by badges, perhaps first under Edward III: with his badge of the white hart Richard II was conforming to contemporary practice. During the Wars of the Roses we hear of the falcon and fetterlock of Richard Duke of York, the Stafford knot, Warwick the Kingmaker's bear and ragged staff, the white swan of Henry VI's son Prince Edward in the 1450s, and the white boar of Richard III. For the 1475 expedition to France all captains down to esquires had their badges. Such badges were worn by the Yorkist army at the first battle of St Albans in 1455, so Gregory's Chronicle says, 'that every man might know his own fellowship by his livery'. Presumably the Earl of Oxford's star with streams would not have been mistaken for Edward IV's sunburst at the battle of Barnet in 1471 had everybody been wearing livery as well as badges.[51] That they were not was presumably because the warring companies contained many who were outside the ranks of those normally liveried and who were enrolled for hostilities only.

All types of retainer received livery: members of the lord's family and household; estate officers, like those of the countess of Aumale in 1261–64;[52] lawyers and clerics; extraordinary retainers; and tenants. Often there were

49. Holmes, p. 59. For the significance and symbolism of livery, see also N. Saul, 'The Commons and the Abolition of Badges', *Parliamentary History* ix.ii (1990), 302–15.
50. Bean, p. 145; M.A. Hicks, '1468 Statute of Livery', *Historical Research* lxiv (1991), 21.
51. P.W. Hammond, *Battles of Barnet and Tewkesbury* (Gloucester 1990), p. 77.
52. English, *Lords of Holderness*, p. 232.

different quantities and qualities of cloth according to different ranks of retainer. All these groups feature in the 130 names on the Courtenay livery roll of the Earl of Devon in 1384–85 and the 143 of that of the lady of Clare a generation earlier.[53] The careful budgeting, bulk purchases, and precise accounting needed to cater for 130 or 143 regular recipients did not leave stocks of spares for casual distributions. Lords did give liveries casually – to one another, as a compliment, for example – but not very many. It was not so much the livery that created a relationship, but the livery that recognised a tie that already existed. The steward of the household was more securely bound to the earl, for example, than the canons of Exeter or royal serjeants at law. The number of liveried retainers could be easily extended in time of crisis to include those with few or no ties on a temporary basis, perhaps more commonly through distribution of badges than of gowns: thus in 1454 Humphrey Duke of Buckingham was reported to have made 2,000 Stafford knots 'for what end your wit will construe'.[54] The intended recipients were probably Stafford tenants. The badges that survive, which are valuable jewels, must always have been exceptional: gowns and badges were a cheap way of retaining and one that did not incur long-term commitments, and hence were popular with lords of limited means. The statutes of livery that sought from 1390 to prevent gifts of livery to those below the gentry were not wholly successful in peacetime; during civil war illegal livery was commonplace. Probably livery was usually given to those already bound to the donor, but possession cannot *prove* such ties; about 1500, servants who were dismissed kept their livery and sometimes used it to cloak their crimes.

. . .

SERVANTS AND WELL-WILLERS

The modern historian can never pigeonhole all the dependants of any aristocrat to his household, extraordinary retinue, administration, or as councillors or liverymen.

53. Holmes, pp. 58–9; McFarlane, *Nobility*, p. 111.
54. Myers, *EHD*, p. 272.

The evidence is never exhaustive and there are always members of these categories known only through other kinds of service. Many, moreover, served in other ways. Every card index of the retinue of every magnate contains additionally feoffees, attorneys, witnesses, servants, creditors and suppliers. For some people, it merely supplements and amplifies unambiguous contracts and commitments, but for others it is everything. The evidence of the past is always imperfect: the perfect source is a delusion. To ignore such data impoverishes the study; to employ it requires interpretation and judgement and risks speculation hard to justify.

All aristocrats had feoffees or trustees, to whom their lands were enfeoffed and whose duty it was to pay the revenues and convey the estates to whomsoever the beneficiary wished, often himself, even after his death. The control of such vital resources implied confidence, not least because the law did not make it easy to enforce the conditions of the feoffment, and so historians have commonly regarded feoffees as committed retainers. Some were, of course; others were kinsfolk; yet others were national notables, mere figureheads who lent weight to the panel; commonly a mere handful of committed administrators or lawyers did the work. Among all Margaret Lady Hungerford's feoffees, including an archbishop, Warwick the Kingmaker, bishops and earls, it was the relatively obscure John Mervyn and Gregory Westby on whom she relied; likewise it was William Berkeswell, dean of Warwick, and Thomas Hugford and Nicholas Rody, mere esquires, who for forty years fulfilled the terms of an Earl of Warwick's will. Again, it was two esquires, William Paston and Henry Robson, and a clerk, Simon Baxter, who kept their faith with Elizabeth Countess of Oxford.[55] The most eminent feoffees could be the most anxious to shrug off the responsibility when difficulties arose.

So too with witnesses to deeds, wills, etc. Given the central importance of land and the need to secure one's title against rivals, did not every aristocrat choose the witnesses with the utmost care from those on whom he could rely? Indeed, should not such decisions carry greater weight

55. Hicks, chs 9, 16, 19.

than mere indentures of retainer or grants of fees?[56] Perhaps: though witnesses were no longer required to warrant or guarantee the transaction. Moreover, they did not have to sign or seal it in person – did not even have to be present, for it could be circulated if necessary – and may not even have known the role that they supposedly performed. People witnessed one another's deeds. To do so implies compatibility: it need not necessitate a firm commitment or allegiance, even among equals, still less a breach with anyone else. Witnessing wills was a commonplace duty that all performed. It need mean no more.

So too with those called servants by others, who called themselves servants, or acted on behalf of aristocrats as intermediaries. Such usage could mean anything or nothing: 'in the fifteenth century the word "servant" was used by the member of one class to express deference to a member of a higher class and does not signify an employer–employee relationship'.[57] Such a category covers everyone from important officials to mere well-willers, to those so titled from employment to those who merely complimented a lord, like those equals who flattered him by wearing his livery.

All such material is evidence of *association*, not commitment. It demonstrates that feoffees, witnesses, servants and well-willers came of the same society, may indeed have known one another, perhaps that they were not at dangerous enmity. By itself, it need mean no more. Some may have made a commitment: many, perhaps most, had not. To make full sense of that data, we need unequivocal evidence of service in household, retinue, administration or livery, which so seldom survives. Historians cannot manage without this data; but they must recognise its weakness, avoid exaggerating its importance – still less rationalise it into the principal bastard feudal bond – and remain ever cautious. By itself such data is always

56. M.C. Carpenter, 'The Duke of Clarence and the Midlands: A Study in the Interplay of Local and National Politics', *Midland History* xi (1986), 24.
57. N.F. Blake, *William Caxton and English Literary Culture* (1991), p. 10.

second best. Round every lord, as we shall see, there were those who aspired to service and those who deferred without being retained. They had not, however, made a binding commitment to him, nor he to them. But, as we shall see, lords hoped for and locally dominant lords secured political and military commitment from many whom they had not retained.

. . .

TOTALITY

All varieties of Bastard Feudalism contributed to a single totality: a connection that served the lord's particular needs. Such needs were never satisfied solely by indentured retainers. Extraordinary retainers, whether tenants by knight service or annuitants, were never the core of the connection, whether in peace or war. That was the role of the household: those with whom the lord lived, who provided not just for his bodily and intellectual sustenance, but much of his administrative and military needs as well. Always to hand, the household comprised a substantial force of combatants, sufficient for most purposes, particularly against lesser men; given time, the lord's estates could supply numbers available from no other source. The central administration, once no more than additional functions taken on by those about the lord, became non-resident, professionalised at the top and thus increasingly independent, and politicised at manorial level. Estate administrators, like extraordinary retainers, were valued both for their own service and for that of their own households and tenantry, to which could be added those merely liveried and, in the most ideal circumstances, the service of servants, well-willers and associates. If the household was the core and the tenantry were the rank-and-file, neither were the equal man for man of the aristocrats, who were better trained, better armed, and were the essential middle managers or company commanders. Such issues of quality and reliability are treated in the next chapter.

Chapter 3

QUANTITY AND QUALITY

Power and influence in feudal and bastard feudal societies derived ultimately from the manpower that lords could effectively deploy. How much manpower is obviously fundamental: those with more, it must be deduced, had an advantage over those with less. However, not all retainers were of the same type. Lords had many different needs, which were served by different categories of men. Scenarios ranged not just from the battlefield to the parliament chamber, but to the kitchen, the council chambers of king and lord, the tournament, the counting house and the lawcourt. Furthermore, the identity and status of such men, the nature of their contracts, and their relative importance changed over time. In spite of all the continuities, bastard feudal connections altered radically between 1150 and 1500, let alone 1150 and 1650. To refine the initial point, it was the number of retainers *in the relevant categories* that determined each lord's capacity for an impressive turnout on any specific occasion. Even that refinement is insufficient: because the numbers alone in each category were not the only factor. Many a great connection failed to meet expectations. The potential turnout of tenants in a Tudor list was probably never entirely fulfilled. Our concern must therefore be with *effective numbers* – with the ties that delivered the intended results – and to identify other influences that could maximise or minimise the actual turnout.

This chapter also considers a range of factors that affected the fulfilment of bastard feudal obligations. The particular circumstances of each case, such as the arrest of a lord or pre-emptive countermeasures, are postponed until later. The influences examined here are locality, tenure, loyalty, and heredity. Did Bastard Feudalism vary with geography? Were there regional variations? Were all varieties of Bastard Feudalism equally binding? Or is there justification for the supposition that households and tenants were particularly stable and loyal and extraordinary retainers especially flighty? Did it matter whether the tie was newly forged, of long standing, or even hereditary? Many historians have identified the most formidable connections with extensive estates, compact lordships, and long association between lords and retainers. How valid are such generalisations and, if valid, how can we then explain the meteoric rise of such effective new affinities as those of William Marshal (d. 1219) and William Hastings (d. 1483)? Were Marshal and Hastings representative, a-typical, or recurrent phenomena; exceptions that prove the rule, compatible or incompatible with conventional Bastard Feudalism? This chapter seeks the answers.

. . .

QUANTITY

So power derived from command over men. In the feudal era, this was often attributed principally to a lord's enfeoffed knight; under Bastard Feudalism, to those the lord 'could recruit *among the gentry*' [my italics].[1] With the almost unique exception of J.M.W. Bean, it is agreed that these gentry, whether feudal tenants, indentured retainers or merely feed men, were themselves landholders residing *outside* the households of their lords.[2] To understand the nature and assess the strength of any connection therefore requires the identification and categorisation of the individual retainers. Often the result is very scanty, as for Aymer Earl of Pembroke (d. 1324), yet assumes without question that 'the permanent basis . . . was composed of men who had made contracts with him for longterm service'[3] because this was what happened in

---

1. Stenton, p. 60; for what follows, see Pugh, p. 101.
2. 'In peace and war the retainer formed part of the lord's household', Bean, p. 55.
3. J.R.S. Phillips, *Aymer de Valence, Earl of Pembroke, 1307–24* (Oxford 1972), 255.

the better documented retinues. But is this assumption valid? Although exceptionally large, the indentured retinues of John of Gaunt and William Lord Hastings have nevertheless remained the model against which others are measured. They were similar in kind to other retinues however different their scale. Such a presumption underlies the work of Holmes for example, who noted that contracts alone provide only 'a very incomplete picture of the Mortimer following' and yet was obliged to base his analysis of fourteenth-century retaining on contracts and fees granted by a handful of the better documented magnates. Their retinues proved, hardly surprisingly, to be similar but smaller than Gaunt's.[4] The numbers of gentry retained are therefore generally accepted as a measure of the relative power of different magnates.

However, the numbers of such gentry were never enormous. If there were ever real knights to match 7,525 knights fees, they cannot have sufficed for foreign war or for both armies in a civil war. The 214 knights due from the earldom of Cornwall and the $127\frac{1}{2}$ from the honour of Clare, still less the 20 of the Count of Aumale, by themselves were insufficient men to dominate politics, particularly when dispersed upon their estates. So, too, in the bastard feudal era. The 'numbers [of indentured retainers] were never, in all probability, very large', observed N.B. Lewis.[5] Jones and Walker have found altogether only about 150 indentures of retainer for all late medieval aristocrats apart from those of Gaunt and Hastings.[6] So, too, with annuities for life. Only 20 are known for Humphrey Earl of Hereford (d. 1373) and 16 for Edmund Earl of March (d. 1381). There were no more: 'There are frequent mentions of payment in the Mortimer accounts but I know of none which adds any names to this list'. Nor were these figures exceptional. McFarlane doubted whether indentured retainers were ever numerous, suggesting fees normally ran at 10

4. Holmes, ch. 3, esp. p. 63.
5. N.B. Lewis, 'Organization of Indentured Retainers in 14th-Century England', *TRHS* 4th ser. xxvii (1945), 30.
6. I am grateful to Professor Jones for this information. For what follows, see Holmes, pp. 60n, 70.

per cent of annual income, which Pugh confirmed from a cross-section of noble tax returns to the income tax of 1436. Lord Tiptoft had granted only £50 in life annuities out of an income of £1,098, Lord Talbot £27 to four individuals out of £1,205, and Lord Beaumont only £8 to three people from £733. Even when vying for power, Humphrey Duke of Gloucester was paying only £280 in fees, less than 10 per cent of his annual income; only two peers were paying more.

> The cost of life annuities granted before 1436 by Humphrey, duke of Gloucester, and 13 other peers hardly suggests that the English nobility as a class was spending too much on retainers in the generation before the Wars of the Roses.

Other evidence for other peers shows that the Duke of Buckingham in 1447–48 had 37 annuitants who cost him £452 a year – no more than 130 retainers of all kinds in total – and the Duke of York feed only 14 in Wales in 1443 at a cost of £170, thus depending for his influence on English politics on 'a small group of devoted followers'. Only 9–10 per cent of the revenues of the Earl of Kent in 1467–68 were spent on extraordinary fees. In such a context, the much higher level of retaining of the Percies and of the Nevilles – northern magnates subsidised by the crown to defend the Scottish borders – look truly exceptional. Whether or not the fee was 'outmoded' by 1441, as declared by Professor Compton Reeves and discussed below,[7] it was never common and therefore was *not* the most important type of retaining.

Such overwhelming evidence demonstrates that extraordinary retainers needed supplementing for many purposes; and it casts doubt on the importance and prevalence of payment for service. It also forces one to ask whether all gentry belonged to a retinue. During the feudal era, such a question was a contradiction in terms. Everybody had a lord and most held land of him, albeit often directly of the king. To be a knight was to serve

7. Pugh, pp. 101–9; A.C. Reeves, 'Some of Humphrey Stafford's Military Indentures', *Nottingham Medieval Studies* xvi (1972), 86; *Grey of Ruthin Valor*, ed. R.I. Jack (Sydney, Australia 1965), p. 56.

a lord. Yet there were also landless knights. New men like William Marshal founded affinities independently of feudal tenure. For the bastard feudal era, tenure alone cannot be evidence of lordship and service, and it is impossible to demonstrate everybody's affiliations. Holmes recognised the importance of the question and responded with a caution borne of profound acquaintance with the evidence: it is 'scarcely ever possible to say with certainty that a man was *not* retained'.[8] Increasing study has shown just how many gentry there were to retain – 500, for example, in Cheshire. Given the uneven distribution of noble estates, the virtual absence of nobles from some shires, the small proportion of land they held, and the low level of fees they granted, it is logical to argue that not all gentry can have been retained. In fourteenth-century Gloucestershire Dr Saul found independent gentry 'outside the embrace of bastard feudalism' and in Sussex he found others 'independent of any formal ties with the nobility'; 'it may be fair to guess that nearer two-thirds than one-half of the gentry were retained in this period'. So, too, in mid-fifteenth-century Suffolk there lived a substantial independent squire in John Hopton. The Stafford indentures were 'a rare Cheshire example of the system of retaining. . . . It can be argued that the lack of a noble presence in Cheshire saved the county from the worst excesses of bastard feudalism'.[9]

Such judgements from silence have not been universally accepted. The reverse can be argued for Hopton and, as Dr Christine Carpenter observed,

> The trouble with 'independent gentry' is that they only remain independent until evidence turns up to link them to a magnate affinity. Two of the Gloucester men for whom Saul failed to find a lord . . . have been found by Julian Turner . . . to be linked to Despenser during the 'Despenser tyranny' of the 1320s.

8. Holmes, p. 78.
9. N. Saul, *Knights and Esquires* (Oxford 1981), esp. ch. 3; N. Saul, *Scenes from Provincial Life* (Oxford 1986); C. Richmond, *John Hopton* (Cambridge 1981); D. Clayton, *The Administration of the County Palatine of Chester 1442–85* (Chetham Soc. 3rd ser. xxxv 1990), pp. 72, 215.

Where hard evidence of commitment is lacking, it can be supplemented by evidence of association.[10] Even so, the statistical argument is difficult to fault. If every one of 37 counties had 500 gentry or more like Cheshire, then each of the 50 or so adult peers needed to retain ten or more times more gentry than those of 1436 and to average 400 per head. We can be sure that they did not. The statistical evidence implies that there were many gentry who were not retained by members of the nobility.

This discussion of the quantity of retaining, however, has overlooked a number of fundamental points.

First of all, both sides have ignored how Bastard Feudalism stretched down the social scale. It was not only the lay tenants-in-chief and the parliamentary peerage who retained the gentry, but also bishops, religious houses, boroughs, the honorial barons and other gentry. Such leading county gentry as the Stonors, Pastons, Plumptons, Vernons, Staffords of Grafton and even John Hopton employed other gentry and indeed those below them. Lords in a position to retain the 500 gentry of Cheshire were not merely the peerage, but the crown as earl of Chester, Chester city and abbey, and the 500 gentry of Cheshire. All could have been retained; the statistical argument does not work and Cheshire was not immune from Bastard Feudalism. *Perhaps* they were not all retained: in the sixteenth century, as the number of gentry explodes, possibly surely becomes probably and eventually certainly.

Secondly, all parties assume that all such retainers were bound by the same bonds and that retainer inhibited independence. Of course, it could; equally it need not. At one extreme, for instance, the learned counsel was retained for law not war, and exclusive commitments were seldom intended or implied. The nature and level of commitment is discussed below.

Thirdly, such calculations ignore other forms of retainer, especially membership of the household. The 130 retainers of the first Stafford Duke of Buckingham do not include the 100 or so members of his household.

10. M.C. Carpenter, 'Law, Justice and Landowners in Late Medieval England', *Law and History Review* i (1983), 206n.

Aristocratic households, as we have already seen, were always numerous and Dr Mertes identifies a 'great increase in average household numbers from the 1380s and throughout the fifteenth century'. If Earl Warenne had a household of only 35 in 1235, probably an underestimate, 'by 1350–80 the average size of an earl's household had increased to about eighty [and] by the 1450s the average household of an earl numbered upwards of 200, an increase of more than 100 per cent since the period 1350–80'. Members of the household of John of Gaunt numbered 115 in 1381 and 150 by the 1390s, of George Duke of Clarence 399 in 1468, and of the last Duke of Buckingham, 157.[11] Whilst the evidence is scanty, too scanty to accept Mertes' generalisations without question, it is clear that most noblemen spent considerably more on their households than on annuities: in the fourteenth century half the total, whilst in the early sixteenth century 'most peers spent between one-third and two-thirds of their income on the household'. Henry VIII's earls of Worcester and Essex spent respectively £250 out of £1,150 and £275 out of £921.[12] There was scarcely any difference between the lesser nobility and top gentry: thus Sir John Howard's household of 70 cost £500 of his £850 in the mid-1460s, whilst Sir John Scott had 60 in his household at Nettlestead under Henry VII, and Sir Thomas Lovell 93 in 1523. The greatest spent most – Humphrey Duke of Buckingham *c.* £2,400 in the 1450s, John of Gaunt between £5,767 in 1376–7 and £7,000 in 1392–93, and Clarence £4,500,[13] – but they had more to spend. Not only did the great have larger households, but they had proportionately more left over for other things. Household expenditure, it seems, took priority. And far more men and probably far

11. Mertes, pp. 11, 135, 186–7; Walker, p. 11; Hicks, *Clarence*, p. 164; see above.
12. S. Gunn, 'Henry Bourchier, Earl of Essex (1472–1540)', in Bernard, *Nobility*, pp. 134, 148; W.R.B. Robinson, 'Patronage and Hospitality in Early Tudor Wales: The Role of Henry, Earl of Worcester, 1526–49', *BIHR* li (1978), 23.
13. P. Fleming, 'Household Servants of the Yorkist and Early Tudor Gentry', *Early Tudor England*, ed. D. Williams (Woodbridge 1987), p. 21; Walker, p. 18; Hicks, *Clarence*, p. 2.

more gentry were retained through the household than through extraordinary fees. The household was omnipresent; annuitants and liverymen were extraordinary, summoned and inflated when required. They and their own followers, though important, were supplementary. And besides them were the administrators, the lawyers, and the tenants who maximised the numbers: tens, hundreds for some gentry, sometimes thousands, tens of thousands in the far North.

And fourthly, it was not necessary to be retained to operate within the embrace of Bastard Feudalism, any more than it was necessary to be literate to live in a literate society.

Probably only a minority of gentry were retained by noblemen and probably most of those were attached to the household rather than by annuities and contracts. Everywhere they were in a minority: in the lord's household, in his mounted escort, and in his retinue of war. That is not to belittle the gentry, but to place them in context. There cannot have been many who served no lord, whether members of the parliamentary peerage or the greater gentry, and few also who had not other gentlemen in their own service. They had a rarity value, were distributed between many different retinues, and were most highly valued as the level of their fees testifies. As individuals they came first in status, were better educated and trained, were more valuable in ceremonial and politics, and more effective in war. The chroniclers were representative of their time when they named only the knights and other gentry from the crowd, for a lord's worship depended more on followers of independent standing than on mere numbers. In most contexts quantity was tempered by quality. Only occasionally was everyone required and the tenantry turned out in force. Even then, it was the gentry who took the lead, advising their lord, commanding their own sub-retinues, and directing their lord's own men. However small in numbers, expensive and hence sparingly employed, gentry were essential to all lords. Hence it was not their presence or absence, still less that of those outside the household, that distinguished the power of the magnates from the rest.

. . .

CHRONOLOGY

Within individual retinues, there was a natural tendency for numbers to increase. Inevitably menials and retainers aged and became less effective and new blood was needed. Lords were understandably reluctant to alienate even superannuated gentry or to consign old servants to penury: perhaps that was why Cardinal Beaufort at St Cross, Walter Lord Hungerford at Heytesbury, and Edward IV at Windsor put time-expired dependants in almshouses. An old lord's death often broke the continuity, whether or not his heir was of age and anxious to retrench. Enfeoffment had been a gradual process that ultimately provided more service than required by the king; rolls of feed men grew and probably livery rolls too. Such conclusions must be tentative: it is only rarely that data reveals clear trends and lets a plan be detected and a lord's strategy emerge. Walker identifies several stages in the evolution of John of Gaunt's retinue, reflecting the stages in his career: as younger son; as military commander in France; as pretender to the crown of Castile; and as elder statesman, perhaps with half an eye on the English succession. Changes are apparent in the connections of Warwick the Kingmaker after he entered his paternal inheritance and of Charles Duke of Suffolk when transferred by Henry VIII from East Anglia to Lincolnshire. Royal policy explains why William Lord Hastings' indentured retainers date so overwhelmingly from Edward IV's second reign. His fall offered opportunities to others. Restoration to his family inheritance and competition with Gloucester help explain how and why the 4th Earl of Northumberland recruited so rapidly after his succession in 1469, focused on Northumberland and the East Riding from 1474, and expanded into the rest of Yorkshire and Cumberland from 1485. Several specific reasons explain the nine Stafford indentures of 1441–51 and Warwick's indentures of April 1462. Richard Duke of York's role in political crises help explain why he was recruiting in 1448–53 and again in 1458–60, as other magnates apparently were; Richard's indentures reveal his dynastic ambitions by failing to reserve the allegiance due to the king.

Such fine-tuning is important within all periods in response to specific circumstances. Changes in the character of retinues over the period 1150–1650 certainly occurred and are obvious in the long term, however difficult to detect over shorter spans of time. Subinfeudation was largely completed by 1166 and had ceased to be significant long before its abolition in 1290. Given that military service was seriously weakened by 1200, it must have been replaced by other ties, but only isolated fees and related devices are recorded for the twelfth century and the earliest surviving fully fledged indenture dates only from 1277, when the retaining of professional lawyers and administrators was already commonplace. It still seems likely that indentures and fees were stimulated by the wars of Edward I. Indentures, fees, and livery were common to all great magnates in the fourteenth century. This was the era when McFarlane, in retrospect, located the age of unbridled livery: a judgement still unsubstantiated. Anyway, it was restricted by the legislation in 1390–1429 that confined extraordinary retaining to peers making lifetime contracts with fellow aristocrats. Illegal livery persisted, but never again on a significant scale. Outside the north of England and the mid-century crises, extraordinary retaining and indentured retaining became ever more modest and had almost disappeared when abolished by parliamentary statute in 1468: that the crown paid Lord Hastings and commanded the marcher wardens to retain makes these genuine, but shortlived, exceptions. Dunham was wrong to use Hastings' indentures as evidence of a move from payment for service to mere good lordship.[14] Extraordinary retaining under the Tudors was undertaken in response to royal licences and not at the initiative of lords, who had no wish to indulge even when it was legal, as in 1509–23. Most of those retained were probably tenants rather than gentry. Lawyers, as always, continued to receive fees.

This trend could indicate a decline in Bastard Feudalism if late medievalists had been correct in their emphasis on the centrality of extraordinary retaining, but, as we have seen, they were not. There were also the household

14. Hicks, ch. 12; '1468 Statute of Livery', *Historical Research* lxiv (1991), 15–28.

and estate offices. Evidence of expenditure and house-hold numbers here is patchy and valid comparisions are difficult to make across time. Mertes is not alone in argu-ing for a substantial increase in household size in the later middle ages and probably there was increasing retainer through the household of those formerly feed outside. The numbers and the pay of estate offices held by gentry grew in the late fifteenth and early sixteenth centuries, in the latter case deliberately to inflate the retinue. As extraordinary retaining and livery diminished, they were evidently supplanted by employment in the household or as estate officials: the size of households and the number of administrators both seem to have been increasing. Tenants of course remained available at times of crisis. Such changes in the *kind* of retaining make it very difficult to measure trends in the *amount*, but it seems unlikely that Bastard Feu-dalism as a whole was declining in late medieval England. What happened after 1500 is discussed in chapter 8.

It is not clear why extraordinary retainers gave way to enlarged households and estate administrations. Such changes could be in response to parliamentary restriction, as suggested by Mertes,[15] but seem instead to run ahead of such acts. Perhaps lords preferred the closer ties and clearer commitments provided by the household and the precise obligations of office to the vaguer understand-ings of annuitants. Maybe multiple retaining, whereby retainers commonly held several fees, did make them increasingly unreliable as late medievalists have often suggested, and prompted magnates to abandon this mode of recruitment. Alternatively, retainer through the house-hold, particularly if personnel were rotated, may have been a more economic and certain way of securing ser-vice at a time when income from land was falling. Firm answers will have to await the results of more research.

.   .   .

LOCALITY

Bastard Feudalism varied not only from time to time but from place to place. If, like Professor Laslett's 'World We Have Lost', it presumed a set of values and relationships

15. Mertes, p. 126.

that were essentially aristocratic and rural, yet everywhere account had to be taken of towns, perhaps 760 in total and dozens per county in 1640.[16] Most were tiny, with populations hundreds rather than thousands strong, yet every county contained a couple with significant populations, often imposing walls and stone-built structures and prosperous and self-conscious political élites, that economically dominated surrounding rural hinterlands. Were they 'largely untouched by Bastard Feudalism', as Dr Linda Clark has argued for 1377–1422?[17] Certainly the inhabitants did not hold by knight service; they did not reside in noble households, nor were many in receipt of fees or liveried, indeed could not be legally retained in these ways after 1390. Fifteenth-century kings frequently ordered towns not to allow lords to retain or livery their inhabitants, cultivated towns as sources of money and manpower, and directed their activities frequently and minutely. Many towns had rights of jurisdiction and managed their own affairs; an increasing number, from Bristol in 1373 to Scarborough in 1484, became county boroughs and thus free from the ministrations of the sheriffs of the shire.

Nevertheless town councils recognised the bastard feudal nature of society and participated in it, both as clients and patrons. They feed their own chaplains, lawyers and judges, as Exeter was already doing in 1342–43, other gentry, and they themselves were included in the calculations of the nobility. Many sought to control towns, to include them in their hegemonies, and clearly valued them as much as did the crown. Many towns, of course, were seigneurial boroughs, often, indeed, planted and still therefore dominated by lords. Some of the largest towns were still seigneurial, usually subject however to undying ecclesiastical corporations, such as Reading, St Albans and Bury St Edmunds;[18] some of the largest, like Salisbury and Hull, had been seigneurial

16. A. Everitt, 'The Market Towns', *Early Modern Town*, ed. P. Clark (New York 1976), p. 168.
17. L. Clark, 'Magnates and their Affinities in Parliaments of 1386–1421' [paper at Durham Colloquium, 1993].
18. Though the resulting relationships between lords and townsmen were notoriously stormy.

foundations. Nobles and gentry did sometimes retain or livery townsmen: for Lord Grey of Codnor (d. 1496) Nottingham was apparently essential to his local power and liverying of townsmen was an indispensable aspect of his influence.[19] Such key men at Newcastle and York as Robert Rodes and Thomas Wrangwish had close ties with Northumberland and Gloucester in the 1470s and 1480s in which mutual business interests, flattering social distinction, and even, perhaps, friendship played their part. Commonly, however, relations were more subtle: lords were important customers, seekers of credit, sources of patronage and mediation with other authorities, representatives of the crown locally, and the dominant local context within which towns plied their trade. However James Blount exercised his rule over Derby in the 1470s,[20] it was not by retaining the townspeople. We can see all this in the ubiquitous offerings of drink, fish, etc., and other marks of deference to lords, whether visiting or resident nearby, in all surviving urban chamberlains' accounts and in the corresponding gifts of bucks with which the recipients responded. It emerges in the appointment of aristocrats to urban office, often admittedly professional experts but increasingly including noblemen as honorific stewards, etc. Most parliamentary boroughs eventually succumbed in the fifteenth and sixteenth centuries to external representation by gentry. Often these MPs were carpetbaggers, without lasting local significance, yet most towns were susceptible, on occasion, to overwhelming external pressure. And the capacity to resist such crude intervention consistently displayed by the most independent mercantile élites did not mean, for example, that Richard Duke of Gloucester did not manage to dominate York in 1476–83.[21]

Feudalism and Bastard Feudalism, it has often been remarked, was stronger in frontier regions, like the bishopric of Hereford or the North in 1215–16, where knights had been settled, often late, in compact blocs with strategic

19. Cameron, 26.
20. Dunham, p. 127.
21. D.M. Palliser, 'Richard III and York', *Richard III and the North*, ed. R.E. Horrox (Hull 1986).

considerations in mind and where mutual interests were reinforced by continuing external threats from Welsh or Scots. The assumption of royal powers by marcher lords in the twelfth century inevitably gave them and their successors greater authority over their subjects. It was not in the dispersed honours of the midlands and the south, but in the compact lordships of the North that Feudalism best survived for James and Smith to find it. The Northerners looked first to the local lord – their feudal lord, near neighbour, the natural source of fees, office, and other forms of further advancement. Yet M.E. James, as we have seen, has argued that neo-feudal loyalty was not confined to peripheral backwaters like the North, but was also experienced in East Anglia and Sussex. But were there not nevertheless important differences? Loyalty itself will be discussed in the next section. From King John to Richard III, Richmondshire has been selected as a particular example of cohesive lordship.[22] What was it that made the North different from other peripheral areas?

One striking difference is the sheer number of men that northern magnates included in their retinue lists and were actually able to turn out, which are far beyond those known for other areas. This was not because there were more people in the North: the border counties and Yorkshire were among the less thickly populated shires in 1523 and 1377 and indeed earlier. Nor is it true that northern lords held a higher proportion of the land than their southern counterparts: that all did at all times is frankly impossible. It follows that northern lords included a higher proportion of total manpower in their connections than their southern counterparts: many were men who elsewhere were included in the county levies and the early modern militia. Potentially this could reach 100 per cent. It is revealing that in 1532, when requiring the 6th Earl of Northumberland 'to put in a readiness and retain of your tenants and servants the number of two hundred able men', Henry VIII continued:

22. J.C. Holt, *The Northerners* (1961), p. 49; A.J. Pollard, 'The Richmondshire Community of Gentry during the Wars of the Roses', *Patronage, Pedigree and Power in Later Medieval England*, ed. C.D. Ross (Gloucester 1979).

Signifying unto that forasmuch as the fewer of the inhabitants of Northumberland [that] be retained in the same
garrison, the stronger shall the country be as ye can
by your wisdom consider, our pleasure is therefore that
there be in no wise above two personages inhabitants of
Northumberland in every hundred of your said number
nor yet of the inhabitants of Cockermouth for disfurnish-
ing of those parts.[23]

Lords were able to do this because they were able
to employ their jurisdiction over men who were not
necessarily their tenants. Rachel Reid long ago stressed
how powerful and extensive were the county palatines
of Durham and Lancaster, the liberties of Hexhamshire,
North Durham, Allertonshire, Howdenshire, Tyndale
and so on, within which feudal and bastard feudal
lords alike exercised on the spot authority delegated
by the crown elsewhere.[24] Even outside the liberties, the
organising principle was not the manor but the lordship, often compact, privileged, and with feudal courts
capable of operating effectively much longer than seems
the case elsewhere. Formal certificates of homage were
frequently composed, preserved and locally registered
into the sixteenth century. And the proximity of the
Scots, the frequency of warfare, and the reliance by
marcher wardens and bishops of Durham on resources
from Yorkshire helped maintain the military potential
of their franchises. To which, of course, was added the
spending power conferred by royal wages as wardens,
reflected both in the exceptional level of fees granted by
the Percies and Nevilles in the mid-fifteenth century[25] –
the 1468 statute of livery allowed the wardens to retain
extraordinarily – and through the wages paid to those
who served. In 1463 Lord Montagu received £6,000
in wartime – probably six times his normal income –
and still £3,000 or double in peacetime. Even in 1488,
after wages had been substantially reduced, Henry VII

23. R.W. Hoyle, 'Letters of the Cliffords, Lords Clifford and Earls
of Cumberland, c. 1500–65', *Camden Miscellany* xxxi (1992), 39.
24. R. Reid, *King's Council of the North* (1919), ch. 1.
25. Pugh, p. 103; A.J. Pollard, 'The Northern Retainers of Richard
Nevill Earl of Salisbury', *Northern History* xi (1976), 52–68. For
what follows, see Hicks, '1468 Statute', 21.

expected the Earl of Northumberland to put 300 men and the Bishop of Durham another 200 into Berwick at the outbreak of war.[26]

It was thus easier for northern lords to deploy much larger numbers of men than their southern counterparts: hence the remarkable influence of the Middleham connection and of the Percies in the Wars of the Roses. How militarily effective they were against fully equipped hand trained troops on formal battlefields rather than against 'naked Scots' in sporadic fighting across the rugged border terrain is another issue.

.   .   .

LOYALTY AND FIDELITY

Numbers, trends and regional variations are all essential when studying Bastard Feudalism, but, by themselves, they are not enough. Beside effective numbers, we need to know about quality. A connection's strength also varied with the occasion, which is studied below in chapters 5–7, and according to their commitment. How far were retainers bound to their lord? How faithful and loyal were they? Under what circumstances, if any, did such fidelity fail? Did the fidelity or effective strength vary with connections or with the particular issues with which they were faced? These are fundamental issues that must be tackled, even though the practical evidence of commitment – turnout rates – is often lacking and at best patchy, and even though they raise imponderable issues rarely divisible from other factors.

The highest standards of fidelity were always expected from members of the household. The household was a family and its head was akin to a father. From at least 1260 living-in servants were equated with children; probably they already owed the unquestioning obedience and suffered the absolute paternal authority of their master assumed in early modern England. This is what post-medieval patriarchalism was all about. Such servants were represented in politics and controlled by their masters: an ancient notion traceable back through

26. Hicks, p. 381.

the lawbooks to Athelstan.[27] In extenuation of his treason against Edward IV, Sir Thomas Tresham pleaded his overriding loyalty to Henry VI as a member of his household, a plea that was accepted.[28] To betray one's master, like the household servants of the last Duke of Buckingham, was particularly heinous; to kill one's master or mistress was not mere murder, but petty treason: the *Laws of Henry I* specified so frightful a death 'that the pains of Hell would seem preferable' and by the fifteenth century they suffered the fiercesome penalties otherwise reserved for traitors against the king.[29] And it was obviously more difficult for members of the household resident with their lord and under his eye not to fulfil the military and other service that he demanded.

Such ties, observed Stenton, originated in that 'early phase of feudal society when the knights and officers of a great man stood alike under his immediate, personal authority'. Early twelfth-century garrisons of household knights, Orderic Vitalis repeatedly shows, took most seriously their obligation to hold out against overwhelming odds until authorised by their lord to surrender.[30] It was such household knights that the Norman baron enfeoffed with knights fees in what Victorian critics of Bastard Feudalism took to be the most binding of contracts. The knight did homage to his lord, swore fealty to him, and was invested with land by him: should his service falter, the enfeoffment was revoked. Here, surely, so it was argued, was the most solemn commitment by the tenant backed by the most effective of sanctions. And it worked. Not only, apparently, did such tenants and their heirs fulfil the various legitimate services required of them, but they also turned out for their lord. They did so against King John: 'Many knights simply followed their lords, for or against the king'. This was true of 30

27. A. Macfarlane, *Origins of English Individualism* (Oxford 1978), p. 150n; G. Schochet, *Patriarchalism in Political Thought* (Cambridge 1975), pp. 66, 82.
28. D.A.L. Morgan, 'The King's Affinity in the Polity of Yorkist England', *TRHS* 5th ser. xxiii (1973), 7.
29. J.G. Bellamy, *Law of Treason in Late Medieval England* (Cambridge 1970), pp. 225–31.
30. Stenton, p. 142.

out of 33 Mowbray tenants against the king and all those of the Earl of Chester for the king. Thus the whole county of Hereford followed the bishop of Hereford: 'They had rebelled when he rebelled and then made peace when he made peace'. Only three had not.

> They were the exceptions that proved the rule, for they achieved independence of the Bishop's faction only because they belonged to another. . . . The rebellion revealed broadly feudal characteristics in that the tie of tenure was still a powerful bond, strong enough in many cases to determine the actions of the tenants of the great magnates.[31]

The strength of the tie and incapacity of tenants to resist it was recognised even as late as the Barons Wars, when the Dictum of Kenilworth treated more favourably those rebels who had been fulfilling their obligations to their feudal lords.[32]

Generally, however, historians take a less absolute view of the efficacy of feudal ties. A comparison of lists of feudal tenants with those who actually fought, even allowing for patchy sources, demonstrates that not all turned out and that some supported other lords. Seigneurial authority was surely reduced from when, in the twelfth century, lords could no longer dispossess disobedient tenants or exact feudal incidents from those holding also of the king: henceforth tenants of the relatively well-documented ecclesiastical tenants-in-chief resisted military service with apparent impunity. Professor Painter considered that feudal ties were already seriously weakened. Moreover, the fractionalisation of knights fees and tenure by the same tenants of fees from different lords has been cited as a cause of decline by M.E. James in the sixteenth century, Professor Ross in the fifteenth, Professor Holt in the thirteenth, and Professor Painter in the twelfth. But this is to oversimplify. That fractional fees were created from the start and that lords bestowed fees on the tenants of others warns that such an explanation is insufficient.

31. S. Painter, *Studies in the History of the English Feudal Barony* (Baltimore 1943), p. 135; Holt, *The Northerners*, pp. 35–6; Prestwich, pp. 33–4.
32. Painter, *English Feudal Barony*, p. 129.

Already by 1135, prime loyalty and liege homage was due to the lord of whom a knight held his principal residence: a system which Stringer considers worked well in practice. Clearly whatever was expected of many recipients of secondary fees, it was not exclusive military service. If we merely compare the turnout of knights for any lord with the number enfeoffed, we are expecting more than was reasonable or ever intended.

So, too, evidently, with indentured retainers and feed men. It is wrong to say that a fee created merely one obligation among many and enjoyed no priority in determining the retainer's actions.[33] The classic indenture of retainer of the thirteenth and fourteenth centuries was not a casual commitment to be shrugged off with impunity. To Bean, it was a natural extension of service in the household – as enfeoffment must have been for feudal knights – and thus involved the same commitment.[34] Composed as the most formal of contracts, the indenture was sealed by both parties, cemented by oath, and reinforced by recognisances. That Sir John Paston, who received livery, prided himself on never being sworn to a lord demonstrates the extra commitment attached to such formal undertakings. Even he, we must presume, rated his faith as a knight – commonly invoked in Lord Hastings' indentures – and the consequent obligation of 'faithfulness' that James has explored two generations later.[35] That such indentures rather than mere grants of fees were so often registered on the royal patent roll indicates the solemnity of the contract: it was a commitment for the life of the retainer, extending beyond that of the lord, which even the lord's suzerain, the king, must respect. The commitment ran both ways: not only could the lord not fail to pay the fee, but the retainer could not fail to come when summoned, whatever the state of his family and business affairs. It was an overriding commitment that such lords as John of Gaunt in the fourteenth century and the Percies in the fifteenth did not fail to invoke. Often it required a landowner with

33. C. Richmond, 'After McFarlane', *History* lxviii (1983), 58.
34. Bean, p. 18.
35. Dunham, pp. 13, 27; James, pp. 53–4.

his own estate, household and family to reside with his lord. Such a commitment, however financially attractive, was only accepted after due consideration, in the light of other commitments material and intellectual, in the recognition that this one took priority and that failure to perform could result, at the least, in the revocation of the fee.

Yet feed men were often retained by more than one lord. As early as 1297, in his indenture with the Earl of Norfolk, Sir John Segrave was allowed to serve under other lords when the earl himself was not on campaign.[36] Where obligations to others were reserved, we must presume that the contracts could conflict and that the lord was satisfied with the residuary compatible service that he had bought. Such exclusion clauses were not common in indentures of retainer. Most probably this signifies that such indentures, like liege homage, normally conferred the retainer's primary loyalty; indeed, such contracts commonly committed him against everyone except the king. Also that the retainer was careful not to take on incompatible commitments. Indentures of retainer evolved over time and varied from case to case. Early indentures commonly focused on service in war, covering such items as replacement horses and the spoils of war. Some specify service in tournaments or in particular countries. Of the nine Stafford indentures, only two specify service abroad. More research is needed on the development of such documents. The variations remind us that the promise of a fee for life was a solemn commitment to the lord as well and that behind every indenture was not just a negotiation or bargain but also a purpose that the indenture satisfied. Sometimes, but not always, that purpose might be the military service of the retainer at all times, in peace and war. The diminishing military character of later indentures and the obscurity of those retained indicates declining interest in retainer for war. We misjudge retainers if we judge them by their absence on particular occasions. Those lords who in 1347 and 1358 expected their councillors

36. N. Denholm-Young, *Seignorial Administration in England* (Oxford 1937), pp. 167–8; see also M.A. Hicks, *Who's Who in Late Medieval England* (1991), p. 31.

to come when summoned lost their cases because counsel could be offered anywhere and carried no obligation to travel.[37] Sir William Skipwith, who lost his fee of 1433 because he failed to turn out for Richard Duke of York in 1460, is often cited to demonstrate that contracts were enforceable: since he was retained of *counsel*, however, he was surely unlucky? Auditors, receivers and lawyers served many men. Sometimes, perhaps, they made a binding tie and respected it, but that was not expected universally or even, perhaps, often.

Most feudal tenants and most indentured retainers were making a solemn and binding commitment with their lord, whose service could reasonably be exacted; it was the administrators, lawyers, and royal favourites who were exceptional. No military service could be expected; if received, it was a bonus. A lord's inability to refuse the succession, which left nothing to reciprocate, emasculated both feudal lordship and service almost everywhere. The outlying areas where compact lordships retained their vitality and homage was still solemnly certified into the sixteenth century were exceptions to the general rule. And yet homage still had meaning. Though Henry V allowed others to take fealty for him, he insisted that homage was rendered to himself; Edward IV's chamberlain still certified the homage of tenants-in-chief to chancery and the king himself exacted homage from feudal tenants, even a royal duke, to his second son, Richard, as Duke of Norfolk.[38]

Indentured retainer at first offered a more precise, targeted and enforceable service for those outside a lord's natural ambit. The best indentured retainers, the bachelors, served partly in the household and reinforced their contract with the more binding fidelity expected of household-men. Retaining to the household by indenture seems to have ceased in the late fourteenth century: perhaps because such men did not take on such obligations unless they conferred real authority and influence; more probably because such men became permanent members of

---

37. Bean, p. 15.
38. C.T. Allmand, *Henry V* (1992), pp. 358–9; Hicks, *Clarence*, p. 131.

the household serving on a rota and hence needed no indenture. As such ties were reinforced by household service, those who were genuinely extraordinary retainers, those resident outside their lord's household and never a part of it, were selected for more specific and limited reasons and felt freer to accept fees from all sides. Such men were surely less securely bound by their agreement: both McFarlane and Saul considered fourteenth-century contracts to be binding and fifteenth-century ones less so. If such fees were to be compatible, the service involved must have been restricted – perhaps highly specific. If it was not compatible, it was surely more advantageous to the retainer to neglect the incompatible obligation rather than to hazard the rest by his zeal. If such considerations caused such contracts to be less effective, they could explain the decline in number and ultimate disappearance of such fees, the tying of such rewards in future to specific duties in the household or on the estate, and the increasing proportion of fees that seem merely to have supplemented other service.

The household, extraordinary tenants and administrators had all bound themselves to their lord to perform certain services for certain rewards, whether specified or understood. They had entered into voluntary contractual commitments and the nature of such commitments determined the quantity, quality, reliability and exclusivity of their service. Their contracts determined how likely they were to accompany their lord into private or civil war. Such an argument cannot apply to agricultural tenants, whom medieval and Tudor lords confidently listed and apparently successfully deployed in internal war. Why and how could lords count on their military service? Medieval peasants commonly owed service as well as rent, but military service was never itemised alongside day-work, merchet or leyrwite in twelfth- and thirteenth-century custumals. Such services were commonly relaxed when demesnes were leased and villeins were *de facto* enfranchised in the late fourteenth and fifteenth centuries, yet military service continued to be expected. Not until the sixteenth century did leases start specifying military obligations and probably only then because peasants were coming to question the obligation;

Lord Bergavenny's mass liverying of his Kentish tenants after 1500 may have been an alternative response.
Although never explicitly stated, military service was apparently understood and exacted throughout our period
and tenants delivered the largest number of men of any
element of Bastard Feudalism.

Yet is this not very surprising? How could lords have
such expectations and why did their tenants perform? Is
it not a historical commonplace that lords exploited their
tenants and lived off their service, that lords and tenants
frequently clashed, and that there were frequent strikes,
riots and even rebellions that culminated in 1381 in the
Peasants Revolt, which was actually symptomatic of landlord–peasant relations? Given this neo-Marxist orthodoxy,
is not the capacity of lords to deploy their peasants militarily something of a paradox? 'This is not to deny that the
relationship between lord and tenant was "conflictual" ',
writes Dr David Carpenter.[39]

One possible explanation is coercion. Lords forced their
peasants to turn out for them. Warwick the Kingmaker
and the Bastard Fauconberg and the Yorkshire rebels in
1489 sought to recruit on pain of death. Giffard tenants in
1321–22 and Strange of Knockin tenants in 1403 claimed
that they rebelled under duress.[40] This certainly fits the
use of estate officers and the compilation of lists of those
liable. Commissions of array played an important part
in recruitment for Edward I's Scottish wars and during
the Wars of the Roses.[41] It was under false pretences,
seeking restoration as dukes, that Henry Bolingbroke and
Edward IV recruited so successfully in 1399 and 1471,
whilst Lord Grey of Ruthin in 1460, Clarence in 1471,
and the Stanleys in 1485 carried their men to the other side
with decisive results. What the study of peasant unrest has
shown is how effectively peasant communities could resist

---

39. D. Carpenter, 'The English Peasantry in Politics 1258–67', *P&P*
    136 (1992), 36.
40. S.L. Waugh, 'The Profits of Violence: The Minor Gentry in
    the Rebellion of 1321–22 in Gloucestershire and Herefordshire',
    Speculum lii (1977), 849–50; J.R. Maddicott, *Thomas of Lancaster
    1307–1322* (Oxford 1970), p. 309.
41. Prestwich, p. 107; A. Goodman, *The Wars of the Roses* (1981),
    pp. 137–44.

seigneurial exactions and the judicial and financial demands of the crown. How could they be compelled to fight against their will, particularly once they had been armed? – except, of course, when the lords had overwhelming force to hand. By itself, therefore, coercion is not enough.

Secondly, they served for pay. There is evidence for this from the twelfth to the seventeenth centuries, see chapter 7, but it is too scanty to support a generalisation and is not incompatible with paternalism or loyalty.

Seigneurial paternalism may have won the loyalty of the peasants. The noble class was expected to protect its tenants: somewhat more cynically, they had an interest in a monopoly of exploitation. Such sentiments were reinforced by the feasts some lords gave for their tenants and by the lands that were probably often leased at less than the market rent. Sir John Paston feared to 'lose his tenants' hearts'.[42] The counter-argument is often cited: that the drastic elevation of rents in the early Tudor period alienated tenants.[43] However, it is difficult to disagree with Professor Dyer, who rejects the notion that 'a few meals could overcome the aggression of the peasantry',[44] – providing, of course, that they were aggressive and the meals were few. That peasants were naturally deferential in the fifteenth to the eighteenth centuries is suggested by their appeals first to their aristocratic governors against famine and only thereafter, failing remedy, that they resorted to self-help, riot and rebellion.[45]

Perhaps we are mistaken in our neo-Marxist orthodoxy that lords and peasants were in natural opposition and that conflict was normal and inevitable? For Dr Barbara Harvey what is surprising is that lords did not exploit their tenants fully.[46] In practice lords did not exact their full rights, e.g. to all their tenants' chattels,

42. Bellamy, p. 46.
43. E.g. James, pp. 160–1, 163.
44. C. Dyer, *Standards of Living in the Later Middle Ages* (Cambridge 1989), p. 55.
45. E.g. *Rebellion, Popular Protest and the Social Order in Early Modern England*, ed. P. Slack (Cambridge 1984), esp. pp. 108–28; Hicks, ch. 22.
46. *Before the Black Death*, ed. B.M.S. Campbell (Manchester 1991), p. 18.

because it was not in their interests to do so. All manors, even before the Black Death, were largely administered by peasants themselves as elected officers and the homage jury, and it was they who defined the custom of the manor. If lords could override their wishes, they did not often do so. Friction did not occur on every manor or every year. It did not break down manorial administration or curtail the lord's income. As with tenants by knights service, the relationship was reciprocal, in which peasants accepted tenancies on terms which were generally performed and presumably therefore acceptable to themselves. And lords, so it appears, recognised the obligations proclaimed by both medieval preachers and Renaissance humanists to foster and protect the interests of their tenants, who accepted them naturally as social as well as tenurial superiors.

. . .

HEREDITY

Feudal and bastard feudal contracts were based on mutual advantage. Lords offered rewards and lordship for the service of vassals and retainers. Originally all such ties were personal: the ties that historians have traditionally regarded as strongest. But personal ties were always temporary, liable to be broken by the death of either party in an age of short lives and unexpected deaths, easily terminated when lord and man fell out. For many a household-man, the death of his lord entailed the dissolution of the household and termination of both service and reward. It was for such men in particular that fears of the future prompted additional contracts, alternative contracts, and the cultivation of reversionary interests that could dilute their existing commitment. Personal ties, in short, were not conducive to wholeheartedness. Casual rewards earned only casual and qualified loyalty, which neither party wanted. Often, however, the change was less abrupt, as the new lord was heir of the old, acquiring not only his resources, but also his commitments and contacts; he, too, needed to fulfil his *servitium debitum* and found it most convenient to accept tenants *in situ* or their heirs. Often, too, extraordinary retainers held their knights fees indefinitely or by inheritance or their annuities and offices for life. These were factors for stability. By making

93

contracts permanent and legally enforceable and thus rendering seigneurial favour automatic or involuntary, such longer terms could erode the reciprocal tie, turn homage and fealty into formalities, and deprive the contract of any force. Ultimately, of course, Feudalism degenerated into random fiscal exactions. So the happy medium, where lords were secure in their service and retainers in their future, lay between the purely personal and the wholly hereditary ties.

The longer relationships lasted, the stronger the commitment on both sides could become. Where the honour or lordship was compact and a natural geographical unit, where there remained mutual interest or external pressures such as defence, where patronage was still offered and lordship sought, then feudal and bastard feudal ties alike could be constantly renewed, and loyalty and obedience was automatic unless powerful forces dictated otherwise. What was rendered might then be the service due to the estate rather than to a specific individual or family, like that secured by King John's Bishop of Hereford or by those who had been granted the possessions of extinct families. The strongest and most durable relationships were those that were hereditary on both sides. Feudal historians have often commented on the force of hereditary ties.

> Naturally the sentimental solidarity of generations of allegiance was an enormous advantage. .... The honorial barons of the honour of Breteuil had lineages as old or almost as old as their lord's [and frequently] demonstrated their corporate loyalty to the house of Breteuil.

Thus they rebuffed Ralph de Gael in 1119–20 'for they favoured their previous lord, Eustace' and later prompted Count Robert to take Breteuil as the surname of his house in 'emphasising the continuity of its rule over the honour'. So, too, Earl David of Huntingdon counted on the hereditary connections of his vassals to his house. And Professor Holt writes of 'the complex bonds of association and common interest which were created by families living together for generations in the same environment and atmosphere'.[47]

47. D. Crouch, *The Beaumont Twins* (Cambridge 1986), pp. 105, 108–9, 110, 114; K.J. Stringer, *Earl David of Huntingdon 1152–1219* (Edinburgh 1985), p. 27; Holt, *The Northerners*, p. 36.

94

Such longstanding connections over several generations reinforced both lordship and service, identified vassals with more than the single lord, prompted each generation to look for advancement to the same family, to look beyond the current lord, and to transfer their loyalty automatically to the next heir; lords chose their men from families that had done them good service. 'In many cases', writes Bean, 'the choice of a lord was dictated by a family tradition built up over generations': comments echoed among others by Given-Wilson, Carpenter, Harriss, James and Coward.[48] The counterpart, not infrequently voiced, is that newcomers – like the new lord of Richmond honour in 1215 – could not count on the same commitment. William Mauduit, who had only recently entered his estate, 'would not at once have the loyalty from the tenants that his predecessor had received', remarks Prestwich.[49] Such an observation is not susceptible to proof, but it is a feeling shared by many feudal and bastard feudal historians, backed in each case with the few fragments of evidence that is all they could expect. Bean, Stone and myself are only three of those who mused when hereditary connections died or could no longer be established.[50]

Probably relatively few household members, annuitants or officers had no prior connection with their lords' estates or other retainers. Mertes has commented on the provincial character of many a household. George Duke of Clarence employed in his household Roger Harewell and Edmund Verney from West Midlands families hereditarily loyal to his duchess.[51] Generations of the same family served generations of the same family. Similarly, John of Gaunt inherited the retainers of Henry of Grosmont, 1st Duke of Lancaster (d. 1361): Sir Ralph Hastings, feed from Pickering by Grosmont, was still drawing his fee in 1391. Many of Grosmont's men descended from retainers

48. Bean, p. 188; C. Given-Wilson, *English Nobility in the Later Middle Ages* (1987), p. 95; G.L. Harriss, 'Introduction', in McFarlane, *England*, p. x; James, p. 2; Coward, p. 86; 'Debate', 187–8.
49. Prestwich, pp. 33–4.
50. Bean, pp. 226, 236; Stone, ch. V; M.A. Hicks, 'Career of George Duke of Clarence' (Oxford DPhil. thesis 1974), ch. 7.
51. Hicks, *Clarence*, pp. 151, 168–9.

of Earl Thomas (d. 1322) and many of Gaunt's served Henry IV and Henry V. Ralph Earl of Westmorland (d. 1425) passed retainers to his son, Richard Earl of Salisbury, whose men feed from Middleham transferred to his own son and granddaughter. The ideal of service to Stanleys 'in some families was passed on from father to son'.[52] Such instances can be multiplied for the gentry. Obviously continuity was normal for peasants on any estate.

Lords were proud of their lineage and anxious to maintain it. Thus Earl Thomas Beauchamp (d. 1369) re-enfeoffed his estates to maintain the male line, and his grandson, Earl Richard (d. 1439), remarried that he might have heirs male. Earl Richard further ordained that should his son Henry become a duke, he would retain the Warwick title, as indeed he did.[53] Such considerations lie behind many of the second marriages, entails, and disputed inheritances of late medieval England. Feudal lords characteristically founded monasteries in which they and their successors were to be buried and which were patronised also by their feudal vassals, like the de Clares and the tenants of the honour of Clare at Stoke by Clare (Suff.). This practice was emulated by their bastard feudal successors. If the Despensers were content to build their funerary chantries around the choir of the former de Clare abbey of Tewkesbury, the Montagus at Bisham Priory, the Etchinghams at Etchingham, and the dukes of York at Fotheringay College founded new houses to act as mausolea, whose inmates commemorated them for ever. Such impressive establishments proclaimed the patronage of their founders and were a focus for dynastic loyalty. Earl Richard Beauchamp refounded the chapel of Guyscliff, which commemorated his supposed legendary ancestor Guy of Warwick, and his son-in-law planned an almshouse there for old retainers. The earls of Warwick sought to improve their inheritance by founding churches and parks, markets and new roads, whilst other lords

---

52. Walker, pp. 25–6; K. Fowler, *The King's Lieutenant* (1969), pp. 183–5; A.J. Pollard, *North-Eastern England during the Wars of the Roses* (Oxford 1990), p. 126; Coward, p. 86.
53. Hicks, p. 339; *Rows Roll*, ed. W.H. Courthope (1859), no. 50.

helped rebuild churches of their patronage and studded them with their coats of arms. However arbitrary in practice, lords identified themselves not just with their predecessors, but with their heirs, for whom they hoped to retain the service that they had found valuable. As Professor Bean remarks, 'it was desirable for a landowner who granted fees and annuities for life to ensure that such dispositions were not interfered with after his death – for instance, in the event of the minority of the heir, when the Crown had the right to dispossess the recipients during the term of the minority': hence in part the development of trusts and wills. Thus Hugh Earl of Stafford (d. 1386) and Henry Earl of Northumberland (d. 1489) wanted fees to be continued after their death, 'he doing his service unto my heirs as [he] doth unto me'; the same sentiment prompted More to place his servants with other lords when he fell from power and Ladies Hungerford and Oxford to agree the same terms with Richard Duke of Gloucester.[54] Even where this could not be guaranteed, it was commonplace to continue payments to household-men until they could secure new employment, and many late medieval magnates provided for old servants by founding fairly luxurious almshouses for them. At Queens' College, Cambridge, Gloucester endowed masses for the souls of retainers who fell in his company at Barnet in 1471.[55]

So, too, the other way. Traditional lords could draw on the insularity of their retainers and tenants, who objected to the introduction of outsiders. In 1557 the Earl of Westmorland and in 1562 Bishop Ilkington noted how much more reliable were the northern tenantry when led by a northern lord. Charles Brandon had difficulties with East Anglians when imposed upon them. Archbishop Cranmer thought south-western rebels naive to suppose that tenants would not follow their masters.[56]

54. Holmes, p. 53; *Testamenta Eboracensia*, ed. J. Raine, iii (Surtees Soc. xlv, 1865), 306, 308–9; Hicks, pp. 176, 305.
55. C.D. Ross, 'Some Servants, Friends and "Lovers" of Richard III in his Youth', *The Ricardian* 4 (1976), 2–4.
56. S. Gunn, *Charles Brandon, Duke of Suffolk, 1484–1545* (1988), p. 53; Bernard, *Power*, p. 181; C.S.L. Davies, *Peace, Print and Protestantism 1450–1558* (1977), p. 55.

The well-known North–South hostility of the Wars of the Roses was fed by Richard III's promotion on northerners in the southern counties: southerners, so the Crowland Chronicle reports, preferred their 'ancient lords'.[57] The succession of heirs was welcomed and husbands of heiresses could call on traditional loyalty. This applies, for example, to Charles Brandon in Lincolnshire and to Edward IV's brothers the dukes of Clarence and Gloucester as husbands of Isobel and Anne Neville.[58] M.E. James draws a sharp distinction between the authority exercised by the 5th Earl of Northumberland and interlopers and between the turnout for the funeral of a long-established magnate and an upstart. It also emerges, as we shall see in chapter 8, in the strength of the military followings levied by old established families at the outbreak of the English Civil War.

However long a family had held an estate, its occupation was hardly likely to be continuous. Lands were held for long periods by dowagers and there were often minorities, when a lord of the main line was not in possession. But estates could carry such interruptions without dire consequences to hereditary loyalties. They could also outlast the dispossession of the rightful lord. The instance of the southerners under Richard III has already been cited. The Cheshiremen rebelled in 1400 in favour of Richard II, the tenants of Pleshey wreaked revenge on the murderers of their erstwhile lord, Thomas of Woodstock, the same year, the exiled Earl of Oxford looked in 1473 for support from his Essex tenants, the Earl of Warwick's name was used to raise rebellion in Warwickshire and Worcestershire in 1486, and repeated attempts were made in the 1480s to exploit loyalties to Richard III as lord of Middleham.[59] In

57. *Crowland Chronicle Continuations 1459–86*, ed. N. Pronay and J.C. Cox (1986), pp. 170–1.
58. Gunn, *Brandon*, pp. 149, 156, 182; Hicks, *Clarence*, p. 167; Hicks, pp. 265–6; for what follows, see James, chs 2, 5.
59. A. Goodman, 'The Countess and the Rebels: Essex and a Crisis in English Society', *Trans. Essex Arch. Soc.*, 3rd ser. ii.3 (1970), 267–79, esp. 273–4; C.H. Williams, 'Humphrey Stafford's Rebellion, 1486', *EHR* xliii (1928), 183; Hicks, *Clarence*, p. 105; Hicks, p. 383; K. Dockray, 'Political Legacy of Richard III', *Kings and Nobles in Later Middle Ages*, ed. R.A. Griffiths and J.W. Sherborne (Gloucester 1986), pp. 205–6.

each case, the figureheads had been absent for only a couple of years, but such loyalties could be much more enduring. The people of the East Riding rebelled in 1469 in favour of the restoration of Percies, the Courtenays and Beauforts recruited successfully in the West Country in 1471 after a decade of exile:

> trusting that their presence-showing in the country should cause much more, and the sooner, the people to come to their help and assistance. . . . In substance, they arrayed the whole might of Cornwall & Devonshire [who were] the more lightly enduced . . . for that they reputed them old inheritors of that country.

The Welshman Jasper Tudor mobilised his supporters repeatedly from 1463 to 1485. The extreme example appears to be the appeal for a resident lord from the lordship of Middleham in 1536, which may be merely a plea for patronage, but more probably harks back to the glorious days of the Nevilles and Richard III:[60] a golden age for the retainers too, despite so much bloodshed and defeat!

Indeed, servants could have stronger loyalties than their masters and acted as custodians of family tradition: apparently quite frequently. We owe the chronicles of the Mortimers and Despensers to the monks of Wigmore and Tewkesbury and the history of the earls of Warwick to the chaplain John Rows, who was perfectly capable of preferring the rights of the dispossessed countess and her son-in-law Richard III. It was the relatively humble Dean Berkswell, Nicholas Rody and Thomas Hugford who implemented the will of Earl Richard Beauchamp, the antiquary William Worcester who strove to fulfil that of Sir John Fastolf, and it was on the blind John Mervyn that Margaret Lady Hungerford principally relied. It was loyalty to his consort Anne Neville, not Richard III himself, that the Neville retainers acknowledged, when they threatened to withdraw their loyalty if he divorced her.[61]

60. M.H. and R. Dodds, *Pilgrimage of Grace 1536–7 and the Exeter Conspiracy 1538* (Cambridge 1915), i, p. 208. *Pace* Dockray, p. 223; *The Arrivall of Edward IV*, ed. J. Bruce (Camden Soc. i, 1836), 23; C.D. Ross, *Edward IV* (1974), p. 127.
61. *Crowland Chronicle*, p. 175.

. . . .

STABILITY

This chapter has stressed the natural and involuntary nature of many ties between lords and men that arose from tenancy arrangements and service over generations and tended to be lasting, hereditary, and even permanent. Does this not fly in the face of the common emphases on the personal nature of the ties with the gentry, whether feudal or contractual, the political independence of the gentry, and the importance of the lord's personality and capacity in creating and maintaining the trust and confidence of his retainers? The gentry – and even their inferiors – were capable of making up their own minds. They were not Pavlovian dogs. Nobody's loyalty was predetermined.[62] Impasse.

How limited is the basis for our cult of the personality! Originally, perhaps, many feudal tenants and annuitants bargained directly with their lords, but surely many domestics were hired by officers, ministers chosen by estate officers, and livery distributed by stewards? How many feudal or indentured retainers, household-men, rustic-tenants or liverymen could know their lord well as an individual or could be in his confidence? It was only the least of lords who could visit all his estates and keep track of all his tenants and vassals in person; even Edward IV's renowned memory for every name and face, we may presume, applied only to men of rank. For most retainers, surely, personal contact was confined to their presence together with their lord or brief contact with him in a crowded hall or on a progress, to communication through his agents or in writing, and to the formal marks of favour, grace, and good lordship.

If we take it for granted that no king could know in person the hundreds of household-men who owed him obedience, still less the thousands of subjects who owed allegiance, and do not consider such obligations weakened by the absence of a personal tie, why do we baulk at such a suggestion about the magnates and gentry? It is clear that the lord's withdrawal from the hall into his private

62. Richmond, 'After McFarlane', 57–8.

100

apartments, first remarked by Langland in the late fourteenth century, did not detract from the commitment and
loyalty of his household men or the significance of the
household as a bastard feudal institution. The convention
that menial service conferred particularly intimate and
binding obligations did not depend on physical proximity
or perhaps even acquaintance. For most it was not the lord
as individual, but the lord as symbol – as with the king's
two bodies – that they served and to whom obedience and
loyalty was due. And since most service was routine, occasions for commitment to be questioned were few and far
between. Most members of most connections most of the
time can have seen only an image, perhaps stereotypical,
they can have heard only what they were told, and they
can have had little scope for critical assessment. It was just
as well. The law of averages dictates that most lords were
intellectually ordinary, merely competent at management,
and uninspiring individually. That loyalty was to the symbol rather than the man enabled lordship to transcend
not just temporary interruptions, but also the blindness
of the Edward Earl of Devon (d. 1419) and John Hopton
(d. 1478), the madness of George Lord Latimer (d. 1469),
the sex of dowagers overmighty or ostentaciously pious,
extravagance or immorality, or merely the mediocrity of
early modern earls of Derby and so many others. The
parallel is with the distinction made between the crown
and the person of the individual monarch encapsulated
by the notion of the king's two bodies.

Regardless of their personal foibles and frailties, therefore, most lords could count on the committed service,
loyalty and fidelity of most of their retainers most of
the time. Relationships based on membership of a lord's
household, management of his estates, and tenure, which
linked precise rewards to specific service, were the more
stable because they were less personal. Inertia favoured
stability. Providing the natural lord was not supplanted
by some interloper, an estate officer like Lord Hastings
who could offer more immediate and better lordship, such
bonds did not have to be constantly nurtured but were
available on demand. It is therefore doubtful whether
William de Valence (d. 1296) and his son Aymer (d. 1324)
or John Duke of Exeter (d. 1447) allowed their local

connections to erode by careers spent at court or in foreign war.[63] Admittedly they chose their *extraordinary* retainers with their careers in mind rather than with an eye to local politics.

Personal ties always mattered for some, the lord's intimates or those whose service he had won rather than inherited. Probably it mattered for the gentry, especially those who contracted into his service without any earlier tradition, the extraordinary retainers. From time to time there were genuinely popular leaders with popular appeals – idols of the multitude. Such idols, of course, were propagandists, whose message need not equate with reality. They presented choices that were seldom on offer. Loyalty to lords that coincided with allegiance demanded no decisions. All lords, of course, were capable of alienating their followers through striking at their interests, through bad lordship or bad policies: Thomas of Lancaster (d. 1322) was one example, Thomas Earl of Devon (d. 1458) another, and the 4th Earl of Northumberland a third. Even Warwick the Kingmaker found his men unwilling to rebel again in March 1470.[64] But the scope for such mismanagement was surely small except in times of crisis. And it is questionable how complete or how durable such alienation was. Just as the house of Lancaster recovered from the disaster of Boroughbridge, so Courtenay loyalties revived in 1471, the Middleham retainers were resuscitated by Warwick's son-in-law, and, though dead, the Percy connection refused to lie down in 1416, 1489, 1537 or 1569. Even a bad lord was a passing phenomenon. A minority of flighty and shortlived extraordinary retainers were alienated, but the stable elements of the connection remained for revival by the next heir.

63. H. Ridgeway, 'William de Valence and his *familiares*', *Historical Research* lxv (1992), 256–7; M. Stansfield, 'John Holland, Duke of Exeter and Earl of Huntingdon (d. 1447) and the Costs of the Hundred Years War', *Profit, Piety, and the Professions in Later Medieval England*, ed. M.A. Hicks (Gloucester 1990), pp. 110–11, 114–15.
64. Maddicott, *Thomas of Lancaster*, pp. 308–9; M. Cherry, 'The Struggle for Power in Mid-15th Century Devonshire', *Patronage, The Crown and the Provinces in Late Medieval England*, ed. R.A. Griffiths (Gloucester 1981), pp. 123–40, esp. 137.

Late medievalists have commonly blamed social and political instability on Bastard Feudalism because it was essentially unstable itself. Whilst Christine Carpenter considers such contracts to be firm and exclusive commitments, she finds them nevertheless transient and fluctuating as retainers transferred from one connection to that of a competitor and kept local politics in a continuous flux. Though Colin Richmond sees retaining as temporary and feeble, he finds retainers fickle and unreliable. In both cases instability bred disorder and made it difficult for lords to mobilise their potential manpower in private or civil war. This is a debate among late medieval historians. Tudor historians have generally accepted that Bastard Feudalism was stable and delivered what was promised.

All the late medieval interpretations equate Bastard Feudalism with extraordinary retaining of the gentry. Mistakenly. The nucleus and bulk of the membership of every connection was made up of the lord's household and tenantry, who had a stable and binding relationship with their lord, which took precedence and was often practicably incompatible with contacts with any other master. They were not susceptible to competitive retaining. The household had strong personal ties with their lord, served under his eye, direction and discipline, and were expected to give overriding priority to their loyalty to him. Tenants were tied to particular estates by a range of inescapable obligations. Both groups carried over from generation to generation and newcomers were frequently recruited from the kinsmen of the old. Not surprisingly, many of those who received fees or livery were also drawn from these categories. Those who were not, those who were merely feed or liveried, had deliberately chosen to contract solemn new obligations and may therefore have been just as committed. Even when not, perhaps because better placed to make up their own minds and act independently, they mattered less because so few in number and mere supplements to a reliable core. Competitive retaining among them was also unusual and occurred only at critical junctures, when lords expanded their resources by granting more fees and distributing liveries *en masse*. At such times, admittedly, desertion or treachery was particularly acutely felt; the reliability of the estates'

103

stewards, on whom lords trusted to mobilise their forces, was perhaps just as suspect. Since lords could not afford high levels of expenditure on fees and livery indefinitely, and since such retainers were much freer to undertake other work and to contract other ties, such retainers were more likely to be dismissed, contracts cancelled, and fees or livery suspended. The total number of such cases known was small, since in normal times the minimal service demanded could be easily accommodated.

If connections consisted mainly of those with firm and stable commitments, it follows that they were stable influences on society. It was only the fringe or periphery of those formally retained, plus the well-willers and fair-weather friends, who changed. Carpenter's shifting loyalties applied merely to extraordinary retainers, if indeed they happened at all: loyalties need not be incompatible and retainers could add to their lords rather than substituting one for another. What use lords made of their men – whether to create order or upset it – is considered in chapter 6.

. . .

AFFINITY

At all times it was possible for men to rise from the dust or near it and to construct connections as powerful or more so than those founded on long pedigrees and continual association. Here, surely, personality, personal standing and personal ability were the key. Such non-territorial *affinities* arose in every generation and deserve separate treatment.

Let us take as our starting point the affinity of William Marshal, the twelfth-century hero who became Earl of Pembroke. Whilst he haled from a well-established baronial family in the Thames Valley, the Marshal was a younger son who entered his inheritance after he had already established his career.

> The Marshal (who inherited little in the way of a landed following) was one of the first great magnates in England to create a political connection not based on landed links and traditional allegiance, but on political interests and more subtle forms of reward; an 'affinity' as the Marshal's contemporaries were already calling it.

Few of his eighteen knights were recruited from his family's territorial base, nor did they originate particularly from those areas of France, Wales and Ireland where he made such a mark. He did not rely on his existing feudal tenants, nor normally did he reward his men with fiefs: that stage of Feudalism was almost past. They entered William's service not because they were his tenants, but because they were attracted by his prowess and by his favour with the Angevin kings that enabled him to reward them. Their tie was personal, not feudal; their rewards were monetary – or bastard feudal – not feudal. Not only was the Marshal an early example of Bastard Feudalism, argues Crouch, but evidence that Bastard Feudalism itself was normal in the twelfth century. Nor was the Marshal the first; a similar affinity was constructed during the Anarchy of Stephen's reign by Roger Earl of Hereford.[65]

Yet neither of these magnates possessed the territorial base that was normally expected both of Feudalism and Bastard Feudalism. In following Crouch there is a danger here that we may mistake a stage in the development of an affinity with the institution of Bastard Feudalism itself. As Coss observed, Marshal and Earl Roger 'were essentially interlopers within the territorial scene' and 'the extra-tenurial retinue, or extra-tenurial elements within a retinue' was 'necessarily aberrant'. Actually there is nothing particularly bastard feudal or anti-feudal in what Crouch has found. If we go back in time, to those lords who invaded with the Conqueror in 1066, none had a territorial English affinity when they arrived. What they possessed were men, often perhaps their feudal tenants back in Normandy, who crossed over as household knights or as barons with attendant households of their own. Some were enfeoffed with estates, yet others remained in the household, and it was only gradually that they put down roots in the locality and that a fluid, personal, money-based affinity took on a concrete territorial complexion. To use Crouch's terminology, Bastard Feudalism developed into Feudalism.

Moreover, this was a recurrent pattern: each individual

---

65. 'Debate', 172–4; D. Crouch, *William Marshal* (Harlow, 1990), esp. pp. 133–4, 161. For what follows, see 'Debate', 200–1.

is unique in his time but such individuals constantly recur. It was always possible to set up a new landed family. Existing aristocratic houses have constantly died out and been replaced by new ones raised from obscurity, usually by fortunate marriages or the profits of trade or the law. The greatest advances were made by those enjoying royal favour: examples like the Marshal and Earl Roger can be found in every generation. Such men could use their national influence to convert provincial potentates into clients; they could enlist them in their factions in national politics; and their own advance and the rewards they could offer attracted others to their service. William Marshal is a twelfth-century example: others are the 'new men' of Henry I. But there were new men in every century. What else were Piers Gaveston and the Younger Despenser under Edward II, William Montagu, Earl of Salisbury to Edward III, William Duke of Suffolk under Henry VI, the first Lord Hastings and first Herbert Earl of Pembroke under Edward IV, Reynold Bray under Henry VII, Charles Brandon, Duke of Suffolk under Henry VIII and Lord Admiral Seymour under his son, Robert Devereux, Earl of Essex under Elizabeth and George Villiers, Duke of Buckingham under the Early Stuarts? Hastings and Suffolk both attracted local men into their affinities, the former apparently for the benefit of his master and the latter to his own advantage. Lord Admiral Seymour 'did vaunt that he had as great a Number of Gentlemen that loved him as any Nobleman in England', whilst Essex built up a following across a dozen counties that included the leaders of the county élites, peers and county gentry.[66] They transcended their actual origins – and all except Villiers started with *some* lands and retainers already – and they constructed affinities that transcended their actual estates. Indeed, where they had estates – like William de Valence – they may have been too provincial or peripheral to be of much use in the indoor manoeuvres that constituted everyday national politics. All were national figures; all, however, were concerned to reinforce their local power-base. We may ask why.

First of all, as Crouch recognised, their new-found

66. Cooper, p. 87; James, p. 416.

power reflected in their swollen affinities was essentially personal and therefore ephemeral. Such affinities depended on them as individuals, on their status as favourites, and their ties with a particular king. Often, indeed, they were made by a particular king: this was true of Thomas Howard, Earl of Surrey, whose power in the North depended wholly on Henry VII's favour, subsequently of Thomas Lord Wharton, and Charles Brandon in Suffolk. There were few, like Marshal and Villiers, whose power outlasted the ruler that made them. Favourites of Edward II, Richard II and Henry VII fell with their masters. Edward III allowed two second earls, Salisbury and March, the heirs of former favourites, to lose ground because their service was valued less than that of their predecessors. Powerful though Queen Elizabeth's Essex appeared, 'once his influence was removed by the queen . . . he found that he had no solid resources of his own to back a credible rebellion'.[67] No wonder that Hastings was apparently so fearful in the aftermath of Edward IV's death. And when Hastings died, so we are told, 'all the lord chamberlain's men are become my lord of Buckingham's men'.[68] As yet, they had no permanent roots. Thus it was easy for Edward IV to revise his territorial dispositions, transferring John Neville from Northumberland to Devon and uprooting his own brother from the North Midlands, for Richard III to flood the southern counties with northerners, and for Henry VIII to switch Charles Duke of Suffolk from East Anglia to Lincolnshire. They had put down no roots and left no permanent mark. Not enough time had yet passed. Many such affinities were still-born because cut short by the death of a lord or of the king on whom his power depended; others collapsed because of loss of favour, like that which befell Brandon or Essex. They did not survive; others pass unnoticed except to the assiduous researcher because their gains were on a lesser scale.

Affinities, impressive though they were, were transient. Every favourite or embryonic magnate – like every townsman sinking his pile in broad acres – sought to consolidate

67. Bernard, *Nobility*, p. 20.
68. Myers, *EHD*, p. 336.

his family's power and wealth by establishing a territorial connection. The Marshal, for example, gave lands in
Ireland to his feed men: 'In this way, what were originally "bastard feudal" connections might be technically
"legitimised" '.[69] So, too, in the sixteenth century: 'But
they usually sought to turn such possibly ephemeral royal
favour into a lasting inheritance for their families – and
they were often assisted in such an aim by the crown's
continuing needs for reliable servants in the localities',
such as the Russell Earls and Dukes of Bedford. This
was not easy: Lord Wharton's funeral shows he had not
yet succeeded and Brandon found it difficult to convert
'his influence with the king into the wealth, landholding,
and "manred" that brought lasting power'.[70] For that was
what he and all the others wanted. To establish a great
family and great connection was to put down roots in a
locality; to establish a resident household or presence in
the locality; to acquire estates, with their tenants and officials; and to forge links with the local gentry as feudal tenants or feed men. Lords thus established themselves and
their heirs, whether as rulers or minor players, as permanent features of local society and politics which endured
even after their own deaths and the disappearance of the
fragile personal influence that they themselves had established. Most lords most of the time were of the permanent
type, even though there were always new men wielding
influence out of proportion to their landed resources,
but in line with their national influence and constructing
affinities that as yet lacked a clear territorial identity.

. . .

PERPETUITY

However wrong Victorian scholars were in their emphasis
on knight service, they were right in identifying the
most permanent ties with tenure of land. It was the
estate, its tenantry, and its administrators that bestowed
a reliable connection on each succeeding lord regardless
of past vicissitudes. Often such stability was reinforced and
changed from inertia to a more positive commitment by

69. Crouch, *William Marshal*, p. 163.
70. Gunn, *Brandon*, p. 18.

the length of association of individual lords and retainers and of their dynasties over several generations. The household, however recruited, was another resource on which every lord could count. Often drawn from the same pool of traditional manpower, extraordinary retainers could extend such natural connections with new service that could not be taken for granted. Noble connections were passed from hand to hand, from generation to generation and via heiresses to new families. Even when broken by forfeiture, such traditions took time to die and delayed their replacement by new ones. Always, however, new ones were being created by new men favoured by the king. The first stage was the affinity, a personal connection specifically tailored to the political needs of the moment, especially the maintenance of power at court and the reinforcement of royal favour. The volatility of such affinities and the difficulties in transmitting them to future generations meant that any parvenu with an eye to the long-term future and to the permanent advancement of his house sought to establish a territorial connection in the localities that would outlast him. Just as land was the safest investment for capital, so too it was the most secure basis for political influence in perpetuity.

Thus far we have dissected Bastard Feudalism, analysed its many varieties, and explored what cemented them into a totality that, ideally, was much more than the parts. Bastard Feudalism created the power for every lord to deploy in so many different contexts. The use they made of their connections is the concern of the rest of this book. First, however, we need to consider how legitimate was its use in any context. Was Bastard Feudalism merely a mechanism, to be exploited for good or ill, or was it inherently illegitimate, illegal, anti-social, and parasitical? Such issues are discussed in chapter 4.

Chapter 4

THE LEGALITY OF BASTARD FEUDALISM

. . .

BASTARD FEUDALISM – THE CASE AGAINST

Traditionally late medieval England suffered from two interlinked evils: endemic disorder, represented by violence, feuding, private and civil war; and everyday corruption of justice. Legal cases were commonly determined by maintenance, embracery and champerty. Cases were influenced or decided by the use or threat of force, the support of third parties, and the bribery of judges, jurors and officials. All these, Bishop Stubbs and his contemporaries agreed, resulted directly from Bastard Feudalism, which gave the great the resources to fight and pervert justice for the benefit of themselves and their retainers. So pervasive was the connection between Bastard Feudalism and subversion of the law that the label 'Livery and Maintenance' was coined to describe them. From 1305 on, complaints were constantly made to parliament and gradually reforms resulted. Particular abuses were outlawed. Yet the problem continued and even escalated, because the root cause – Bastard Feudalism itself – remained. Attempts to outlaw retaining also were thwarted by the lords, who continued to practise it despite a succession of ordinances and acts from 1390 on, and thus conditions did not improve. 'For the statutes of "Livery and Maintenance" were not properly observed', remarked Mowat (1913), 'and consequently public order was not very good'. Only with Henry VII's act and the Tudor Star Chamber, however, was the system brought properly under control, civil war ceased, law and order was restored and justice was purified.[1]

1. R.B. Mowat, *The Wars of the Roses* (1914), p. 37; Hicks, pp. 3–6.

Many historians agree that Bastard Feudalism was integral to society – as essential to it as the open fields.[2] Abuse was not inevitable, McFarlane thought, but secondary and dependent on circumstances. For Storey and Bellamy, for thirty years the principal castigators of Bastard Feudalism, reform was slow and achieved only by the Tudors. For Coss, however, society could have taken a different form. Abuses were not peripheral to a system that was fundamentally sound, but were central to the system itself. Bastard Feudalism was the response of an aristocracy threatened by the substitution of royal authority, jurisdiction and courts for their own. To retain their power, the aristocracy had to take over the new system, which they did by subverting it; the crown weakly conceded control of local government and justice to those who represented the greatest threat. Late medieval government and society were forced along a different course. 'So intractable and enduring were the problems created by bastard feudalism', observes Bellamy, 'that the government was forced increasingly into developing that law in a direction quite distinct from what had obtained before the later fourteenth century'.[3] For Coss, the later fourteenth century was a missed chance to change direction. The emergence of a bastard feudal society, when subversion of the law and abuses achieved a new scale, occurred in the mid-thirteenth century: the first full description dates from 1261.[4]

. . .

THE IDEOLOGICAL FRAMEWORK

Concepts like legality, illegality, corruption, and abuse imply the existence of accepted standards against which actual practices can be measured. To have any meaning or validity, these standards must be those of the time, standards of which those involved were aware, to which they could comply, and by which their contemporaries could judge them. It is no use condemning them because they

2. Holmes, pp. 2–3; G.R. Elton, *The Tudor Constitution* (Cambridge 1965), p. 31.
3. Bellamy, p. 9.
4. 'Debate', 182, 195.

fall short of our own very different ideals, as Plummer, the Whig historians, or Marxists do. Their notions of inevitable progress are anachronistic. Bastard Feudalism, like any other social institution, operated in a concrete context: it presumed contemporary society and operated within a framework of law and government, accepted values and conventions. This context was not, however, immutable, neither monolithic nor for all time, but was constantly shifting. Bastard Feudalism changed with it and indeed had to do so. This sense of movement is essential to discussion of the legality of Bastard Feudalism.

England was ruled by a monarch who controlled an ever burgeoning and ever more effective central administration. But he was never absolute. His actions were ruled by conventions and the need for consent from his principal subjects, increasingly formalised through council and parliament. Decisions made jointly and laws to which he consented were binding on him and procedures for the exercise of his powers were increasingly prescribed: justice was done, for example, through the royal lawcourts. There were things that the monarch could legitimately do, things that he could not, for which he required consent or not, all of them gradually elaborated and codified into a complex system. All these regulations and statutes, it must be stressed, required the consent of the aristocracy, at first outside and later inside parliament.

Magna Carta (1215) is our earliest schematic depiction of relations between the crown and aristocracy. It regulated the operation of Feudalism as it affected the king, his tenants-in-chief, and their tenants. Magnates accepted that the king had feudal rights over them, but sought to regulate them – to take out the arbitrary element – in the light of accepted values and standards. Central to these standards is a concept of law: an abstract standard with many concrete expressions that all accepted as binding. They appealed also to custom, to precedent, and to what is reasonable. And when they had offended, they were to be subject to judgement by equals both for the verdict and the sentence. Changes could be made only by consent of all those involved.

Note here especially the respect for law and for due process that is present throughout our period. Such respect, of course, did not prevent Englishmen then, as now, from seeking to interpret the law in the way most favourable to themselves or to get around it. They could play the system and manipulate, for example, the plethora of alternative suits and alternative courts available in Tudor England. The law defined crime as an offence against the king's peace: to burgle someone's house or to kill him was not merely an offence against the victim, but against the king, whose right it was to try and punish him. Such powers could be delegated to others through grants of franchises subject to royal supervision and correction. The law forbade resort to violent acts of revenge and blood feuds. It forbade private warfare except within the marches and even there, in 1291, Edward I outlawed it by the exemplary punishment of the earls of Gloucester and Hereford: when private feuds escalated into the Wars of the Roses, they were thus illegal. The law that governed title to land was increasingly the king's law orchestrated through royal procedures in royal courts. The law, it was agreed, should be applied without fear or favour on all parties, however great; sometimes it was. The law was an abstract standard to which all appealed and to which all classes resorted in ever larger numbers. It regulated the conduct of both lords and retainers and was a legitimate route through which they could pursue their ends.

But the law was never static. It developed constantly in flexible response to social and ideological changes. The assize of novel disseisin that the magnates supported in 1215 was only fifty years old and time immemorial dated back less than thirty years. They accepted the legal reforms of Henry II that substituted better remedies in royal courts for their own courts and jurisdictions. They demanded, indeed, more than the crown could deliver.[5] Royal law and equity was what they administered in their own courts and as arbiters. As society became more complex, as new developments like trusts demanded new remedies, so new laws were created to regulate them. Activities that had been legal and unregulated came to be seen as anti-social, ceased to be tolerable, and were

5. R.W. Kaeuper, *War, Justice and Public Order* (Oxford 1988), p. 135.

prohibited or restricted. The law extended ever further into everyday life and regulated the use of property and relations between subjects. Before laws were passed against retaining, livery and maintenance, no crime was committed by undertaking these activities. Once such laws were promulgated, new crimes were created and new lines were drawn between what was permitted and what was not. Hence claims that lords and retainers flouted the law are frequently incorrect. Even the statutes against livery and maintenance never prohibited *all* retaining, *all* livery, or *all* maintenance. There remained legal forms of these activities. Historians are wrong to condemn practitioners of these legal forms. Tax avoidance is not the same as tax evasion. Admittedly some contemporaries, such as Chief Justice Husy, interpreted the law unduly strictly, Henry VIII went beyond the strict letter of the law, and Queen Elizabeth sought to apply extra-legal pressure to outlaw even what was permitted.

The authority of English kings was never confined to feudal relationships and was extended gradually into a notion of overriding sovereignty. Royal claims to the prior loyalty of their subjects developed gradually into a notion of allegiance that took definite precedence over lesser loyalties. As early as 1086 William the Conqueror had summoned to Salisbury all significant holders of land 'whosoever's vassals they might be' to make them swear 'oaths of allegiance to him that they would be faithful to him against all other men', including their immediate lords. What this could mean emerges from the trials at Rouen in 1124 of knights captured when fighting for their lord. 'My lord count [of Flanders]', observed King Henry I,

> what I do is just . . . With their lord's consent, [they] became my liege men, and they broke faith with me. . . . Therefore they deserve to be punished by death or mutilation. They ought to have sacrificed all they possessed to preserve the fealty they swore to me, rather than supporting any rebel and breaking their covenant with their liege lord.[6]

6. D.C. Douglas, *William the Conqueror* (Cambridge 1964), p. 355; M. Chibnall, 'Feudal Society in Orderic Vitalis', *Proceedings of the Battle Conference* i (1978), 42.

Under Henry II allegiance to the king was formally given precedence over loyalty to some intermediate lord. Aristocrats could legitimately use their men only to support the king, not against him. Another century was to pass, however, before the feudal notion of defiance, whereby subjects could renounce obedience and rebel, gave way to the notion of rebellion that was punishable by death. Whereas no rebels were executed in the thirteenth century, two earls suffered such a fate in 1322–23, one being the king's cousin and of the blood royal. The first Statute of Treasons in 1352 prescribed levying war on the king and plotting his death and was gradually extended to imagining his death by sorcery, to treasonable words, and to offences against members of the royal family.

Treason became the most heinous of crimes: it became conventional to liken traitors to Judas Iscariot. Traitors were worthy not just of death, but of the most heinous death; they were dishonoured and degraded from knighthood; their chattels and lands in fee simple were confiscated; and the taint was held also to have corrupted the blood of their progeny, so that wives were deprived of their dowers and children of lands entailed on them. The Tudor concept of order denied any right to rebel, even against a tyrant: only passive resistance and submission to whatever ensued was allowed. The duty of allegiance took precedence over honour, and family ties and horror of treason colours much sixteenth-century political theory and such Shakespearean plays as *Richard II* and *King Lear*. The taint of treason compelled those accused to hazard their lives to clear their names or, in the case of Edmund Duke of York, to sacrifice his own son. Such provisions were invoked in civil war, when aristocrats serving in the army of a defeated king were executed and attainted. Not surprisingly, lords and retainers became so much less willing to commit themselves publicly, to call out their retinue of war or to serve in one in domestic conflict, that Henry VII's 1495 parliament felt obliged to declare that service in the army of a *de facto* king was not treasonable. Whereas only a couple of John of Gaunt's retainers reserved their allegiance to the king when sealing an indenture of retainer,[7] next century it became customary. It was therefore significant that in 1460 this reservation was omitted from new indentures of Richard Duke of York and in 1478 and 1521 the omission of such clauses became the basis of treason charges. Allegiance to the king's heir was often added: George Duke of Clarence in 1464 and Henry Duke of York in 1501.[8] There was suspicion when forces were raised without royal commission or consent – or even with consent, in the case of the last Duke of Buckingham – and the crown secured a near veto on an activity that remained perfectly legal.

. . .

LAW AND ORDER

Bastard feudal abuses are merely a facet of contemporary crime and disorder. Historians have generally supposed that crime and violence were endemic, that some periods were particularly bad, and that there was overall deterioration. Such was the message of Bellamy's *Crime and Public Order in the Later Middle Ages* (1973). 'Early Lancastrian England was not a well-ordered society', observes Professor Allmand.[9] The blame is traditionally attributed to the backward state of English law and to the abuses of Bastard Feudalism. The more sensational crimes were committed by the great and so 'the accent falls on the nobility', says Coss.[10] But nobody has yet tackled the voluminous records of the central courts over a long period. If they did, they would have serious difficulties. New crimes were constantly created, the relationship between crime, recorded crime, indictments and convictions shifts, appropriate jurisdictions changed, and the records of all the relevant courts virtually never survive.

7. *Statutes of the Realm*, ed. A. Luders and others, 11 vols Record Commission 1810–28, ii.568; 'Indentures of Retinue with John of Gaunt', ed. N.B. Lewis, *Camden Miscellany* xxii (1964), 79.
8. Cooper, p. 82; Dunham, p. 27.
9. C.T. Allmand, *Henry V* (1992), p. 300. Dr Rawcliffe takes for granted 'the high level of crime in late medieval English society', 'Parliament and the Settlement of Disputes by Arbitration in the Later Middle Ages', *Parliamentary History* ix.ii (1990), 318.
10. 'Debate', 195.

The traditional interpretation is thus impressionistic and seriously misleading.

Actually, most serious crimes were not committed by aristocrats. Walker's view that 'the magnates' responsibility for much of the violence of the period can now be discounted' is amply justified.[11] Most recorded crimes were property offences committed by the lower orders against the lower orders: they increased in famine years and decreased when times were better. Violent deaths were more frequently accidental than political and the level of violence was actually unimpressive. A late Stuart *cause célèbre* in Cumbria – the 'Black and Terrible Troop' – proved quite unimpressive when investigated by Dr Alan Macfarlane. That it was nevertheless notorious reveals the sensitivity of contemporaries and their low shockability threshold.[12] Only very low expectations of violence could cause such relatively tame crimes to stand out. So, too, in Tudor and Early Stuart England[13] and even in the early fifteenth century. Whilst historians have long realised the conventional language of many indictments and bills, which were designed to qualify cases for particular courts and actions, Dr Philippa Maddern has now demonstrated references to violence to be generally unfounded and trivial and the actual level of violence to be slight. Her broad definition of East Anglia witnessed only two occasions in twenty years when Bellamy's truncated procedures were invoked – for the only two major riots.[14] What evidence there is, Bellamy concluded, reveals the incidence of serious crime to be diminishing in the fifteenth century: it certainly was in the early seventeenth century, when most crimes were minor misdemeanours.[15] That there was so much concern about public order merely demonstrates how much standards and expectations were rising.

Nobody had more interest in law and order, of course, than those with property to protect and nobody had more

11. Walker, pp. 117–18.
12. A. Macfarlane, *The Justice and the Mare's Ale* (Oxford 1981).
13. See below ch. 8.
14. P. Maddern, *Violence and the Social Order* (Oxford 1992), pp. 175, 209.
15. Bellamy, p. 100.

property to protect than the aristocracy. It was they, above all, as legislators and petitioners, who were behind the new laws, the new courts and legal remedies, and the summary procedures of the later middle ages. Society was more regulated and the courts were made more effective as a result. These innovations, in a period long considered legally backward, involved co-operation between lawyers and aristocrats, often out of court through arbitration. Violence or corruption were far from usual ways of set-tling cases; settlement out of court was the norm.

Of course aristocrats did commit crimes – their own sort of crimes – what Professor Hanawalt has called 'fur-collar crime'. Usually committed in support of prop-erty suits, they were trespasses or misdemeanours rather than felonies, were deliberately focused and carefully limited. Forcible entries, for example, had their own rituals and conventions and employed the language of violence rather than the reality. Armed gangs sought to overawe rather than to fight and avoided confron-tations whenever possible. When they did occur, they were strangely bloodless: how could the Duke of Norfolk's three-day siege of Caister Castle in 1469 and why did a five-day siege with cannon in 1578 each result in only one death?[16] The real *causes célèbres*, like Radford's murder in 1455, were always exceptional. Again, disorder was diminishing. If 'robber barons' really committed havoc from 'adulterine castles' during Stephen's reign and if the Cotterell and Folville gangs and Sir John Moleyns operated with apparent impunity in the untidy aftermath of Edward II's fall, the restoration of normal government was accompanied by a return to order. When the crown intervened in the locality with its judicial commissions, it was commonly responding to the demands of local property-owners.

'Fur-collar crime' was 'social crime': the crime of a particular class, that was acceptable and understood by members of that class. Aristocrats were prominent among the poachers in Duffield Frith, Needwood Forest, and the New Forest in the fifteenth century. Other localities acted

16. Ibid., p. 124; *Paston Letters and Papers of the 15th Century*, ed. N. Davis, i (Oxford 1970), p. 346.

in ways that were legally criminal, but acceptable locally: this was true, in the eighteenth century, of poaching in Waltham Chase, smuggling in Sussex, and wrecking in the West Country. Aristocrats identified themselves with their local societies, whose interests they knew best, and resisted external interference. Hence the men of Norfolk rejected the Suffolk knight, John Howard, as knight of the shire in 1455 and the intrusions of Sir Arthur Heveningham a century later. Elizabethan Lord Chancellors and Lord Keepers enjoined returning MPs in vain to enforce the laws, for they would implement only those in the local interest. So, too, in 1414 the North Midlands jurors declined to convict those indicted before Henry V's impressive judicial commissions and Devonshire jurors similarly protected Devonshire pirates.[17] It was the royal judges and royal officials that the Peasants Revolt struck at first. Local abuses were lesser evils: though always acutely resented by those affected.

. . .

CORRUPTION OF JUSTICE

Prosecutors, defendants, plaintiffs and criminals always want to win their cases, often desperately, and the best means are not always above board. 'Every medieval man of property wanted to obtain preferential, if not openly partial, treatment at law'.[18] Maintenance was the means. It could involve violence, the threat of violence, blackmail, influence or bribery; it could be applied to judges, jurors, or legal officials; and those engaged in it could be the parties themselves, their lords, servants or allies. 'All legal authorities, including sheriffs, judges and juries, were likely to be corrupted or intimidated by them'.[19] There were officers who colluded with wrongdoers, sheriffs who did not serve writs, and bailiffs who did not make arrests. The great could secure royal commissions made

17. E. Powell, *Kingship, Law and Society* (Oxford 1989), pp. 201–2; McFarlane, *England*, p. 10.
18. C. Rawcliffe, 'Baronial Councils in the Later Middle Ages', *Patronage, Pedigree and Power in Later Medieval England*, ed. C.D. Ross (Gloucester 1979), p. 94.
19. J.F. Baldwin, *The King's Council in England during the Middle Ages* (Oxford 1913), p. 265.

up of their own nominees to coerce their enemies. All these abuses can be illustrated with concrete examples that certainly happened. This chapter takes the existence of such cases of bastard feudal corruption for granted. There is no need to elaborate, since Bellamy selected the worst cases and many others are cited elsewhere. Yet the evidence leaves much to be desired. We have to rely on allegations and anecdotes, the preambles to statutes, the denunciations of preachers, satirists and poets, much of it literary, conventional, even fictional and traditional, full of bias and special pleading, and far from literal. How can we establish what is typical and the trends? And how crucial to them was retaining? 'The livery of a great lord', wrote Stubbs, 'was as effective security to a malefactor as was the benefit of clergy to the criminous clerk'. Itself 'a political mischief', 'this evil system of "livery" soiled all chances of law and order in the country during the Lancastrian period', observed Mowat.[20] For such historians, corruption of justice was a symptom of Bastard Feudalism: there could be no justice without the abolition of livery.

The logic is impeccable, but not necessarily convincing. It assumes the existence of modern standards, in which maintenance is illegal, at times when it was not. Legislation in this area need not mean that the problem of maintenance was increasing, as Saul for example deduces,[21] but that it was coming to be seen as a problem requiring action. The phenomenon existed before it became a crime and the fact that it became a crime indicates a growth in sensitivity – a growth in intolerance towards an activity hitherto legal if perhaps antisocial. There was nothing criminal about either livery or maintenance before they were legislated against and even then neither was completely outlawed. There was legal maintenance – the support of a just cause – and there was legal livery, for instance of menials. Denunciations, whether contemporary or modern, do not always make

20. W. Stubbs, *Constitutional History of England in the Middle Ages* (Oxford 1880), iii.575; Mowat, *Wars of the Roses*, p. 251.
21. 'Maintenance was on the increase', N. Saul, 'The Commons and the Abolition of Badges', *Parliamentary History* ix.ii (1990), 313.

such precise distinctions; indeed, it may have been difficult to apply them in practice. Many cases of maintenance involved neither livery nor lords; from the days of King Cnut and no doubt earlier, royal officers had often manipulated the law to their own personal profit. Much maintenance was the work of conspirators of equal rank, of relatives, friends and neighbours. Indeed Saul argues that in the late fourteenth century livery and maintenance were increasingly abuses of those socially inferior to the county gentry.[22]

Moreover the chronology does not fit the argument that associates Bastard Feudalism with disregard for the law. The abuses existed before Bastard Feudalism. There was judicial malpractice in Anglo-Saxon England. Livery was recorded in the mid-twelfth century. Magna Carta, Holt observes, already reveals a society 'in which powerful men tried to turn the law and the operations of government to their own ends'.[23] Moreover, the abuses persisted after Bastard Feudalism. It was in 1621 that Lord Chancellor Bacon was successfully impeached for accepting bribes from both sides in a lawsuit and that his defence, that they had not affected his decision, was rejected. The proverb 'best ended best frended' is sixteenth century in date. Far from being curbed by the Tudors, writes Professor Aylmer,

> the present tendency is to suppose that a good deal went on until the turn of the 17th to 18th centuries. ... We can only say that *some* Embracery and *some* Maintenance, under whatever names, probably did persist through the Stuart period, and that royal officials may on occasion have profited thereby.[24]

Because Bastard Feudalism is now seen as originating earlier and ending later than McFarlane and his contemporaries supposed, that chronological argument has now as good as failed. There is now a much nearer match in chronology between the emergence of Bastard Feudalism and the start of bastard feudal abuses. Indeed,

22. Ibid., p. 311–12.
23. J.C. Holt, *The Northerners* (Oxford 1961), p. 6.
24. G.E. Aylmer, *The King's Servants* (rev. edn 1974), p. 180.

Coss has argued that it was the need for such abuses that prompted Bastard Feudalism itself. If some abuses existed earlier, argues Carpenter, they were on an altogether smaller *scale* from the large-scale maintenance of the mid-thirteenth century. An argument difficult to combat, not least because it is then that evidence first exists in any quantity.

Whilst ostensibly attractive, the argument rests on at least three fallacies. Given that evidence for the twelfth century is much less than for the thirteenth – and especially evidence of the uses of aristocratic connections and judicial corruption! – the alleged increase in scale may result from an increase in documentation. With any increase in the activity and records of royal courts should one not expect a proportional increase in corruption? Was it proportional? Secondly, the alleged increase in scale may reflect other changes. Private justice preceded royal justice: is it not likely that there was as much malpractice in the eleventh and twelfth centuries in the private, honorial courts in the form of pressure, bribery, and arbitrary exercise of judicial power? We know that the unfree peasantry experienced it. And what makes the abuse of power of royal officials so preferable? 'It would be naive to believe that the "public authority" of the crown was consistently exercised for the common good', writes Harriss. Perhaps in 1261 curial sheriffs could protect against greater men,[25] but who would provide protection against curial sheriffs and their underlings? Thirdly, why did the magnates of eleventh–thirteenth centuries have to use Bastard Feudalism to pervert justice? Why not feudal tenants? For Coss, of course, this does not matter, as he has neither a fief-centred view of Feudalism nor a retinue-based notion of Bastard Feudalism. It is not the nature of the bonds that matters, not their use to subvert justice, but to subvert *royal* justice, in which he sees a special significance. What is at issue here is not the role of the bastard feudal retinue in perverting justice, but lordly dominance and manipulation of royal justice: since the latter is new, so by definition is the former. It is the

25. Ibid., p. 182; G.L. Harriss, 'Political Society and the Growth of Government in Late Medieval England', *P&P* 138 (1993), 33.

hierarchical nature of society to which he objects. 'What I wanted to stress was that it arose out of the existing power structure and here, inevitably, the accent falls on the greater lords'.[26] It does not follow that Bastard Feudalism in the retinue-based sense used in this book was the prime cause of judicial corruption or that judicial corruption itself resulted from the change from a feudal to a bastard feudal society.

The growth in complaints in the mid-thirteenth century may indeed indicate a growing problem and certainly suggests that problems were becoming politically more significant. But it need not. Perhaps those who suffered were now the politically important, those magnates, now subjected to the royal courts, who had not hitherto complained about any injustices perpetrated by the private courts that they ran themselves. They had suffered in the twelfth century at the hands of the royal sheriffs who had been curbed. Again, new voices were certainly being raised in the thirteenth century – the voices of the knights – that had not hitherto been heard: not because they had no complaints, but because they were of no account. The apparent peaks of complaint in the literary evidence *may* indicate real peaks in judicial corruption, but the relationship is not a simple one.

For an essential context, as we have seen, is that law and order was improving and expectations of order were rising among the very class guilty of bastard feudal abuses. Modern historians have concluded that there was not much bastard feudal abuse in fourteenth-century Sussex, early fifteenth-century East Anglia and late fifteenth-century Cheshire.[27] Complaints of disorder occurred when order was improving. Should not the succession of legislative enactments against corruption be seen as part of this increasing regulation of anti-social activities? And why should it be supposed that the legislation against livery and maintenance alone was ineffective, that 'it failed to curb such practice', and that the enactment of subsequent statutes is proof that earlier ones failed?[28] After all, the statutes are not identical. If they indicate that livery was not legislated against for a century after the first

26. 'Debate', 195.
27. Maddern, *Violence*, pp. 226–35; ch. 3 above.
28. Powell, *Kingship*, p. 113; Bellamy, p. 85.

complaints about maintenance, why must we treat this as evidence of myopia among those unable to trace abuses to their bastard feudal roots and recognise them instead as a correct ordering of the problems? Can we not deduce a gradual progression towards less partial administration of justice? Early legislation did indeed focus on maintenance in a variety of scenarios and on the oppression of the great. The ordinance and statutes of livery of 1390–1407 were not an attack on the great themselves, who were allowed to continue retaining, still less on the categories of retaining that really mattered to them. First non-resident liverymen were outlawed, who mattered little to lords, but were certainly less easily controlled. Then, in 1468 and 1504, it was the turn of extraordinary retainers, who mattered even less, but were the logical next step. Perhaps it was no longer deliberate maintenance by the lords, but unlicensed abuse by their men that was the problem. The data is compatible with the progressive and successful restriction of abuse: though never, of course, to the extent that we find acceptable today. But much more research will be needed before this or any other interpretation can be substantiated.

. . .

THE STATUTES OF LIVERY

The first outburst of complaint against bastard feudal perversion of justice, when 'the magnates influenced and corrupted in their favour the whole working of the legal system', was in 1258–65.[29] Legislation against maintenance was followed by attacks upon livery – livery of hats was forbidden in 1377 – and then on retaining itself. A first attempt in 1384 was thwarted by John of Gaunt, who protested that lords could control their own retainers, but succeeded in 1390, when the lords' protestations were rejected and their capacity to retain was restricted to members of their households and gentry whom they retained for life. The act of 1393, which blocked a loophole, and those of 1401–29 demonstrate that the law was not being enforced. A further, somewhat ambiguous statute of 1468, which stopped retaining for life and which even modern

29. Coss, 38.

historians cannot agree on, had little effect: Chief Justice Husy reports illegal retaining by the lords in 1486 almost as soon as they swore to stop it. Henry VII also legislated in 1504. Despite all this legislation and repeated official intervention, illegal retaining took a long time to stamp out and was a cause of concern in every Tudor decade.

This orthodoxy, however, is difficult to accept. It presents a picture in which those retained – principally the gentry, represented in the House of Commons – repeatedly overrode the opposition of their lords and passed acts that restricted their capacity to retain. Such legislation, it seems, whether re-enacted or modified, could not be enforced, so the evils remained. It is far from obvious, however, that such legislation was opposed by the lords, that it restricted the lords, or that it was not enforced. An alternative scenario is that it achieved its objectives, which were more limited than the traditional orthodoxy suggests, and that successive acts were supplementary, gradually restricting activities hitherto acceptable in line with rising expectations and with royal aspirations.

It is not hard to find examples of retainers who committed crimes or perverted justice, with or without their lords' consent. Not surprisingly, therefore, many historians have rejected the claims of Gaunt in 1384 and the lords in 1486 that they could control their retainers. Yet there is nothing novel, original or surprising about such claims. As Stubbs long ago observed, good lordship 'was a revival, *or possibly a survival* [my italics], of the ancient practice, by which every man was bound to have a lord and every lord had to represent his men or be answerable for them in the courts'. Lords were made into sureties for members of their households in the laws of Athelstan, Ethelred Unraed, Cnut and William I. So, too, in the mid-thirteenth century, heads of households were responsible for the actions of their domestic servants and lords for their bondmen and could also claim damages done to them. Their relationship to their master was identical to that of his children: already, as in the seventeenth century, living-in servants were represented politically by their masters, who exercised absolute authority over them. The absolute authority of the Stuart kings was identical to the absolute authority of a father over his family and living-in servants.[30] Why, then, are we unimpressed by the assertions of Gaunt and his 1486 successors?

Not only did the great have households, but most young people spent periods in service in the households of others, even labourers keeping servants in sixteenth- and seventeenth-century England. This was the mechanism that deployed workers where they were needed and permitted sexually fertile youngsters to marry late. To restrict living-in service was not only to attack the hierarchical organisation of society – the features that distinguished the aristocracy from the rest; it struck at the heart of society itself and at the operation of both agriculture and industry. Such restrictions were obviously unthinkable: even Thomas More, who thought noble households excessively large, lamented the loss of household employment. Nor were such measures seen to be necessary. It was not menial servants who were the problem. Masters who claimed to control them were well placed to do so, since they lived under their roofs under their eyes and subject to their discipline. Household ordinances and courtesy books reveal servants subjected to their lords' overriding will, in which a good impression, economy, and decorum were all required. Recruitment was selective – be careful to enrol only honest servants, urged the thirteenth-century *Rules of St Robert* [Grosseteste] – and unsatisfactory servants could be sacked: indeed, to Thomas More's thinking, they were too often sacked, with unfortunate repercussions for public order. To take one example among many, George Duke of Clarence ordained in 1468 that the steward, treasurer and controller of his household should summon all household servants before them and 'straitly' charge them:

> to be of worshipful, honest, and virtuous conversation, abstaining themselves from vicious rule and suspected places; and also restraining themselves from seditious language, variances, dissensions, debates, as well within the said Duke's court as without, wherethrough any dislander or misgovernment might grow . . .

30. Stubbs, iii.574; A. Macfarlane, *Origins of English Individualism* (Oxford 1978), p. 150n; L.R. Poos, *A Rural Society after the Black Death* (Cambridge 1991), pp. 200–1; H.M. Jewell, *English Local Administration in the Middle Ages* (Newton Abbot 1972), p. 160.

Nor was this mere lipservice: for the first offence, the penalty was a month's wages; for the second, a month's imprisonment; and for the third, dismissal.[31] Faced with hordes of vagrants and masterless men, potentially criminous or seditious, and with occupations of such dubious social value as acting and peddling, parliament and government in 1572 provided for the punishment of offenders unless taken into service by men with taxable incomes of £5 or honest householders, who would take them out of circulation and vouch for them.[32] To the Elizabethan Commons, therefore, menial service offered guarantees against crime and perversion of justice. It is no wonder, therefore, that none of the statutes of livery sought to restrict this type of retaining.

Lords also had responsibilities to non-resident retainers. Anglo-Saxon lords had responsibilities for all their men, resident or not. Feudal lords had a right and a duty to do justice on their men, in manorial or honorial court, and, as we shall see, their late medieval successors commonly arbitrated their disputes. They could be held responsible for the conduct of their retainers. Thus the government ordered lords in 1346 to expel any maintainers in their service, in 1461 to help arrest them even if they were retainers, and in 1486 the council decreed that 'every Lord and gentleman, if any of his servants make a riot or other excesse, the master of the same trespasser shall have in commandment to bring forth the same servant' or else answer for the servants' offences himself.[33] The sureties for good behaviour, sometimes of retainers, that Henry VII developed into a system had earlier parallels under Edward II, Henry V, and the Yorkist kings.[34] Roger Damory guaranteed that his followers would share his attitudes in 1321 and Cheshire gentry vouched for

31. *Collection of Ordinances of the Royal Household* (1790), p. 89.
32. *Proceedings in the Parliaments of Elizabeth I*, i, ed. T.E. Hartley (1981), p. 344.
33. Baldwin, *King's Council*, pp. 438–9; Dunham, pp. 69, 72.
34. J.R. Lander, *Crown and Nobility 1450–1509* (1976), ch. 11; P.M. Barnes, 'Chancery corpus cum causa file, 10–11 Edward IV', *Medieval Legal Records*, ed. R.F. Hunnisett and J. Post (1978), pp. 430–41, esp. 438–40; J. Conway-Davies, *Baronial Opposition to Edward II* (Cambridge 1918, repr. 1967), 36, 321; see also Mertes, pp. 176–8.

their servants, tenants and kinsfolk in 1642. This notion of surety should also come as no surprise, for the whole population was arranged in tithings, in which each was bound for the good behaviour of his neighbours, and it was commonplace to act as pledges in manorial courts or to require sureties when granting pardons, leases, or financial offices. The gentry of fifteenth-century Cheshire were frequently called on to act as sureties for their social inferiors: it was a form of patronage.[35] Neighbourhood and good lordship were equally long-lived and were complementary.

Despite such mechanisms, livery and retaining were still seen to be problems connected with maintenance, and so Richard II's Commons repeatedly pressed for restrictions and parliament reluctantly conceded rather less than was sought. The problems related to non-resident or extraordinary retainers, who were the objects of all the statutes of livery. The service of legal counsel, exempted from livery legislation, administrators, menial servants, and tenants was not affected. The first prohibitions, in 1390–1429, forbade the retaining of non-residents for terms of less than life, if below the rank of gentleman, and by lords who were not peers of the realm. Whereas hitherto there had been no restrictions on who retained or who was retained, henceforth only peers had 'the invidious privilege' of extraordinary retaining as 'the presumably dependable members of society'.[36] But remember that the restricted notion of parliamentary peerage, merely a fraction of the aristocracy, was only a creation of the fourteenth century. Henceforth the holders of feudal baronies, the overlords of knights, who had been several hundred strong and liable to occasional summonses to parliament in 1300, were no longer eligible. The restriction of 1390 is therefore much greater than it appears at first sight. Richard II's parliaments, it seems, accepted that all lords could control their households, but that only peers could control non-residents. Non-residents had to be bound for life – thus creating a lasting and

35. D. Clayton, *The Administration of the County Palatine of Chester 1442–85* (Chetham Soc. 3rd ser. xxxv 1990), p. 257.
36. Stubbs, iii.577–9.

binding commitment, both financial and disciplinary – and should come only from those who were gentlemen, who understood the conventions of legitimate service. All these could be clad in livery. Tenants could be arrayed, but not liveried. Gentry could be retained, but could not retain. Such measures enhanced the authority of the peerage at the expense of the gentry.

Why, then, did the gentry – as the parliamentary Commons – approve measures that apparently disadvantaged them? Of course, they were still eligible to be extraordinary retainers, which they wanted – 'retaining for life explicitly received their approval', observes Saul[37] – and to serve in the households and as estate officers. Receipt merely of livery was comparably unattractive. Again, they themselves were allowed to have household servants, estate officials, and learned counsel and to clothe them in livery. They certainly paid less and smaller fees than the peerage and perhaps also gave less livery to non-residents. No doubt they wished to prevent maintenance, but it is hard to see how the new legislation seriously limited potential abuse by the *lords*: they had the most legitimate retainers; they could call on their tenants; and surviving livery rolls do not suggest that many of those liveried were not otherwise retained or that those who were added significantly to a peer's connection. More probably, as Dr Saul has suggested, the legislation on livery was aimed at those below the parliamentary gentry. Maintenance, he suggests, was spreading down the social scale and so too was livery, to those who were not interested in permanent ties and gave livery only with criminal objectives in mind. Perhaps hats and badges were most restricted because they were cheapest and most accessible to men of moderate means and caught the eye less than the cloth that peers gave their men? If so, this legislation was designed to restrict the giving of legal livery to the aristocracy, nobility and gentry alike, and to shut out their social inferiors. If so, as Saul suggests, it should perhaps be seen alongside contemporary sumptuary legislation – which denied aristocratic dress to non-aristocrats – and indeed statutes that created substantial property

37. Saul, 'Abolition of Badges', 311–13.

qualifications to vote in parliamentary elections, to become a JP, and to hunt.[38] In short, the statutes of Richard II and Henry IV limited non-aristocrats to household servants, allowed gentry to give livery to their households, lawyers and officials, and left the most expensive type of retaining – to non-residents for life – to the peerage. Gaunt won.

The statute of livery of 1468 seems clear enough. It explicitly outlaws retaining for life, including indentured retaining by the peerage. Since historians could find very little evidence for its use for purposes not covered by the earlier legislation, they have doubted whether it meant what it apparently said. New evidence, however, has recently demonstrated that the act was passed because of the misuse of *legal* retainers for violent feuding and private war in the North Midlands in 1468. The act did aim at the peerage and was immediately used to prosecute the dukes of Norfolk and Suffolk and their private armies for the siege of Caister Castle and other offences in East Anglia. The act specifically forbade all extraordinary retaining by the peerage except on the northern marches, where the wardens in effect were retaining on behalf of the crown for national defence.[39] Even they stopped retaining by indenture during Edward IV's reign: hence the infrequency of prosecutions under the statute of 1468. As enforced by Henry VII, the act often penalised peers, was re-enacted in 1504, and was essentially the law until 1628, when all such statutes were annulled.

Why did the peers agree to the statutes of livery? The earlier statutes, as we have seen, prevented them only from retaining outside their household-men who were not gentry and from casual distribution of livery, neither of which seems to have been common. Prosecutions of peers for illegal livery in 1390–1468 are very few and commonly involve only handfuls of recipients. The peers were able to manage very well without casual livery because legal means of retaining supplied their manpower needs. Why

38. I. Harvey, 'Was there Popular Politics in 15th-century England?' [Durham Colloquium paper, 1993].
39. Hicks, '1468 Statute of Livery', *Historical Research* lxiv (1991), 15–28; for what follows, see Cameron, p. 27; Cooper, pp. 81sqq.

did they submit to the statute of 1468? The answer, it seems, is that by that date the numbers of indentured retainers and feed men retained for life was very low, except in the North which was specifically excluded; many of those who were so retained, moreover, may have served in the household. The lords gave way because they were conceding nothing of value. Why? McFarlane said that it was because fees were no longer securing undivided and exclusive loyalty. This could be because non-resident recipients failed to see themselves as akin to household men and had no intention of living in.[40] This need not mean that there was less retaining, but merely that retaining was concentrated in areas recognised to be legal. The reduction in fees may have been compensated for by an increase in household size, perhaps a rota of attendance, and by the multiplication of estate office. Such alternatives may have been less costly and offered more commitment. They were also legal: powerful though he was, there is 'no hint that the fifth earl [of Northumberland] retained or gave his livery illegally'.[41] Those of his contemporaries who were prosecuted – with the great exception of Lord Bergavenny! – were guilty of retaining only a handful of followers illegally. All this later legislation, as Dunham so wisely observed, 'distinguished between maintenance (the evil to be eradicated), livery (the psychological stimulus to many of the abuses), and retaining itself (the institution to be preserved)'.[42] Livery retained many legitimate uses – ceremonial, corporate, and military – which were explicitly listed in the 1468 statute.[43]

Indentured retaining ceased during the fifteenth century, when the small numbers prosecuted for illegal livery suggest that these laws were successfully reinforced. The figures for prosecutions were never large when peers were involved. The more serious breaches occurred in Staffordshire in 1412, when seven gentry apparently liveried 44 yeomen and tradesmen, who can hardly have contributed substantially to their riotous conduct with

40. McFarlane, *Nobility*, p. xxxiii.
41. James, p. 51 & n.
42. Dunham, p. 12.
43. Hicks, '1468 Statute', 21.

retinues allegedly ranging from 80 to 1,000 men. No wonder Dunham considered it 'quite evident that these prosecutions did not affect the strength of any particular retinue' and that McFarlane supposed that after 1399 'the problem of livery was at least temporarily solved'.[44] That, however, is not the impression given by contemporary observers, who deplored the continued malpractice and seem consistently to exaggerate the amount of illegal retaining that was going on. There is therefore a serious discrepancy that can only partly be explained by increasing sensitivity among contemporaries.

Undoubtedly there were problems in distinguishing between legal and illegal livery. Maintenance and private war could result from livery that was entirely legal; large, indeed excessively large, companies could be raised by legal means. The legitimate categories of household, officers, and counsel, particularly when inflated, were quite big enough. Moreover, observers could not easily recognise to which categories particular individuals belonged. Four defendants in 1429 proved not to be recipients of illegal but of legal livery, because they were estate officials (steward, parker and receiver) and menials.[45] If the lords did indeed retain new men the moment they had sworn to keep the statutes in 1486, as Husy CJ claimed, perhaps they fell into legitimate categories? Might not the livery denounced by Elizabeth I's Earl of Leicester have been quite legal?

It may well be that the decline in illegal retaining identified by Dunham and McFarlane made little difference on the ground. Such retainers merely swelled the impressive retinues of the nobility and were only a fraction of the numbers (probably exaggerated) in the plea rolls. Such evidence minimises the importance of illegal retainers. For lesser men, however, with smaller households and few tenants, for those below the lesser gentry, the lesser gentry themselves, or even the greater gentry, the numbers were not insignificant. Half a dozen able-bodied men were a substantial increment of strength. And though these cases

44. Dunham, p. 27; McFarlane, *Nobility*, p. 107n; Powell, *Kingship*, pp. 213–16.
45. Dunham, pp. 71n, 72n.

are not numerous or frequent, they nevertheless persist throughout the fifteenth century and beyond. Draconian fines did restrict peacetime livery, but at crises – in these cases, local rather national – men were still given livery or badges wholesale.

That the situation had improved is suggested by the fact that the statutes of 1468 and 1504 resulted from royal initiatives rather than popular uproar. Moreover, kings disapproved not only of those that breached the law. They and their judges seem to have interpreted the law ever more strictly in contravention of its literal meaning and the original intention of the legislators. Edward IV, for example, certainly overstepped the law in 1461 when he forbade the use of badges except for his own benefit, against his enemies or rioters.[46] If membership of the household made livery of cloth legitimate in 1390, which was not revised by legislation, later it became a breach of the statute to wear such livery out of the household. Was the Talbot retainer who appeared liveried in Henry VIII's presence really illegal? It became very difficult to avoid breaches of the law. If wearing livery outside the household or after dismissal was illegal, were retainers expected to change when going outside or lords expected to reclothe the staff they dismissed?

· · ·

UNFAIR COMPETITION

Kings did not seek to abolish Bastard Feudalism. Even their most vigorous attacks on it can be interpreted as the self-interested actions in the bastard feudal market-place of a new competitor with significant advantages: the crown. And by the sixteenth century the crown sought to be the sole beneficiary from retaining, whether by itself or any other lord.

Anglo-Norman kings had exercised lordship directly over their tenants-in-chief, only indirectly over their vassals. They and their late medieval successors had possessed resources in the localities, but they did not seek to construct their own local connections, or to participate in local power politics. When estates came into their hands,

46. Dunham, p. 72.

they commonly granted them out. They were generally content to work through such intermediaries.

The royal household contained lots of knights and other potential soldiery, which was readily increased in wartime by kings as chronologically separated as Henry I, Edward I, Henry V and Edward IV. As their knights aged or died, new ones were recruited. The adult Edward I, Edward II, Henry IV, Henry V, and Richard III brought their own men and the relatively young Richard II and Edward IV brought their fathers' men into royal service on accession. Edward II bound many of his magnates directly by indentures sealed with generous annuities,[47] but systematic retainers of the gentry in the localities, according to Dr Given-Wilson, were an innovation of Edward III. Coss placed it a century earlier and we have already seen that the Norman kings were paying mercenaries by 1102.[48] Whenever the practice began, it continued and apparently increased in the later middle ages. Not content merely with the service for which they had paid, kings cultivated loyalties personal to themselves. The Lancastrian dynasty kept the duchy of Lancaster apart and sought to maintain the Lancastrian connection as peculiarly their own. Edward IV kept his duchy of York separate and Richard III relied heavily on his northerners after his accession. Edward IV allowed, authorised, encouraged and even financed extraordinary retaining by those whom he particularly trusted, the Prince of Wales, the wardens of the marches, and probably additionally his chamberlain Lord Hastings, and the Tudor monarchs, as we have seen, also licensed retaining. The Commons about 1400 feared that the creation of a royal retinue could spell the destruction of the king's relationship with his subjects.[49] M.E. James, in contrast, saw Henry VIII's retaining of traditional Percy retainers as decisive blows at the family's power. Actually, it was a recurrent, short-term phenomenon, that ebbed and flowed, just as the Lancastrian

47. J.R.S. Phillips, *Aymer de Valence Earl of Pembroke, 1307–24* (Oxford 1972), pp. 148–51.
48. C. Given-Wilson, 'The King and the Gentry in 14th-century England', *TRHS* 5th ser. xxxviii (1987), 42; see above ch. 1.
49. Saul, 'Abolition of Badges', 313–14. For what follows, see James, pp. 66–7.

affinity died away during the minority of Henry VI and not before.

In theory, direct retaining should have meant that everyone who was anyone – certainly all those engaged in county government – were bound to the king not just as sovereign, but as bastard feudal lord. How effective such ties were in practice is debatable. Recipients received rewards and office, but the king could not be continually engaged in local politics; they were infrequently in his household or in direct contact, and the immediate lord was obviously often more important. Kings had to delegate their authority to local officials, generally local notables themselves. Royal retainers commonly accepted fees from others, perhaps regarded their ties with others as taking priority, and interpreted their obligations more narrowly than the king might wish. As James I complained to his recalcitrant House of Commons, 'There is none, or scarcely none of you, who has not had something of me, whether of office or profit'; but he still encountered their opposition.

Some monarchs, at least, were dissatisfied by this and sought to make more of the obligations incurred by their patronage; and the Tudors made this into the norm. When Henry V gave property to Englishmen in Normandy, he imposed feudal-style obligations to perform military service. Monarchs sought to make more of existing relationships with the citizens of their towns and the tenants of their estates. In theory, each was subject directly to the king's officers – members of borough corporations, stewards and other ministers – and could not be retained by anybody else except as menial servants. The practice, however, was different, as lords recruited townsmen; and stewards were either non-resident or diverted tenants' loyalties to themselves. From Henry IV on there were repeated letters to towns such as Coventry, Southampton and York forbidding retainer of the citizens; Henry Lord Grey of Codnor was prosecuted three times for recruiting citizens of Nottingham.[50] So, too, with tenants. Margaret of Anjou sought to restrict the tenants of Leicester honour to her service and Lady Margaret

50. Cameron, 26.

Beaufort did the same. Richard III instructed the tenants of Tutbury and Tonbridge to be attendant on the steward Sir Marmaduke Constable, who was instructed to prevent them from being retained by anyone else.[51] We have already seen how from 1346 royal judges were allowed to be retained only by the king. From early in the sixteenth century, it seems, the same applied to members of the royal household. The privileges of royal service were extended at the price of other ties and retaining fees. Undoubtedly there were many breaches of these novel rules, which went beyond the requirements of the law and threatened to make retaining exclusive to the monarch, but they were part of the successful competition of the crown with other lords. They deserve to be seen alongside the Tudor development of the militia, and its gradual extension at the expense of bastard feudal retinues, and in terms of its fruits. Tudor aristocrats were no longer free to use their manpower as they wished, but only as the monarch or the state permitted. From mere assertion of the priority of allegiance over service to national lords, Tudor monarchs sought to make themselves the sole beneficiaries of Bastard Feudalism.[52] That, however, still lay in the future for their predecessors in the later middle ages, who sought only to regulate and maximise the value of aristocratic retinues, in particular to ensure that they were not used against them, and to make their own men into the most powerful connection of all.

51. Dunham, pp. 72n, 73n; Cooper, p. 82; *British Library Harleian Manuscript 433*, ed. R.E. Horrox and P. Hammond (1982), iii, pp. 116–17.
52. See below, ch. 8.

Chapter 5

BASTARD FEUDALISM IN PEACETIME

. . .

THE LORD'S PERSPECTIVE

The typical connection comprised a household, tenantry, estate officers and learned counsel, extraordinary and the liveried retainers. Numbers varied from lord to lord according to rank, estate, wealth, age and many other variables; they could be concentrated in one locality or dispersed across many. Such categories help us to arrange the connection in ranks and relationships. It is not clear how important such distinctions were to the lords themselves. Categories were far from watertight. Feudal tenants served in the household, cooks and minstrels were retained by indenture, and lawyers doubled as stewards. Earl David of Huntingdon and William Marshal granted both fiefs and annuities. Lords used whatever rewards were convenient, seeing all categories merely as servants, and required them to perform highly miscellaneous tasks regardless of the particular offices they held. Those eleventh-century household knights, 'endlessly pursuing a round of gentlemanly activities, practising arms, riding on the count's business, acting on his behalf in law-suits, and dining in hall', had much in common with the Italian Renaissance Courtier depicted by Baldassare Castiglione; Dr Horrox describes the equally varied range of activities required of fifteenth-century retainers.[1]

The connection was a flexible unit that could be used

1. R.A. Brown 'Status of a Norman Knight', *War and Government in the Middle Ages*, ed. J. Gillingham and J.C. Holt (Woodbridge 1984), p. 24; B. Castiglione, *Book of the Courtier*, ed. G. Ball (Harmondsworth 1967), bk I; R.E. Horrox, *Richard III: A Study of Service*, (Cambridge 1989), ch.1.

as appropriate in different combinations, at different strengths, and with varying levels of military equipment. Display was often the object. 'Traditional feudal ideas', observed Painter, 'tended to measure a man's importance by the number of his vassals': literature rated him by 'the number and quality of the noblemen who entered his court or rode in his train'. Five centuries later he still 'made manifest his greatness by the number of gentlemen whom he could, on occasion, summon to follow him'. Big turnouts, like open-handed hospitality, were facets of the magnificence, liberality, and 'contempt for moderation and any form of meanness' expected of the aristocracy.[2] But there were times and places when display was not the prime object – when lords withdrew into their private chambers; when Edward III was at Sheen with Alice Perrers 'sitting at the end of the bed' and a mere handful of others; when noblemen went hunting; or when the noblest of ladies stayed with only two or four attendants in an enclosed house of Minoresses.[3] When calling up his extraordinary retainers in 1489, Northumberland instructed them to come 'privy harnest'; on another occasion it might be important that they came fully equipped or without weapons. It is important to remember such occasions precisely because they were *not* the staged events that the great wished to record or dispassionate observers thought worthy of commemoration. However widely dispersed geographically, lords always possessed the capacity to focus their connections at particular times and places for specific purposes. On such occasions different varieties of retainer were merged into the lord's entourage, his retinue of war, or his affinity. It was the use of such resources – for defence or for rebellion, for enforcement or perversion of the law – that the case for

2. S. Painter, *Studies in the History of the English Feudal Barony* (Baltimore 1943), p. 29. F. Heal, *Hospitality in Early Modern England* (Oxford 1990), esp. pp. 23–5; J.E. Neale, *Essays in Elizabethan History* (1958), pp. 70, 83.
3. C. Given-Wilson, *The Royal Household and the King's Affinity* (1986), pp. 33–4, 144; M.A. Hicks, 'English Minoresses and their Early Benefactors', *Monastic Studies*, ed. J. Loades, i (1990), pp. 162–3. For what follows, see Hicks, p. 400; Bellamy, p. 47; A. Goodman, *The Wars of the Roses* (1981), p. 148.

and against Bastard Feudalism rests. 'By their fruits shall you know them'.

Our data on turnouts is certainly not comprehensive. Few lords, if any, expected everyone to appear and seldom were the numbers and composition recorded. Whilst such material survives more commonly for the sixteenth century, Tudor heralds were interested only in the more conspicuous displays; likewise medieval chroniclers remarked only on the most outstanding examples – such as the army that customarily accompanied Hugh Earl of Chester in the late eleventh century![4] – and ignored the company of the common or garden earl, let alone the knight or mere gentleman. Relatively few household accounts survive and rarely for the important occasions. Admittedly the Tudor evidence is probably applicable both to earlier and to lesser aristocrats: it was the evidence, not the phenomenon, that changed and lesser men also employed display to impress the humbler provincial communities in which they moved. They tailored their conduct and their companies were commensurate to their station and aspirations.

All lords had households. Sometimes a distinction was made between the great household and the smaller and more selective riding or foreign households; sometimes only a proportion of the household was present on a rota system and many households periodically divided into those attending the master and those with the mistress. The precise membership varied from place to place. Always, however, a lord lived in his household, took it with him, and ensured that it corresponded to his station. The 'custom among the Anglo-Saxons' of the time of King Edgar for a lord to be accompanied by a 'large mounted company' persisted into the seventeenth century. Indentured retainers contracted 'to sojourn and ride' with the Duke of Buckingham in 1441–51 and to 'ride, come and go' with the Earl of Warwick in 1462.[5] 'Ride always with a notable company of servants and orderly apparelled', advised George Clarkson.

4. P.R. Coss, *The Knight in Medieval England 1000–1400* (Stroud 1993), p. 19.
5. Ibid., p. 12; T. Madox, *Formulare Anglicanum* (1702), pp. 104–5; PRO E 101/71/5/945; E 315/49/157; E 326/6402; BL Cotton Charter V.39.

139

If the size of an entourage reflected directly on the reputation of the lord, so too did its quality: it really mattered whether it consisted of mere servants and peasants or members of the gentry. To be poorly attended was disparaging: to be nobly attended was to impress. Thus the entourage was often out of proportion with what we, anachronistically, regard as actual domestic needs. In 1293 Edward I's daughter Joan of Acre, Countess of Gloucester, was attended by 200 knights, servants and maids of honour; next year Henry Earl of Lincoln travelled with a hundred men and twice as many horses. George Duke of Clarence's riding household was to comprise *only* 188 out of the full total of 399! Lower down the aristocratic hierarchy, retainers contracted to bring attendants appropriate to their station and lords to house and feed them and their horses. Merely when visiting the Earl of Warwick for lunch in 1431 the young Duke Richard of York took four knights, 12 esquires, and 14 yeomen with him; Sir John Howard, his wife and daughter brought a damsel, two esquires, two valets, and two grooms when visiting Alice de Brian in 1412; and in 1421 Sir William Mountford was accompanied by three valets and two pages and John Throckmorton by six grooms when they visited Elizabeth Countess of Warwick.[6] Hosts, too, needed to ensure an impressive turnout of their followers when receiving important guests. It was more impressive, of course, to bring a large meinie without any attempt to afforce it: Humphrey Duke of Buckingham's riding household of 56 in 1439 and 85 in 1458–59 was impressive enough and a Yorkist chronicler claimed, somewhat improbably, that York and Salisbury in 1458 'came merely with their household men'.[7] All lords, however humble, had men to hand in their household whether on their estates or not; for a great lord the force could be very considerable. From time to time, however, the household was afforced to make a more impressive entourage with extraordinary retainers, officers, and/or tenants,

6. A.R. Myers, *Household of Edward IV* (Manchester 1959) p. 94 [duke]; *Household Books of Dame Alice de Bryene 1412–13*, ed. V.B. Redstone and M.K. Dale (Ipswich 1931), p. 7; Hicks, *Clarence*, p. 164.
7. Bean, pp. 174–5.

140

who might be re-clothed in more striking livery to make a more impressive display.

Early tournaments, which were not dissimilar in scale to battles, demanded large retinues of good fighters for the leading participants. Having reached its political apogee under Edward II, the tournament became even more of a spectacle and was nationalised, being used principally to mark national events and organised by the crown. Total numbers could be large, e.g. at Dunstable in 1309, where the 235 participants were all knights:[8] how many squires, grooms, and pages were in attendance? The royal takeover was even clearer in the fifteenth century, for example the famous tournament of the queen's brother Anthony Lord Scales and the Bastard of Burgundy in 1467 and the set-piece jousting dominated by the king's in-laws that accompanied the marriage of his second son and the execution of his elder brother in 1478. Sir John Howard, who was acting marshal, had an entourage of 67 at the former occasion. Though ever less realistic, tournaments continued to be held throughout the Tudor era.

Bishops, of course, were spiritual lords, with estates and incomes matching secular lords and a need to impress churchmen and the secular élite alike. The household of Richard de Swinfield, Bishop of Hereford was as large at 40 on average and as elaborately organised as any lay magnate of comparable means; in 1406–07 there were 13 gentlemen and 29 grooms in the household of Robert Mitford, Bishop of Salisbury. Bishops made a particular show of their enthronement feast, which was often delayed for precisely this reason: those of Bishops Raleigh and Sandale of Winchester in 1238 and 1317, Shrewsbury of Bath in 1337, Archbishops Neville in 1465 and Warham in 1504 were particularly splendid.[9]

8. Coss, *Knight*, pp. 117–20.
9. *Household Rolls of Richard Swinfield, Bishop of Hereford*, ed. J. Webb, ii (Camden Soc. lxii, 1858), xxx; J. Leland, *De Rebus Britannicis Collectanea*, ed. T. Hearne (1770), vi. pp. 1–35; *Household Accounts from Medieval England*, ed. C.M. Woolgar (2 vols, BA xvii, xviii, 1992), i, no. 14; E. Roberts, 'Bishop Raleigh's Banquet', Hampshire Field Club *Newsletter* n.s. xii (1989), 1–2; C. Dyer, *Standards of Living in the Later Middle Ages* (Cambridge 1989), p. 54.

Expenditure varied with the Christian calendar and lords made a particular show on the great feast days: it was at Epiphany 1508 that Edward Duke of Buckingham hosted 519 people to dinner and 400 to supper. In 1462 Robert Perrot promised attendance on the Earl of Warwick at Christmas, Easter, Whitsun and All Hallows.[10] Everybody celebrated rites of passage, such as baptisms, betrothals, declarations of age, marriages, churchings or funerals, though of course it is the greatest who tend to have left records behind. Striking examples are the two particularly grand ceremonial reinterments of two victims of the battle of Wakefield (1460): the Earl of Salisbury at Bisham Priory in 1463, which was recorded as a model for subsequent interments, and the Duke of York at Fotheringhay in 1476. Following the death of Isobel Duchess of Clarence, her bereaved husband organised an elaborate series of services and ceremonies conducted by important clerics imported for the occasion; he himself kept vigil with his household and principal clerics. But then, as for that of the last Earl of Warenne in 1347, the numbers were not recorded. Wills often sought an impressive turnout both for funerals and subsequently for obits. The funeral at Beverley in 1489 of Henry Percy, Earl of Northumberland inaugurates a series of grandiose Tudor wakes: M.E. James has examined those of the Lords Dacre and Wharton. In 1539 120 gentry preceded the Earl of Shrewsbury's coffin from Wingfield to Sheffield, whilst in 1572 the cortège of the Earl of Derby included 80 gentlemen 'on comely geldings in their gowns and hoods', 50 knights and esquires on horseback, and the earl's chief household officers. The coffin itself was surrounded by esquires and gentlemen ushers of good families and 500 of the earl's yeomen took up the rear.[11]

It was customary for the earls of Derby – and no doubt others less well-documented – to be met by the élite of their native 'country' on their return to the north-west. In 1597 the earl was met by the sheriff of Cheshire and

10. McFarlane, *Nobility*, p. 208; BL Cotton Charter V.39.
11. *Collection of Ordinances of the Royal Household* (1790), pp. 131–2; Hicks, *Clarence*, p. 114; N. Saul, *Scenes from Provincial Life* (Oxford 1986), p. 35; Coward, p. 120; James, ch. 5.

500 horsemen and next day by a further 700 horsemen from Lancashire. In 1630 the earl's mother-in-law was greeted at Chester by 600 mounted gentry from the counties of Flint, Cheshire and Denbigh. Returning from France in 1566, the Earl of Arundel was met by 2,000 friends, retainers, servants and tenants in London. Such impressive displays could mark a royal visit: thus in 1486 on his first visit to York, Henry VII was escorted by the Earl of Northumberland with no less than 33 knights: scarcely more impressive, however, than the legendary (and perhaps apocryphal?) reception for the king from the Earl of Oxford. County elections, county courts, and quarter sessions could be very well-attended: we lack the data to assess quite how exceptional were the companies of 200 of Sir Richard Empson at York assizes in 1505, the 500 each taken by the Berkeleys and Russells to the Worcester quarter sessions, and the 80 taken by Sir James Croft in 1590.[12]

Just as much care was taken for national events like coronations, parliaments, and councils. None, surely, was more important to Henry Lord Daubeney than his creation as Earl of Bath in 1538, when he was accompanied by 80 men in new liveries. For Anne Boleyn's coronation in 1533 the 6th Earl of Northumberland intended taking 'seven score horse and not above', the gentlemen clad in tawny with black velvet trimmings 'as they use now at court' and his yeomen plain tawny with red caps and black feathers. In 1553 the Earl of Derby's escort to London comprised 80 gentry in coats of velvet and a further 218 liveried yeomen, in 1562 the Duke of Norfolk brought 100 liveried horsemen, and in the 1570s 80 men accompanied the Earl of Oxford to London. Splendid though the Earl of Shrewsbury's entourage was in 1555, when he had 120 horsemen, 30 gentry in velvet caps, and his barge-crew were decked out in blue coats, white stockings, red caps with white feathers and his talbot badge, he was nevertheless overshadowed by the Earl of Pembroke, who in 1560 brought 200 men to

12. Coward, p. 119; Leland, *Collectanea*, iv. pp. 186–7; Cooper, p. 88; F. Bacon, *Works of Francis Bacon*, ed. J. Spedding et al. (1858), vi. pp. 219–20; Stone, pp. 214–15, 231; Bellamy, p. 96.

parliament, all mounted, in velvet coats, and with his badge of the green dragon.[13] This last example stresses the competitive elements in such displays that forced everyone to participate. There were inescapable costs in wages, keep, clothes and accoutrements. Not to participate was to encourage unfavourable comparisions that undermined one's political standing. If one could not compete, it was better not to come: thus in 1471 the Duke of Suffolk felt unable to attend parliament 'to his worship' because his entourage was insufficiently numerous, many household-men being on leave over Christmas in Suffolk. So, too, in 1483, when Richard III conducted an impressive progress north to the city of York, his secretary urged a splendid reception to overawe the southern lords in his company.[14] However ostensibly peaceful, such displays had their significance for the political standing of the relevant peer. To stand aside from such competition was hardly possible without detracting from one's worship and reputation.

Such turnouts therefore had some political significance, even when they did not coincide with political crises. Often, however, they did: the magnates brought particularly large companies to the stormy parliaments of 1303–21; Thomas of Lancaster brought 1,000 horse and 1,500 foot in 1312.[15] So, too, during the 1450s. Thus the Earl of Devon brought 300 men and the Earl of Warwick 400 men to the crisis parliament of 1450. For the parliament of 1454, when the king was mad and the country on the verge of civil war, all parties brought as many as they could make, the Duke of Somerset additionally commandeering all the lodgings near the Tower for his retainers. In 1456 York and Warwick each brought 300 men in coats of mail; and in 1458, for the so-called loveday at St Paul's, Somerset and his

13. Coward, p. 92; Cooper, p. 88; H. Miller, *Henry VIII and the English Nobility* (Oxford 1986), pp. 25–6; Stone, p. 208; Bernard, *Power*, pp. 85–6.
14. *Stonor Letters and Papers of the 15th Century*, i, ed. C.L. Kingsford (Camden Soc. 3rd ser. xxix 1919), p. 117; M.A. Hicks, *Richard III: The Man Behind the Myth* (1991), p. 122.
15. J.R. Maddicott, *Thomas of Lancaster 1307–1322* (Oxford 1970), pp. 43–4.

adherents came 'with a great power', whilst York brought 140 horsemen, Somerset 200, and Salisbury 400 including 80 knights and esquires.[16] In 1483, to prevent discord, the royal council *restricted* the Wydeville escort of young Edward V to a mere 2,000 men, which Lord Hastings approved because he was confident that the Dukes of Gloucester and Buckingham would bring no less with them.[17] The threat of violence sufficed both in 1397, when Richard II's archers overawed parliament, and in 1483, when Richard III's northern army ensured his smooth usurpation and coronation.[18]

It is salutary to consider how varied were the uses to which lords put their connections and how few were military. War, foreign or civil, was exceptional: most of the time was peacetime and most of the services required were peaceful. That does not mean that retaining had not a warlike objective – that recruitment was not undertaken in case of war, as Thomas More reports – but that the principal uses of retaining were peaceful and that most retainers were civilians. Such instances, of course, are unrepresentative. They relate to special occasions, when lords made a particular effort, but not to those when the chips were down, when a lord was fighting for his life at Evesham (1265) or Neville's Cross (1346) or Towton (1461), and when retainers risked death and ruin and were torn by divided loyalties. Attendance at the household sets the minimum that a lord could count on: but how many would turn out in crises and how many would stay? When he confronted a rebellious rabble with the flower of northern chivalry in 1489, the 4th Earl of Northumberland was abandoned to die alone. On reflection, however, how special were these special occasions? Were not some quite frequent or even regular, such as sessions of parliament or quarter sessions? And whilst they seldom involved tenants and did not carry much physical risk for retainers, did they not test the conflicting loyalties of the gentry? The emphasis on display and reputation prompted lords to maximise

16. Bean, pp. 174–5; Myers, *EHD*, 272.
17. *Crowland Chronicle Continuations 1459–86*, ed. N. Pronay and J.C. Cox (1986), pp. 154–5.
18. Hicks, *Man Behind the Myth*, p. 106.

the turnout of the gentry, who could only serve one lord on the great feasts, at quarter sessions, parliaments, coronations or other set-piece events. At such times the more important retainers publicly acknowledged their prime loyalties to all their lords, if, of course, they had ever been in doubt. Such commitment carried a price: not, admittedly, the death and ruin that accompanied civil war and therefore inhibited turnout. But rebellion and civil war raised other issues beyond the nature and enforcement of contracts: most notably allegiance and the rule of law.

.   .   .

THE RETAINER'S PERSPECTIVE

What was in it for the retainers? What did Bastard Feudalism offer to persuade men from all walks of life to serve, depend, defer and even to commit crimes and risk their lives for their lords, to give priority to such obligations over their own interests and comfort, often at short and inconvenient notice and for long or indefinite periods? If Bastard Feudalism was indeed the reciprocal and voluntary contract so easy to terminate that some historians claim, the question of incentive is an important one. Did the lords receive the commitment that they paid for? And did Bastard Feudalism exist for the benefit of the lord or for that of those retained?

Historians have spilt little ink about most categories of retainer because the incentives were so obvious: members of the household, whatever their status, received their keep and pay; feudal knights were granted the land that supported them and their family and conferred social standing and a measure of independence; estate officials and lawyers had salaries, expenses or fees; and tenants had their holdings and hence their livelihoods. They could not have made a living (tenants and menials) or lived up to their aspirations (knights) or practised their skills (estate officers) without taking service. The perennial younger sons found one of their few avenues of social mobility in service to lords. Such people had little choice: they could not afford to be independent, were individually of small account, and lacked the worship by which contemporaries judged the great connections. Moreover there seemed no ambiguity about what they owed. Members of the household lived under the lord's eye and were readily disciplined or dismissed; peasants were little better off; estate officials were painfully accountable for the exercise of office at audit; they and lawyers owed specific and limited service that was understood on both sides. It was those aristocrats of standing with the resources to be independent who carried most weight: the established gentry, who were honorial barons, indentured retainers, annuitants and estates stewards. They surely had a choice. Could they not have lived peacefully on their estates, as backwoods squires practising country sports, as John Hopton of Blythburgh (Suff.) is supposed to have done? Why did they choose to serve lords? And how strong was their commitment?

The most obvious reason for service is stated in most surviving patents of appointment, indentures of retainer, and estate accounts. Financial reward. All retainers, at all levels, were paid: sometimes as little as 6s. 8d. (33p.), occasionally £100, far more often 2d. a day (£6.66), 10 marks (£6.66), £10 or £20. Such sums need to be related to the means of the recipient: there was many a gentleman with 10 marks (£6.66) to his name for which the smaller sums were enticing; the great Earl of Shrewsbury received £200 from Richard Duke of York. Whatever their rank, lords had other calls on their expenditure – the household, diet, and dress deemed appropriate to their rank – and spent only a small proportion of their income on fees and annuities which, in turn, constituted only a fraction of the income of the recipient: insufficient incentive, historians have argued, to stake the rest. The actual value to the recipient is not to be measured in such stark terms. Was not this hard cash, over and above the normal budget, free from other commitments and unmortgaged? When all other income was committed, additions at the margin are particularly welcome. Such sums should not be taken in isolation or regarded as the limit. One fee led to another: secure in the household of the Duke of Clarence, James Norreys accrued officers in Ireland, the Channel Isles and Somerset. On the Duchy of Lancaster estates in the North Midlands William Lord Hastings was steward and constable of

147

Tutbury, Castle Donington and High Peak, and master forester of Needwood and Duffieldfrith in 1472–83. Stewards, in particular, were paid expenses and could take out leases. In the 1470s it was as their estates steward that Sir Richard Verney ran up arrears of rent to Warwick College and it was the ministers of Tutbury and Duffield honours who poached their master's deer.[19] It is hardly likely that estate officers alone among late medieval officials overlooked the potential profit from patronage and blackmail arising from their duties. Peasants were 'adread as of the death' of the reeve.[20] Even offices that carried with them duties could be turned into pure profit. Most of the higher offices appointed deputies in the fourteenth and fifteenth centuries. At the highest level in the county palatine of Chester, it was normal for both the chief officers – the chamberlain and chief justice – and also the deputy justice to be exercised by deputy.[21] The estates steward, who had once held all the courts of an estate, was replaced by multiple stewards, each responsible for a group of manors, and each, also, commonly with a deputy who did the work. Such offices could be seen as sinecures. And besides the potential profit attainable from one annuity or office from one estate, many aristocrats accrued similar grants and appointments from other lords. Humphrey Stafford of Grafton in 1449–50 received 18 per cent of his total income – £57 from £331 – from seven stewardships and annuities.[22]

Estate offices could be exploited in other ways. They were sources of patronage. The official who acted in person could appoint to inferior offices or grant leases at his own initiative and advise on the appropriate destination for rewards outside his gift. The appointment of a deputy was itself an exercise in patronage. They were also sources of authority. To hold such an office bestowed authority over other men's tenants, for example as their commander in case of war. It extended

19. Hicks, pp. 141–2; *Clarence*, pp. 167–8.
20. Saul, *Scenes*, p. 128.
21. D. Clayton, *The Administration of the County Palatine of Chester 1442–85* (Chetham Soc. 3rd ser. xxxv 1990), p. 159.
22. BL Add.Roll 74169 m. 2.

the officer's authority and standing beyond the bounds of his own estate and added to his local importance. This was why Sir William Plumpton wanted to be steward of Knaresborough (Yorks); it was in this capacity that Sir John Malliverer was exercising authority in the 1460s. Such enhanced weight could be recognised by equals and superiors alike, even by the crown: in the fourteenth century, Dr Payling argues, shire elections were commonly made by the stewards of the great lords and still were in fifteenth-century Sussex and Yorkshire, where the selfsame stewards were always justices of the peace.[23] Such advancement could be more deliberate. Lords patronised their followers at the expense of others: they recommended their clerks to church livings to the prior of Durham and other ecclesiastics, proposed laymen as office holders to towns and other landholders, secured remissions of geld, royal appointments and pardons at their own instance and petitioned the Pope for all kinds of favours. Advancement in one service could lead to advancement in another: many successful royal officers started off with other lords. Military service especially opened all kinds of doors that were otherwise closed and was an important source of social mobility.

Service also conferred on the retainer some of the respect due to his lord. It enhanced his prestige and authority. Minstrels and messengers were well-received, fed, fêted and tipped by towns and recipients of their messages. Lords were better able to influence royal and other decisions that affected themselves and to secure such favours as portable altars, private chapels, and licenses to alienate. Because they served a lord and wore his livery, retainers were emboldened to act more forcibly and perhaps illegally than they dared on their own. Private

23. *Plumpton Correspondence*, ed. T. Stapleton (Camden Soc. iv 1839), p. 25; 'Debate', 184; J.S. Roskell, *The Commons in the Parliament of 1422* (Manchester 1954), p. 11; S. Payling, 'The Widening Franchise – Parliamentary Elections in Lancastrian Nottinghamshire', *England in the 15th Century*, ed. D. Williams (Woodbridge 1987), pp. 171–2; L. Clark, 'Magnates and their Affinities in Parliaments of 1386–1421' [paper at Durham Colloquium, 1993]; C. Arnold, 'Commissions of the Peace for the West Riding of Yorkshire 1437–59', *Property and Politics*, ed. A.J. Pollard (Gloucester 1984), pp. 116–33, esp. 119, 126, 132.

enemies and public law-officers, who were not at all in awe of a gentlemen in himself, hesitated before attacking, distraining, arresting or otherwise punishing his officer because of his powerful connections and the potential repercussions of their actions, even when legitimate. They feared support for the retainer from his lord, by force or maintenance, and their apprehension owed little to actual backing of the lord or even his knowledge of what was going on. David Esseby notoriously paid Earl Richard de Clare for protection against his feudal lord, Sir Henry de Hastings. During the 1470s Essex men of Duke Richard of Gloucester invoked his name in private quarrels unbeknown to him.[24] Dismissed household-men wearing the livery of former lords overawed unfortunate rustics in the 1490s. Retainers entered service for protection against their enemies: the Pastons were advised to get a lord if they wished to stand up to their enemies. Retainers could also use lordship to cover a career of crime.

. . .

MUTUAL PERSPECTIVE

Bastard Feudalism existed for the mutual advantage of lords and retainers. Thus far we have considered cases where the advantage to each – particular services and specific rewards – were clearly defined and compatible. But their interests could also clash. The aspirations of the retainer could conflict with those of the lord, a lord might wish to prioritise his own concerns over those of the retainer, and yet, in both cases, the retainer could demand and expect his support. How lords handled this crucial issue of good lordship determined who was master and how they performed on the wider local and political scene.

Bastard feudal lords were expected to support their retainers in their just causes. Many indentures of retainer specifically said so; Lord Hastings promised little else. Traditionally this has been taken to mean that the lord backed his man in all his quarrels, just or not, took his side, if necessarily backed him by force and/or in the

24. Horrox, *Richard III*, p. 245.

courts, and was ultimately drawn into conflict with his opponent's lord. Such exercise of lordship contributed to corruption of the law, to violent episodes, to private war, and ultimately to rebellion. The initiative lay with the retainer, who embroiled his lord in his own quarrels and determined how his lord's power was deployed. The exercise of such lordship was a threat to public peace on a progressively wider scale. Such lords may well have attracted criminals to his connection: it is striking that Robin Hood before 1262, the notorious Folvilles and Cotterels in the fourteenth-century, and Sir Thomas Malory a century later, had noble connections. Secure in good lordship, those with powerful protectors could decline to agree with their neighbours or to try their differences in the courts since violence and immunity against prosecution offered more certain results; the intervention of a lord became a threat that was invoked to get their way; opponents and victims had either to give way or concede or to seek the protection of a lord of equivalent standing; such lords were drawn into conflict on issues of little concern to themselves; and every petty quarrel had the potential to escalate out of hand. Far from taking a broad view of his interests, the lord had become a puppet, whose personal interests were overridden by those of his retainers.

That scenario is backed by concrete examples. Alternatively, however, promises of good lordship were interpreted more literally. The lord need back his retainer only when his cause was just and not otherwise; he guaranteed neither wholesale nor unrestrained nor illegal support. The lord might confine his support to legal forms – quite a broad category, since maintenance could be legal; he could disown those using his livery or name in their own cause, as both Cecily of York and her son Gloucester did in their Essex case in the 1470s; he could advocate a peaceful settlement – compromise, mediation, arbitration – and impose a solution; and he could exercise his authority to restrain or even discipline his retainer – Dr Rawcliffe records rebukes, humiliation, and even imprisonment.[25]

25. C. Rawcliffe, 'The Great Lord as Peacekeeper: Arbitration by English Noblemen and their Councils in the Later Middle Ages', *Law and Social Change in British History*, ed. J. Guy and H. Beale (1984), pp. 41, 45, 49.

If many modern historians have condemned good lordship as wholly bad, many contemporaries saw it as an ideal
to be sought. The reality surely lies in between.

All quarrels that had wider ramifications involved members of the landed aristocracy. Surviving ordinances and
courtesy books show the economy and decorum that lords
expected of their households. So, too, on their estates,
where bondmen in particular were subject to arbitrary
interference. Since lords had the right to correct their
menials and villeins, to beat or dismiss them, they were
able in practice to impose peace and settlements on both
servants and bondmen. Probably there were many quarrels, rivalries, brawls and disturbances within aristocratic
households, but we know little of them, except that household ordinances and courtesy books show them not to be
tolerable. Aristocratic retainers were different. They were
not so dependent on their lord – had private incomes and
independent standing – and did not have to submit to
punishment. Most of their quarrels, it is now agreed, arose
from their estates, which were the basis of their rank,
status, lordship, and wealth. Disputes about titles, rights
of inheritance, boundaries, or about such appurtenances
as advowsons or tenancies, were too important to permit
easy compromise. Such disputes caused many quarrels
and escalated easily: they determined many political
alignments in the civil wars of both King Stephen and
Henry VI. When historians discuss good lordship, they
are concerned overwhelmingly with disputes involving
this one numerically small category: the extraordinary
retainers.

Most quarrels were limited to particular districts. Not
only did they relate to estates that were relatively small
and concentrated, they commonly involved neighbours
with contiguous properties or relatives. Few gentry had
estates that were even county-wide or contracted marriages beyond a limited radius. Disputes with strangers
or outsiders were less common. Since, moreover, most
retainers came from the estates, neighbourhood or natural sphere of influence of their lord, most such disputes
were between members of a single connection subject to a
single lord and were thus theoretically capable of resolution by him alone. Henry I recognised that the quarrels

between vavassours of a single lord should be settled in his honorial court. Following the decline of such courts, late medieval lords commonly mediated between their retainers or arbitrated the disputes of retainers whether willing or not. It is not clear how sharp a distinction can be made between the earlier exercise of formal jurisdiction and the subsequent voluntary and informal conciliation processes. Many feudal courts must have been small, informal, almost domestic affairs much concerned with custom; baronial councils and arbitration panels had professional membership often including judges, formal processes for receiving, vetting and sifting evidence, applied the same law as the royal courts, and relied on the royal courts and the lord's physical power for the enforcement of their decisions. Infinite pains were taken with fairly trivial cases.[26]

Disputes between retainers of different lords, of course, were always more complex. Henry I provided that they should be handled by the local royal courts and that the king, as longstop, should settle quarrels between lords. The monarch continued to be good lord of all good lords into the seventeenth century – effective monarchs imposed peace, obedience and settlements on their magnates – and increasingly delegated such business to Star Chamber and other conciliar courts. Lords need not have been drawn willy-nilly into their retainers' quarrels. Most commonly they left them to the courts. Lords could refuse to back them – should refuse to when in the wrong – or could abandon them to the tender mercies of their rival. They could also mediate or settle disputes together, as Gloucester and Northumberland did in the 1470s.[27] Most lawsuits were settled out of court, often by arbitration, and the thorniest cases were repeatedly taken to arbitration. Arbitration was commonplace at all levels of society. Friends, kinsfolk, and neighbours were more commonly involved than lords. The parties seldom secured all they wanted from it: it was a process of conciliation, that produced compromises in which the losing party however wrong was protected from complete defeat; the winner

26. Rawcliffe, 'Great Lord', pp. 45–6.
27. Hicks, p. 375.

was confirmed in possession and freed from further dispute; and peace was restored.

The role of the lord, in such cases, was a delicate one. If he was to be well-served, he had to be seen to be a good lord, able to protect his men, perhaps also able to secure them what they wanted, but he also had to take a wider political perspective, to exercise restraint and authority, to remain in control of his own affairs. Protection, of course, was essential: no lord could allow his retainers to be molested with impunity. The 4th and 5th Earls of Northumberland sought to protect their people against royal interference.[28] Disputes had to be resolved or at least quietened. And it was essential that any solution was seen to be just. Just as arbitrary and self-interested judgements by kings did not last, so unjust settlements revived when coercion was relaxed. It was probably this need to appear just that prompted magnates to employ lawyers and even the royal judges, whose legal expertise could not be questioned, and to place such stress on the principles of equity and fairness. Lords thus avoided personal resentment. 'It is evident', observes Dr Rawcliffe, 'that any lord who failed to offer justice . . . ran the risk of . . . loss of reputation and eventual disgrace which overtook the most unpopular of the Staffords'.[29] The ideal, perhaps rarely attained, was that both parties approved the result; often indeed, neither noblemen, king nor parliament could make their awards stick.[30] A lesser, more commonly attainable, aim was that potentially disruptive differences were quietened without serious ramifications.

28. M.E. James, 'The Murder at Cocklodge', *Durham University Journal* lvii (1964–5); James, pp. 61–2.
29. Rawcliffe, 'Great Lord', p. 51.
30. Ibid., esp. p. 52; 'Parliament and the Settlement by Disputes by Arbitration in the Later Middle Ages', *Parliamentary History* ix.ii (1990), 336–7, 340.

Chapter 6

POWER AND POLITICS

Much of the debate about Bastard Feudalism has concerned its role in politics and society: was this role malign
or was it merely a mechanism, available for 'good' purposes as well as abuse? Fundamental to this debate is our
understanding of Bastard Feudalism itself. Earlier chapters in this book have established the nature of Bastard
Feudalism and hence of the bastard feudal connections
that operated in society and politics. Henceforth it is the
connections rather than the Bastard Feudalism on which
they were based that is our concern. The next stage is to
apply our knowledge to the political systems within which
Bastard Feudalism occurred.

The last chapter treated the role of the bastard feudal
connection in uncontentious circumstances: when there
was no resistance to overcome and when there were no
conflicts in loyalty. This chapter considers how it operated
in the more acrimonious spheres of local and national
politics; which inevitably involved contact with other connections, co-operation or competition with potential rivals;
and which forced retainers to balance their loyalty to one
lord against their self-interest, against ties with other
lords, their political principles and even their allegiance.
It commences with a lengthy discussion of the political
power structures in which such connections played major
parts and with the character of local government and
local justice. These enduring structures are then examined
under strain in sections focusing in turn on equilibrium,
friction and finally crisis. They examine the ways in which
bastard feudal connections could contribute to crises and

cope with them – issues of prime concern to so many modern historians! – but they also recognise crises to be exceptional. Hence appropriate attention is devoted to equilibrium and to Bastard Feudalism's role in creating and maintaining it. Civil war, which broke out when political crises escalated beyond peaceful resolution, is specifically reserved for the next chapter.

. . .

LOCAL POWER STRUCTURES

Twentieth-century historians have generally agreed that the English provinces were dominated by the nobility, that their dominance rested ultimately on force derived from landholding and retainers, and therefore that each area was dominated by the nobleman with the largest lands and feudal/bastard feudal connection. England was, for Given-Wilson and Bernard, 'a federation of lordly spheres of influence': what was called their *terra* or *potestas* in the twelfth and thirteenth and their *country* in the fifteenth–seventeenth centuries.[1] This was so from the Norman Conquest: it was not, *pace* Coss and Carpenter,[2] a creation of the mid-thirteenth century. This longstanding and hitherto unquestioned orthodoxy has now been challenged. The 1436 income tax revealed that peers held only a fraction of national wealth. Resident magnates, it is now apparent, did not exist everywhere. In many counties, perhaps most, there was no single dominant figure. 'In practice', writes David Carpenter,

> in the thirteenth and fourteenth centuries, [there was] never ... uniform magnate rule in the shires. Structures of power were kaleidoscopic in their variety. In some areas the gentry were able to create their own order or chaos; in others there were competing magnate factions; in yet others a lord might exercise for a time more or less stable rule.[3]

1. Bernard, *Power*, p. 180; C. Given-Wilson, *English Nobility in the Later Middle Ages* (1987), p. 1; D. Crouch, *William Marshal* (Harlow 1990), p. 161n; see also R. Virgoe, 'Aspects of the County Community in the 15th Century', *Profit, Piety and the Professions in Later Medieval England*, ed. M.A. Hicks (Gloucester 1990), pp. 4–7.
2. 'Debate', 179–80, 200–3.
3. 'Debate', 184; Cooper, p. 19.

Such comments apply also to the fifteenth, sixteenth and seventeenth centuries. Counties varied: if magnates dominated fifteenth-century Devonshire and Warwickshire or Northumberland and Norfolk before 1569–70, power was shared among lesser aristocrats in fifteenth-century Derbyshire and Nottinghamshire and in early-seventeenth-century Somerset. Society was kaleidoscopic also over time: magnate rule gave way to gentry rule in mid-fifteenth-century Devonshire, the gentry to magnates elsewhere. A century of gentry rule separated the extinction of the Beauchamps of Bedford in 1265 and the emergence of the Greys of Ruthin. In the late fifteenth century the Stanleys, Talbots, and Hastings asserted their dominance over Lancashire, Derbyshire and Leicestershire, relegating gentry rule to a passing phase following the waning of the house of Lancaster.

> The rise of the Stanleys was obviously not an unmixed blessing: their power and influence inevitably served to undermine the vigorous independence of the county communities.[4]

Such examples remind us that change was not in one direction only. The emergence of the earls of Newcastle and Warwick in Early Stuart Nottinghamshire and Essex indicate that there was no time within our period when noble hegemonies ceased to be created.[5]

Post-Conquest magnates were never dominant landholders in the sense that they held all or most of the land in any area. Much of what the Norman nobility were given was subinfeudated to knights, leading inevitably to an eventual loss of control, and even the most powerful magnates held only a proportion of the land in their areas of greatest strength. This emerges clearly from the maps on which Given-Wilson has plotted the holdings of such magnates as the Berkeleys in Gloucestershire and

4. K.S. Naughton, *Gentry of Bedfordshire in the 13th and 14th Centuries* Leicester University Occasional Paper 3rd ser. ii, 1976), p. 11; M. Bennett, *Community, Class and Careerism* (Cambridge 1983), pp. 248–9.
5. B. Manning, *The English People and the English Revolution* (2nd edn 1991), p. 230; C. Holmes, *The Eastern Association in the English Civil War* (Cambridge 1974), p. 38.

the Beauchamps in the West Midlands.[6] Though their estates were worth more than those of neighbouring gentry individually, the incomes of the Berkeleys and Beauchamps were certainly exceeded by those of the lesser landholders of the locality taken together. Surely they lacked the resources to overawe all the gentry or to fee them all at a level sufficient to secure their commitment? Hence historians have reinterpreted local politics as the interaction of many lords among whom, perhaps, the magnates were most important but not in charge, perhaps indeed an intrusive or disruptive element in a system that was working well. They have read back into the middle ages Professor Everitt's vision of Early Stuart England as a federation of autonomous county communities run by the local gentry. And the gentry themselves are now seen as men of substance, who were politically independent and able to make up their own minds.

Such new ideas have much to commend them. The greater gentry were the successors of feudal barons and honorial barons who had always carried weight, all the leading gentry were men of substance and standing, and from the 1250s at least their political support could no longer be assumed, but had to be solicited. Hence the propagandist manifestoes and songs that mark each successive political upheaval. With the early break up of some honours and the demise of feudal military service and of honorial jurisdiction over feudal tenants almost everywhere, many gentry found themselves without local superiors. Furthermore, the greater gentry – the Vernons of Netherhaddon or Staffords of Grafton, Sir John Pelham or Sir John Fastolf – often had larger estates and higher incomes than the lower ranks of the peerage. They had no need to defer to them and could manage local society themselves. But such observations make too much of the artificial distinction between nobility and gentry, a new creation of the fourteenth century, that gave particular weight to one criterion and one scenario: rank in parliament. It minimises what these two elements

6. Given-Wilson, *Nobility*, pp. xiv-xv, xvii; N.J.G. Pounds, *The Medieval Castle in England and Wales* (Cambridge 1990), pp. 132, 134.

of a single class (the aristocracy) had in common, such as education, recreation, aspirations, and source of income. The Vernons, Staffords or the knightly families of Sussex managed their estates like the nobility, had relatively large households, estate officials and learned counsel, tenants and extraordinary retainers. They too were lords and/or masters. Why should the gentry in a county without a dominant lord – say Dr Wright's Derbyshire – behave differently from the nobility? Why should those where there was a dominant lord behave differently in their little patch? Was there no room for the gentleman to dominate his parish because an earl dominated the whole region? The distinction between nobility and gentry has been overstressed. All counties were dominated by the aristocracy.

More seriously, the new interpretation explains away what dominance did exist. We know that magnates *did* dominate certain areas. Some examples have been cited. We can deduce dominance ourselves from the use they made of it. Thus the earls of King Stephen's Anarchy made treaties that recognised one another's spheres of influence: Robert Earl of Gloucester with Miles Earl of Hereford (1141 x 1143) and Robert Earl of Leicester with Ranulf Earl of Chester after 1147. Three centuries later the parliamentary representation of Norfolk was divided up between the dukes of Norfolk and Suffolk and the North of England was parcelled out between the Duke of Gloucester and Earl of Northumberland in 1474. Contemporaries tell us so. They leave us in no doubt that Thomas of Lancaster dominated Edward II's North or that the Duke of Suffolk ruled Henry VI's East Anglia. It was no accident that George Duke of Clarence bore Ankarette Twynho through three several shires to his town of Warwick for her judicial murder. Correspondents, petitioners to parliament, and parties in chancery from the twelfth–seventeenth centuries constantly complained of enemies too powerful in their own countries to oppose. Even allowing for the special pleading, it is striking both that some such petitioners were themselves powerful – like Matthew Paris's St Alban's Abbey or Ralph Lord Cromwell – and that their overmighty opponents are small men whose importance must have been geographically restricted. Edward VI's Lord Admiral Seymour, as we have seen, parcelled the country out in noble spheres of influence.[7] Justices of the Peace often served only in their quarter of their home county.

Of course, certain parts of the country experienced more lordship than others. We have seen how in certain localities the feudal map comprised compact lordships with natural focuses, which were less susceptible to erosion and escaped partition, and that a common purpose was reinforced by external threats, by continued private jurisdiction, and by resident lords with funds of patronage. Examples are the marcher lordships in Wales, the counties palatine, lordships in Yorkshire, and the borders which were subjected to martial law. The county palatine of Chester is a particularly striking example. Contemporaries and modern historians alike have looked further afield, to the Courtenays in the West Country, Talbots in Derbyshire, to the Berkeleys, Beauchamps, Staffords, Mowbrays and so on. As M.E. James observed, such hegemonies did not exist just in the highland periphery – they could occur anywhere and on different scales. The gentry themselves had their own, much smaller, countries: they were large fish in smaller or very small pools. Often it was *their* stifling power in particular districts against which litigants petitioned. If local potentates did not hold most of the local land or dispose of most local resources, what was the mechanism that gave them their power?

A fundamental presumption for everybody is that there was a direct relationship between landholding and retainers and power. Authority was exercised by magnates on their own lands, ceased at the boundary, and derived from the service of gentry, however retained. Dr Christine Carpenter has charted how Richard Beauchamp, Earl of Warwick (d. 1439) extended his influence in parts of Warwickshire and lost it elsewhere in a continuous process of alliances, retaining, and quarrels with gentry on a day-to-day basis.[8] Unfortunately her analysis is mistaken. At the bottom, perhaps, the minor gentleman

7. See above p. 106.
8. M.C. Carpenter, 'The Beauchamp Affinity: A Study of Bastard Feudalism at Work', *EHR* xcv (1980), 514–32.

with a single manor exercised authority only within it or within his parish or immediate locality: he possessed a very narrow circle of acquaintances and was *primus inter pares* among peasantry. Those with more land, however, stood out in wider area – beyond the boundaries of the land – and demanded deference and respect there, had wider horizons and acquaintance, and perhaps also exercised authority through various kinds of public or private service or office for greater lords, lay or ecclesiastical, boroughs, or for the crown. Simon de Montfort (d. 1265) dominated much more of the Midlands than his own honour of Leicester. Henry VII's Earl of Oxford and Charles I's Earl of Newcastle relied for their 'regional hegemony' on 'the vaguer goodwill and co-operation' of the 'most ancient families' of gentry whom they had not retained as well as on those they had. The Stanley contingents in Scotland in 1482 and at Bosworth in 1485 included many gentry whom they had not retained and so too, self-evidently, did the massive turnouts of gentry that met them when returning home in the sixteenth and seventeenth centuries. If Dr Saul's Sussex knights were not retained by Earl Warenne in 1347, they nevertheless attended his funeral:

> The importance which they and others not directly of the earl's affinity attached to being present that day gives some insight into the sense of loss felt by a community that had known his lordship for as long as forty years. His influence in Sussex society was not to be measured exclusively in the number of life-retainers who took his livery.

So, too, at Lord Dacre's funeral in 1529[9] and doubtless those other similar set-piece occasions. Those royal boroughs who appointed officers or elected MPs at the behest of local aristocrats in the fourteenth–seventeenth centuries were acknowledging a power that extended beyond the boundaries of their estates. At the

9. Prestwich, pp. 39, 57; S. Gunn, 'Henry Bourchier, Earl of Essex (1472–1540)', in Bernard, *Nobility*, p. 158; Manning, *English People*, pp. 330–1; W.C. Metcalfe, *Book of Knights* (1885); N. Saul, *Scenes from Provincial Life* (Oxford 1986), p. 35; James, p. 181; 'Ballad of Bosworth Field', *Bishop Percy's Folio Manuscript*, ed. J.W. Hale and F.J. Furnivall, iii (1868), pp. 233–59.

top the great magnate with the largest estate in the locality carried weight extending well beyond the bounds of
land and exercised a genuinely *regional* authority. Earl
Richard Beauchamp was the dominant magnate in the
West Midlands: it mattered not at all that he had no
lands or retainers in certain corners of Warwickshire
and his hegemony was unaffected by minor manoeuvres
around the fringes. His rank secured respect from his
social inferiors, whether or not they were his retainers.[10]
So, too, the Percies in Northumberland, the Courtenays
in the south-west, the Talbots, Somersets, Howards,
and the rest. Such lords were 'cohesive forces' in late
fourteenth-century Essex, fifteenth-century Richmondshire and Devon, Lancashire and Cheshire, and the
sixteenth-century North, contributing to 'further inte-
gration', local solidarities, stability and order.[11] But
sometimes also to 'local tyranny'.

Ultimately such power rested on the capacity to deploy
the resources that made the magnate individually more
powerful than his aristocratic neighbours. Medieval aristocrats lived up to their income and had to: their standing was measured by consumption and not to live at the
appropriate level was derogatory and invited disrespect.
It was particularly difficult to keep up appearances for
those earls, barons or knights whose incomes were near or
below the qualifying level: that is why certain barons, earls
and dukes abandoned their status and many potential
knights preferred distraint to the acceptance of additional
responsibilities and expense. Though living in every way
at a higher level and at greater cost, it was the great who
had the largest margins left for subinfeudation and other

10. It is possible that Beauchamp's hegemony did not cover the whole
     county and therefore that county government could be disputed
     in crises.
11. A. Goodman, 'The Countess and the Rebels: Essex and a Crisis in
     English Society', *Trans Essex Arch. Soc.* 3rd ser. ii.3 (1970), p. 272;
     M. Cherry, 'The Courtenay Earls of Devon: The Formation and
     Disintegration of a Late Medieval Aristocratic Affinity', *Southern
     History* i (1979), esp. 71, 79–80; A.J. Pollard, 'Richmondshire
     Community of Gentry during the Wars of the Roses', *Patron-
     age, Pedigree and Power in Later Medieval England*, ed. C.D. Ross
     (Gloucester 1979), p. 52. For the next phrase, see Walker, p. 3.

forms of extraordinary reward. Moreover, between 1390 and 1468 only the peerage were allowed extraordinary retainers. The annuitants, estate officers, and other gentry in such connections were generally of higher rank, carried more weight individually, brought more followers with them and extended the lord's influence further afield. They mattered, but were not the core of the retinue. The great estate had more tenants than any of its neighbours. More important yet, the magnate's household was many times more ostentatious, prestigious, and numerous than his neighbours. An earl had always with him a small army of 50, 80, 100 or 200 able-bodied men who conferred immunity from violent attack or robbery and whom he could focus at a particular time or place to influence a lawsuit or election, to pull down an enclosure or a house, or to strike at a specific enemy. At such points he deployed his whole resources – not just those of local origin – on a local problem. It was the household especially, his tenants and extraordinary retainers, who gave him the initiative and created his local dominance. The manpower of household and estates far exceeded that of any individual opponent and he was protected against the united opposition of disparate enemies by the habits of deference and by ties of loyalty among them to himself. His men could be deployed anywhere that he had estates and, indeed, where he had not. And the lesser aristocrat had the same advantage *vis-à-vis* his own inferiors: a household of ten and a dozen tenants made him a giant in his village.

But did it work? Recently it has been argued that it did not. Magnates could not persuade their retainers to turn out and even the greatest could not enforce their will in the localities. Power depended to some extent on respect and deference, on trust and acceptance of authority, and where that was missing power was flouted. Illustrative failures include Thomas of Lancaster in 1322, the Earl of Devon in the 1450s, the Percies in 1403, 1405, 1489 and 1569, and Warwick the Kingmaker in 1470. Even John of Gaunt could not get his way in Sussex: he abused his influence at court to secure a special commission of oyer and terminer that duly indicted his opponents and yet his will did not prevail.[12] If even Gaunt could not dominate, one asks how could any lesser aristocrat?

It is a fundamental question that requires an answer. It suggests that our whole notion of how medieval society, politics and local government worked is wrong. Was politics not in fact a debate between great men, as McFarlane and his successors have argued for sixty years? There are at least two convincing arguments against it: first, that John of Gaunt could get his way but chose not to do so. Secondly, that we are applying the wrong standards. Tied up with these answers are other important issues.

If lords ever travelled around all their manors and showed their faces everywhere, they were surely petty knights of the Anglo-Norman era: even the late medieval bishops of Winchester, with as many residences as anyone, did not have them everywhere, keep them all up or use them all, even before they leased out their demesnes. There were few major estates concentrated in a single area or region and without outliers. The natural processes of marriage and inheritance that swelled the larger estates created several centres and many peripheries. Thomas Grey, Marquis of Dorset had three baronies with focuses in Leicestershire (Ferrers of Groby), Lancashire (Harrington) and Somerset (Bonville) and many outliers. The principal estates of Richard Duke of York were in Ireland, the Welsh marches, south Yorkshire, Northamptonshire, and East Anglia: his son Clarence had property in thirty counties with centres at Tiverton (Devon), Tewkesbury (Gloucs), Warwick, and Tutbury (Staffs). All great and many lesser aristocrats had estates they seldom visited and valued primarily for their revenues. John of Gaunt, for example, gave much less time to Castle Rising (Norf.), King's Somborne (Hants), Pevensey (Sussex), and Embleton (Northum.) than to the Savoy and Leicester even when national and international commitments permitted. He cared enough about what happened in Sussex to use his influence at the centre to secure a favourable commission of oyer and terminer, but not

12. Ibid., pp. 117–41; C. Richmond, '1485 and All That, or what was going on at the battle of Bosworth', *Richard III: Loyalty, Lordship and Law*, ed. P.W. Hammond (1985), p. 177.

enough to take a hand in local affairs himself. What he
did not do was bring his own power to play, through
his household and tenants and himself, and concentrate
his overwhelming force, nor devote the time to win the
compliance and co-operation of the local gentry. Sussex,
in short, was never sufficiently high on his list of priorities
for that. No lord, however great, could pursue all his
interests to the full everywhere all the time. If even the
king's most decisive interventions only transformed local
political systems in the short term, how much more true
was this of a great lord? A sustained presence over a
considerable period was necessary to convert Gaunt from
an occasional, though admittedly formidable, intruder
into the dominant player in the local political game.

We need also to consider what is the standard of
success or failure we are applying to John of Gaunt. Is it
realistic or anachronistic? How much was meant by Tudor
statements that the North knew no lord but a Percy,
that the Earl of Shrewsbury was prince of two Midland
counties, or that 'the keys of Lancashire . . . hang from
the earl of Derby's old girdle'? What did contemporaries
mean by the 'rule' of a particular country? Did any
of them mean the *complete* dominance that we tend to
assume? And when we judge them ineffective because
they were disobeyed or their arbitrations failed to stick
or because there was disorder, crime or feud, are we sure
that contemporaries accepted such criteria as appropriate?
Are we not elevating a model of complete authority
and effective peace-keeping that was not accepted by
contemporaries and not even current in our own day?
May we not be placing too much emphasis on such
evidence? How can we judge the effectiveness of the
rule of the borough of Derby granted by Lord Hastings
to James Blount in 1474 when we know nothing of
what either *did*? Can we justifiably attribute the absence
of evidence to successful peace-keeping or the absence
of evidence? Even Richard Duke of Gloucester's rule
over York was not without exceptions.[13] And do we
not assume that conflict means failure? If Clarence's

13. Dunham, p. 127; D.M. Palliser, 'Richard III and York', *Richard III
and the North*, ed. R.E. Horrox (Hull 1986), pp. 67–70.

retainers poached in his forest, was not their prosecution, settlement out of court and future compliance evidence of successful enforcement of his authority rather than of the limits to his dominance? Undoubtedly even the greatest encountered determined criminals and malefactors who were not susceptible to reason, as indeed there are today, but are not the dire fates of John Lord Moleyns, Sir Thomas Malory, John Cockayne, and Sir William Lisle warnings that even such offenders could suffer their come-uppance?

Sometimes, it seems, historians are inclined to blame medieval magnates for their inability to preserve order when nobody could. Kaeuper, Lander, Harriss and Powell have stressed the limits of royal authority.[14] Justice was imperfectly administered and many laws were seldom or never implemented. Yet we expect of lords 100 per cent achievement in control of the localities. Did lords want 100 per cent? Did they see their role that way or want a finger in every pie? Was their dominance active rather than passive, did they intervene in every quarrel, and was their authority constantly enforced? Were they everywhere proactive or were they drawn into other's quarrels only when the parties solicited it? Instead of suggesting that contemporaries have got it wrong, we should seek to understand their criteria and expectations. The massive amount of litigation in the central courts brought by the magnates and gentry demonstrates how few civil cases lords sought to settle directly. They did not see themselves as responsible for preventing crime. No magnate, even where most dominant, could expect 100 per cent dominance and 100 per cent local peace. If this was not present, may it not be that the level that was achieved was *sufficient* – met expectations – and tolerable? Even Earl Richard Beauchamp in the West Midlands and Duke Richard of Gloucester in the North did not get it all their own way. In Sussex, where John of Gaunt decidedly did

14. R.W. Kaeuper, *War, Justice and Public Order* (Oxford 1988) pp. 2–3; G.L. Harriss, 'Political Society and the Growth of Government in Late Medieval England', *P&P* 138 (1993), pp. 28–57; J.R. Lander, *Limitations of the English Monarchy in the Later Middle Ages* (Toronto 1989); E. Powell, 'Arbitration and the Law in the Late Middle Ages', *TRHS* 5th ser. xxxiii (1982), 50.

not, matters were not so bad as to be intolerable and to demand his personal intervention. Such standards of tolerance were variable and depended on how central were the interests and priorities, geographical, temporal or whatever, that were involved.

There were many outlying estates that were regarded primarily as sources of income, which sometimes indeed were granted to cadet lines, mortgaged or leased for lives or long terms of years. What happened? 'Absentee lordship', suspects Saul, 'was little different in practice from no lordship at all';[15] historians often use the words 'void' and 'vacuum'. Of course absentee lordship did not mean no lordship: it was exercised by someone, not necessarily the landholder. Peasants and ministers saw little difference: rents were collected and courts held, accounts written and audited, and revenues paid over regularly despite the non-residence of the lord and the absence of seigneurial oversight backed by physical force. Any void was filled by the estate officers, who exercised the patronage, controlled the manpower, and generally wielded the authority themselves within the fairly limited framework of seigneurial expectations. In every locality the sway of resident notables were extended by such estates, many of which were ecclesiastical. The fees and authority of most small priories, university colleges, and cathedral canons were exploited by the aristocracy most of the time; by the Reformation – and perhaps much earlier – the same was true of large monastic estates. Such officers were chosen in part at least because their local roots and local standing bestowed the authority to run the estate and defend it against marauders. In return lords had to accept standards of conduct that they would have disciplined on properties closer to hand. And if they chose to reside or manage the estate directly, their assertion of authority could be thorny and time-consuming.

.   .   .

LOCAL GOVERNMENT AND JUSTICE

About 1150, aristocrats had rights of jurisdiction over all their tenants through manorial, baronial, and honorial

15. Saul, *Scenes*, 29.

courts. Disputes between vavassours of a single lord were tried in his court. From late in the twelfth century, thanks to Henry II's legal reforms, business passed to the royal courts and the feudal courts withered and eventually died. It was this victory of royal justice, argues Coss, that forced the aristocracy from sheer self-preservation to subvert royal justice. Henceforth aristocrats exercised jurisdiction only over their households and agricultural tenants: the latter dwindled to insignificant proportions as the middle ages expired. Henceforth, until 1889 or perhaps 1974, the aristocracy exercised local power through the crown's own administrative and judicial institutions.

Coss envisages too complete a transformation from honour to county. Some honorial courts – those studied by Stenton and Chew – were effective, but many surely were not. Honours were new creations, the result of the Norman Conquest, which needed time to acclimatise and were adversely affected by minorities and partitions. Often without geographical coherence, sprawling over several counties interspersed with the lands of others, they did not constitute a *system* of local government. Many knights always held of more than one lord and many disputes between neighbours must always have been handled by the county courts as Henry I had envisaged. Local royal courts always existed: before the feudal courts, at the same time, and afterwards. Aristocrats had always to take account of such courts and even in the twelfth century needed to exercise influence over them and good lordship through them. The changing map of aristocratic spheres of influence never coincided with local government districts, for twelfth-century honours and baronies and late medieval and early modern estates did not observe county or hundred boundaries. Estates were concentrated in particular districts, so that Tudor JPs sat only in particular divisions, or straddled adjoining shires. To influence royal justice and administration, men had to work through units of royal jurisdiction and it was these, moreover, that recorded their activities most fully.

The Anglo-Saxons bequeathed a system of local government based on the shire, county court and sheriff, and its constituent hundreds, wapentakes, rapes and lathes, all with their own courts and their bailiffs; escheators, administering royal feudal rights, and coroners were newer, lesser officials. Actually royal authority was often exercised in particular places by local notables, to whom particular franchises, whole hundreds and even shires had been granted. Until about 1330 royal justice was exercised by periodic judicial eyres (sessions of the royal justices locally) and thereafter by occasional commissions (trailbaston, oyer and terminer) as required. Private rights dwindled in importance from the fourteenth century, when the old system was increasingly supplanted by a new one. The sheriff, so powerful in the twelfth century and so prone to abuse of power, was repeatedly downgraded and restricted. Starting about 1327, there were keepers of the peace, later justices of the peace (JPs), who tried lesser cases four times a year, perhaps also conducting investigations; they were given more effective summary procedures in the fifteenth. Finally, in the sixteenth century, the creation and repeated upgrading of a militia run by Lords Lieutenant and Deputy Lieutenants and the 'stacks of statutes' that imposed ever more responsibilities on the JPs enormously expanded the functions and personnel of local government. The JPs now became the real county administration, meeting for ever longer quarter sessions, acting daily out of court, and from 1631 holding petty sessions as well.

Twelfth-century kings appointed trusted men as sheriffs, paid them, and maintained them in office for long periods. Such sheriffs wielded real power and often abused it. Since they were often outsiders, independent of local factions, and thus potentially impartial, such appointments are seen by Coss and Carpenter as more appropriate than the local notables who replaced them and perverted royal administration and justice in bastard feudal ways. It is a matter of opinion and preference whose abuses were worse. To the local élites, who were actually subject to such government, local men were to be preferred, even if their abuses also had to be corrected and external intervention sometimes invoked. Royal interference was often unwelcome. It was the protests of the local aristocracy that caused the emasculation of the sheriffs and created the alliance between crown and the local aristocracy that endured into the nineteenth century. From the thirteenth century on the officials of local

169

government – sheriffs, escheators, coroners, JPs, and commissioners of all types – were unpaid amateurs chosen by the crown from local aristocrats to their mutual advantage. Apart from saving on salaries and securing a permanent and continuous administrative and judicial activity locally, the crown reinforced its own authority and respect with their own. It was their local standing that enabled royal commands to be executed and royal policies to be implemented. Since the most valuable and effective administrators were naturally those with most lands, tenants, and standing locally, it was the local magnates and the heads of the leading county families who were normally sheriffs and JPs. As such men were not readily replaced – they had no counterparts – dismissal from office was not really an option and the crown lacked effective sanctions for negligence, disobedience, or obstruction. From the officer's point of view, such appointments legitimised their authority as local aristocrats over tenants and non-tenants alike, extended the range of potential favours they offered, and could avert actions detrimental to themselves and initiate or direct actions to their own advantage. We have already touched on the scope for influencing legal cases, but there was much else, from manipulating the militia to determining tax assessments: 'a light subsidy assessment was a way of showing favour to their friends, tenants and dependants', observes Professor Russell.[16]

By the late fifteenth century such office-holding was expected by the county leaders and was sought by those aspiring to such status although, in practice, it was a handful of legal experts who were most active JPs. The sixteenth century, however, witnessed a change in emphasis. To hold office became an essential mark of status; not to hold it was a blow to reputation. 'If thou hast no command in the country', observed Sir John Oglander, 'thou wilt not be esteemed of the common sort of people, who have more of fear than of love of thee'.[17] Demand for office increased and spread far beyond the local élite, so

16. C. Russell, *Parliaments and English Politics 1621–1629* (Oxford 1979), p. 50.
17. A. Fletcher, *A County Community in Peace and War* (1975), p. 128.

that membership of commissions of the peace multiplied several times between 1500 and 1640. Men competed to be JPs, for higher places on the commission, to be members of the quorum, and to be *custos rotulorum*, which were rated equally with rank, birth, and ancestry:

> *Shallow*: Sir Hugh, persuade me not; I will make a Star-chamber matter of it; if he were twenty Sir John Falstaffs, he shall not abuse Robert Shallow, esquire.
> *Slender*: In the county of Gloster, justice of the peace, and *coram*.
> *Shallow*: Ay, cousin Slender, and *Custalorum*.
> *Slender*: Ay, and *Ratulorum* too; and a gentleman born, master parson; who writes himself Armigero; in any bill, quittance or obligation – *Armigero*.
> *Shallow*: Ay, that we do; and have done so any time these three hundred years.[18]

The power they exercised swelled also. The balance of advantage thus changed from officer to crown. Monarchs insisted on active participation and weeded out the idle drones. They required ever more work from them: 'I am weary of the burden and charge of it already', lamented one Elizabethan JP, 'It is sessions with me every day all the day long, that I have no time for my own occasions, hardly to put my food into my mouth'.[19] The Privy Council supervised local government more closely, demanded propitiation with ever more paperwork, and required compliance with ever less popular policies. When the crown insisted on having its way with the forced gift (1613), the forced loan (1626) and shipmoney (1636), its wishes prevailed. Only on the very eve of the Civil War did local government break down as local officers realised that they were paying too high a price for their prestige.

. . .

POLITICAL EQUILIBRIUM

Peacetime politics were generally peaceful. They involved the aristocracy, who counted for something individually. They were a coherent caste who shared a

18. W. Shakespeare, *Merry Wives of Windsor*, Act I, scene 1.
19. T.G. Barnes, *Somerset 1625–40* (London 1961), pp. 302–3.

common education, military training, and family back-
ground and who inhabited the same sort of households
and lived off estates organised in the same sort of way.
They shared the same outlook, expectations, aspirations,
and values, such as a faith in rights of property and
inheritance and their consequent respect for the law.
Any crimes that they committed were 'fur-collar crimes',
infractions appropriate to their status and condoned in
their circle. Their shared world-view emerged, when they
come together to discuss heraldry, to hunt legitimately
or to poach, or when they embarked on pilgrimages,
foreign campaigns, or the tenure of royal offices. That
they were influenced by the same fashions we can see in
the proliferation of crenellated houses, individual chambers, private oratories, parks, chantries and monumental
brasses, jointures and enfeoffments for use.

Each of these aristocrats had his accepted sphere – his
little kingdom, where he was supreme. An Englishman's
house was already his castle. An aristocrat had a conservative view of his possessions. Having inherited estates,
castles, towns, churches and even servants, he saw it as his
prime responsibility to preserve them for his heirs, to consolidate, to modernise, and to improve, rather than to add
to them. He did not compete for retainers – there was no
competitive retaining by the peerage in 1436 – and others
did not interfere in the management of his household or
estates, in his relations with his servants or his menials,
and left him unchallenged in his own locality. Even the
most insignificant gentleman sought office in the militia
that gave him command of his own men and resisted
their command by others. Where they could not command or successfully enjoin, the law offered a remedy:
most lawsuits, by magnates and gentry alike, were against
such social inferiors as defaulting bailiffs, rustlers and
poachers, who quickly submitted and made their peace.

Relationships between aristocrats were defined by their
rank, ancestry and family connections, the extent of their
estates and fortune, and their estimation in the eyes
of local magnates and the crown. There was a social
hierarchy, that rated each in importance, and local society
was small enough for each to know his place. There was a
natural order. It was a stable system that altered slowly, by

the natural processes of succession, inheritance, majority
and death, sale and purchase. Noble houses failed naturally in the male line after only three generations on average. Minorities may temporarily have removed particular
lords from the scene, though their interests were often
represented by dowagers and trustees, but their estates,
their officials and tenantry remained in being to furnish
the household and feed men when they came of age.
The Norfolk connection was revived after the disasters
of 1405, 1485, and 1547 and the Percy one after those
of 1403–08, 1461, 1489 and 1537. Continual exercise of
lordship was not essential. Hence most alterations passed
off peacefully and their sum total left society essentially
unchanged. Members of this society met together on many
formal occasions, entertained one another at home and on
the hunting field, co-operated as neighbours and office-
holders, acted as sponsors for children and trustees, and
intermarried, generally in narrow geographical spheres.
If Pollard's fifteenth-century Richmondshire gentry were
a network that was tightly meshed, so too were Professor
Everitt's county communities in seventeenth-century Kent
and Suffolk and Devonshire. Mary Honeywood's 367 living descendants of 1620 had their earlier counterparts.[20]
The vast majority of relationships were with others within
a socially and geographically circumscribed circle. Frictions arose, inevitably, the consequence of close proximity
and over-close acquaintance, and neighbours, kin and
friends sought to mediate and reconcile differences, at
first and frequently thereafter. When they failed, there
were accepted channels of settlement in the common law
and in good lordship. Most disagreements were settled out
of court.

Lordship was an element in the richly textured networks of local society. It was yet another cement to bind
together people already associated and those who were
not, in a particular locality and in different ones, social
equals and of varying ranks. Its geography seldom if ever
coincided with that of local government districts. That
disparate and heterogenous elements came together on

20. Pollard, 'Richmondshire', pp. 47–9; A. Everitt, *Community of Kent
    and the Great Rebellion 1640–60* (Leicester 1960), p. 36.

regular occasions in household, entourage, tournaments and retinue of war and on infrequent ceremonial occasions, gave them a further common interest in the service of a particular lord and commitment to him, and directed their activities in his service – often overriding, when summoned at an hour's warning or committed to foreign war. The respective importance of such ties varied, but it should not be forgotten that many of these other ties, such a brotherhood in arms, co-membership of commissions, business transactions, friendships and marriages were actually forged *within* connections. Lordship was a natural element in society; integral, not an intrusion. The circles that were united varied greatly in size, strength and cohesion, and density, depending on the greatness of the lord, whether a duke or a mere esquire. They overlapped, for aristocrats were generally both lords and retainers. They could overlap, because they were compatible and non-competitive, the lesser lords deferring to the greater and the greater accepting the lesser. Just as everyone's family was unique to himself, so too was the society to which each belonged. Lords offered all kinds of self-advancement and further means to resolve disputes through arbitration. Aristocratic society, in short, was stable and contained its own self-righting mechanisms: its own means to reconcile disputes.

The amount of time spent in exercising lordship or serving lords, in local government, and in local politics was relatively small: surviving household accounts often suggest it was insignificant. Only a minority of aristocrats were active in local government. Sheriffs and JPs were chosen from the leading gentry and escheators and coroners from lesser ones. Historians have often analysed such appointments along bastard feudal lines to identify the balance of political power in any county: so many were retainers of the Duke of Gloucester, so many of the Earl of Northumberland, and the trend over time reveals the former prevailing over the latter. Such analyses are valuable where magnates can be shown to be competing and where their influence determined appointments. Such evidence is usually lacking. Almost always those appointed were natural nominees on grounds of their local standing whoever was lord – like Sir John

Stanley in Staffordshire[21] – and sometimes they prove to be *ex officio*, serving because they were stewards of some great lordship. In times of crisis, admittedly, the position changes, as some were omitted from commissions and others added, but such decisions emanated from the monarch, doubtless acting on local advice; even then, not all these political nominees actually officiated.

A prime example of these considerations is the election of knights of the shire to parliament. Here, surely, was an opportunity for local aristocrats to assert their dominance locally and to exercise influence in national politics through packing the House of Commons. Most, if not all, MPs had noble affiliations and many sat for seats susceptible to noble influence, whether pocket or rotten boroughs or shires that they dominated. Cases are known where elections were fixed or names inserted in blank returns or over deletions. For the parliament of 1478, which was scheduled to destroy the king's brother Clarence, a particular effort was made to secure a compliant Commons by maximising the electoral potential of the crown, the royal family, and the court nobility. Sometimes similar results were sought by particular noblemen, such as Clarence himself in 1472 and Earl Rivers in 1483.[22] The Paston Letters and electoral lawsuits record bitter divisions, votes, riots and clashes between aristocratic connections. Such instances, however, are exceptional, for most elections were uncontested: perhaps all were uncontested before the 1420s, when majority voting and qualifications to vote were introduced. Hitherto – and perhaps often thereafter? – only the magnates or their stewards were consulted. At the least there was frequently a consensus already, based on agreement between magnates and/or the county gentry, who valued the reality and appearance of unity.[23] MPs elected by consensus presumably

21. Hicks, *Clarence*, p. 169.
22. Ibid., pp. 139–44, 202–3; E.W. Ives, 'Andrew Dymmock and the Papers of Antony Earl Rivers, 1482–3', *BIHR* xli (1968), 222–3.
23. E.g. S. Payling, 'The Widening Franchise – Parliamentary Elections in Lancastrian Nottinghamshire', *England in the 15th Century*, ed. D. Williams (1987), pp. 171–7; A. Hassell Smith, *County and Court* (Cambridge 1974), pp. 314–32, esp. 316, 318, 322–3; see also M.A. Kishlansky, *Parliamentary Selection* (Cambridge 1986).

represented that consensus and continued to respect the society, governing élite, and noble connections that had put them there. Whether formally retained or not, they were the product of local political society and operated within it. 'Could Warwick, Plympton, Poole, Ludgershall or any other seigneurial borough choose anyone hostile to their lord . . .?'[24] Before the early seventeenth century, when counties mandated their MPs to work for political programmes,[25] there was no *necessity* for lords to put in their own men or to require particular conduct from them. Retainers who served as MPs were generally qualified by birth and wealth. Often they wanted election for their own ends, particularly through boroughs – many borough constituencies were *created* to provide electoral representation for particular families – and sought the backing of their lords where appropriate. Then lords intervened, instructed, courted, or begged the borough council on their candidate's behalf. Sometimes seigneurial pressure was effective, sometimes not, but little hung on the result. Only occasionally did lords care enough for their local or national standing to risk it in an election.

All gentlemen were masters in their own houses and on their own estates and had independent incomes. They had their own affairs to manage and family strategies to plan. They were the leaders of their local communities, were often office-holders in their own right, and had both administrative and military duties. Such men, it is argued, had standing and experience. They were not to be taken for granted by their lords, whether in honorial courts, parliament or in private war. From the thirteenth century, so it is argued, their views had to be taken into account; hence their summons to parliament and the care of barons in watching over their interests. Edward III felt it necessary to win their approval for his war on France and participators in the Wars of the Roses solicited their support: because their views mattered. Tudor proclamations and homilies addressed an ever wider audience. The gentry were capable of speaking frankly to the greatest of

24. Hicks, *Clarence*, p. 171.
25. D. Hirst, *The Representative of the People?* (Cambridge 1975).

lords and correcting them[26] and they themselves had too much to lose to follow blindly in politics. There is truth in all this. However, most service involved no difficult choices, merely routine activities predicted when they were first retained. The interests of lord and retainer were compatible. However experienced and independent, retainers were customarily subordinate to their lords, used to deferring to social superiors, to serving under their command, and to seeking their lordship. Only bad lordship, divisions within their community or political crises beyond its boundaries could force such choices on them and such events were by definition rare. Essentially backwoodsmen, their appreciation of the nuances of national politics should not be exaggerated. It is hardly surprising that so often they accepted the judgement and followed the lead of their lords.

. . .

POLITICAL FRICTION

Yet political friction occurred. Why? Of what, indeed, did local politics consist? Undoubtedly of the private warfare, feuds, ambushes and forcible entries so often recounted, but their very notoriety – their status as *causes célèbres* – remind us that they are exceptional. Moreover, such incidents are not themselves what is at issue, but the symptoms or consequences. What factors caused such results?

Different historians have different explanations. For Stone and James they arise from childish quarrels, which James attributes to a cult of honour, that made aristocrats assertive, quarrelsome, and unduly sensitive and constantly embroiled them in quarrels that could only be settled violently.[27] Both historians exaggerate the levels of violence. Perhaps such quarrels and consequent duels developed towards the end of our period, but earlier feuds had more substantial causes. Coss sees the causes in a will to dominance – surely only disruptive when resisted? – and over jurisdiction over tenants.[28] Did thirteenth-century

26. E.g. C. Rawcliffe, 'Parliament and the Settlement of Disputes by Arbitration in the Later Middle Ages', *Parliamentary History* ix.ii (1990).
27. Stone, pp. 233–44; James, p. 309.
28. Coss, 'Debate', 200, 203.

aristocrats really seek to exploit other people's serfs? Whilst private franchises clearly mattered much more in the thirteenth than later centuries, such disputes are surely an aspect of the property disputes – Bellamy's 'land wars' or 'gentlemen's wars' – that were endemic from the fourteenth to the seventeenth centuries? Such disputes could threaten the whole landed basis on which wealth and rank depended.

There was always potential for political friction, but it occurred only occasionally. There were three important local factors, which interacted rather than being self-contained. By far the most common cause, to be found everywhere, were disputes about the ownership of land. Secondly, disruption arose from disruptive newcomers. Thirdly, there were clashes between established magnates. To such local causes could be added external factors – clashes arising from royal intervention or civil war – and from the withdrawal of restraint, through the removal of a dominant lord or the virtual collapse of central government in the 1330s or 1450s. Disorder occurred everywhere from time to time. It occurred almost everywhere in times of national crisis.

Land disputes occurred everywhere all the time. Estates grew and divided with inheritance: it was commonplace for different portions to have different heirs. Land-law was ill-defined and made it hard to establish watertight titles. Landlords created entails and trusts beyond their legal powers. Litigation offered hope to those with little right. Most common, perhaps, were disputes between heirs male and heirs general: thus in the great Berkeley lawsuit James Berkeley, against justice and all odds, saved peerage, castle, and estate for the male line. There are Berkeleys at Berkeley Castle still. Sometimes such differences arose from attempts to favour children of second marriages over their seniors, as in the Neville vs Neville and Talbot vs Lisle disputes, or even to favour bastards over collaterals. Sales of land by the impecunious or childless were liable to challenge from residual heirs: not only could the latter win, but purchasers had to buy out the most vestigial claims. In their long struggle for the Fastolf estate the Pastons were obliged to confront and surrender lands to rivals with little or no right.

Most cases were settled relatively easily at the inquisition *post mortem*, in the courts or by arbitration. That some rumbled on was because the issues at stake were so fundamental, the estates at issue so important, and the parties so well-connected. Magnates were not embroiled in every petty dispute, which could be accommodated without polarising local society, but they could not overlook the major feuds.

Property disputes were generally defensive, about the protection of real or imagined rights. Established families tended to be conservative and uncompetitive, accepted the status of others, planned advancement through peaceful intermarriage, and operated within existing social networks. There were many purchasers of land who sought no more than acceptance by local society. Important newcomers, however, were often assertive, acquisitive, and disruptive. Supplanting reluctant sellers, searching for viable estates to pass on to their heirs, they had strategies for development that impinged on others and were in a hurry not merely to be accepted but to lead or dominate local society. Characteristically such parvenus erected grandiose status symbols as marks of their local eminence well before they had integrated themselves into local society: new religious foundations at Bisham Priory, Caister and Middleham Colleges; new castles at Farleigh Hungerford and Caister; new mansions at the Rye House and Layer Marney Towers. Many such intrusions, promotions, and recoveries from minorities and forfeitures passed off peacefully, but all had potential for disturbance that sometimes materialised. The forceful assertiveness of Lord Fanhope in Bedfordshire in the 1430s, of Lord Bonville in Devonshire in the 1450s, and of the Duke of Gloucester in the North in the 1470s are good examples.

Clashes arose, thirdly, from overlapping jurisdictions and spheres of influence: perhaps over dominance of a particular town, such as York in the 1450s, over competition for particular retainers, or from backing retainers in their disputes. Such clashes surely point to some underlying cause or change: a more expansionist policy, perhaps, or weakness that made refusal of a retainers' wishes impossible. All lords did clash with other lords – hence the constant litigation between them – but such cases did not necessarily have political ramifications or even always involve the lord himself. Did Clarence's lawsuits with Lord Audley or Lord FitzWarin's men really determine political alignments? Lords lived with a good deal of low-level friction without proceeding to extremes. So many men were able to serve several lords because their demands were compatible. There were conventions about who to retain and who not. Warwick the Kingmaker was authorised by Richard Duke of York to employ Walter Blount at Calais. The rules were broken, however, when Gloucester retained Northumberland's undersheriff, John Widdrington, and when Sir William Plumpton sought appointment as a JP from Lord Hastings. But each time the potential aggressor withdrew rather than rupture relations with the retainer's original lord. Warwick, Gloucester, and Hastings recognised legitimate interests of York and Northumberland with which they would not tamper.[29] Edward IV's queen declined to arbitrate one dispute fearful lest it 'cause a grudge' between her and Warwick.[30] Whilst there were many occasions for dispute, most were controlled by mutual restraint.

Even when differences were pursued, they could be prosecuted well short of private war. At manorial level, it was possible to establish seisin or interrupt that of another. Rents could be collected, fences broken, and hay mown. In 1472 John Paston III obstructed another's manorial court.[31] All stages of legal process could be manipulated. Lordship was invoked to protect, to intimidate, to support and to mediate. Royal authority was applied in private disputes through suits in the central court, whether common law or prerogative, through appeals to king or council or parliament, and through the purchase of writs, pardons and commissions. Even the intervention of the king could be the tactic of an influential partisan without right on

29. *Original Letters Illustrative of English History*, ed. H. Ellis, 2nd ser. ii.i. (1827) ii.i.125–6; Dunham, p. 140; *Plumpton Correspondence*, ed. T. Stapleton (Camden Soc. iv 1839), p. 33.
30. C. Rawcliffe, 'The Great Lord as Peacekeeper: Arbitration by English Noblemen and their Councils in the Later Middle Ages', *Law and Social Change in British History*, ed. J. Guy and H. Beale (1984), p. 38.
31. Bellamy, pp. 45–6.

his side. So many stages and tactics could be tried that the crown was bound to be offered the chance to impose peace well before quarrels got out of hand.

. . .

POLITICAL CRISES

There were two origins for political crises: local and central. In one sense, national politics was the sum of all the different local politics, which could all coalesce and sweep away king and national government alike. This happened with the escalation of private feuds in the 1450s[32] and with the revolt of the provinces in the 1630s. Each, however, could have been prevented, by a firmer hand in the earlier instance and by greater conciliation in the latter. Few local differences had the potential to explode on the national scene and none could not be quelled by the concentrated deployment of national resources. In 1473, for example, Edward IV's progress through the North Midlands imposed peace in the Welsh marchers, on his two brothers, and on rival magnates in the North. Backed by the whole military might of the kingdom, he was too powerful to withstand.[33] Kings commanded a fearsome array of judicial commissions. As good lord of all good lords, they arbitrated disputes and imposed settlements, fined, imprisoned, disinherited and frankly terrorised their greatest subjects. Such powers were not effectively used to control trouble by such kings as Henry III, Edward II, Richard II, Henry VI, and Charles I. Their failures allowed crises to develop – indeed, caused them to develop by denying them just remedy – but could themselves result from crises at the centre.

Great political crises 1150–1650 all had national causes. Power was concentrated in the hands of the monarch provided it was exercised to the satisfaction of the aristocracy, who had the resources in manpower to impose their wills

32. R.L. Storey, *End of the House of Lancaster* (2nd edn Gloucester 1986), esp. p. 27; M.A. Kishlansky, *New Model Army* (Cambridge 1979), p. 4. For what follows, see J.S. Morrill, *Revolt of the Provinces* (2nd edn Cambridge 1980), pp. 21–31.
33. Hicks, *Clarence*, pp. 107–8.

by force. Generally they were content to stand aside. Relatively few attended court before the Tudors and many absented themselves from parliament too. Their power was dormant. But ineffective kings, unsuccessful kings, or arbitrary kings, who were unable to keep peace and order, could overcome aristocrats' disinclination to rebel, could unite their naturally loyal subjects against them, and cause them to overthrow them. It took a long time, commonly a decade or more, for frictions and tensions to produce decisive conflict. Not only had the rebels to make up their own minds – to overcome their own prejudices and fears – but they had also to persuade those peers who normally stood above politics and their own advisers of the course they were to take. They knew what was at stake, were rational in their decisions, and deployed their manpower only as a last resort. Their objectives, also, were limited. Such revolutions changed the identity of the king and always resulted in the restoration of stability within the same system by a more effective and acceptable alternative. If civil war was a drastic remedy, the political system nevertheless contained within it the means to correct its own imbalances. And the means that the aristocracy deployed were bastard feudal.

It was only at such times that retainers too were faced by political choices. There was no problem when self-interest, one's lord's wishes and the dictates of allegiance agreed – for the suppression of rebellion or war in France, for example – or when they were compatible, as they normally were. Rebellion brought them into conflict, presented real risks and perhaps demanded the political nous with which they are now credited and which historians have pushed back to the fifteenth and even mid-thirteenth centuries even for the peasantry. Where past historians too readily assumed an unquestioning obedience to lords, it is now commonplace to state that they were not Pavlovian dogs. 'Press a button ... and you have won the North Midlands'.[34] It is not difficult to find

34. C.F. Richmond, 'Fauconberg's Kentish Rebellion of 1471', *EHR* lxxxv (1971), pp. 691–2; D. Carpenter, 'The English Peasantry in Politics 1258–67', *P&P* 136 (1992); Bernard, *Power*, p. 182; C. Richmond, 'After McFarlane', *History* Lxviii (1983), 58.

evidence for both positions: qualitative rather than quantitative, it helps us very little with the generalisation. Obviously the chronologically final position was our own – that everyone of whatever class made up their own mind on the basis of the facts available to them, personal advantage was balanced against loyalty and allegiance, and retainer became a matter of bargaining rather than 'unconditional faithfulness'. But had this occurred within our period for some, for most, for everyone? And did it necessarily follow, as from our vantage point it does, that the rational answer was always allegiance rather than bastard feudal loyalty? For some, certainly, advantage prevailed, at all times: for example Sir Robert Holland, most trusted betrayer of Thomas of Lancaster in 1322, or Henry Vernon in 1471. That others interpreted the fidelity of others as due to fear, like Clarendon over the Stanley tenants,[35] may have been because they found their conduct otherwise difficult to understand and less advanced, mature and sophisticated than their own?

At the other extreme, among the 'poorer and meaner sort', we have every reason to doubt their capacity to choose. Christopher Hill has collected a wealth of references demonstrating the universal belief of the Tudor and Early Stuart élite that the people were 'a many-headed monster' that thought and behaved irrationally, especially in rebellion.[36] Many thought that they did follow their leaders blindly, not least Richard III and Charles I, who were consequently prepared to be lenient towards them.[37] Holinshed stands in between, testifying both to their 'soldier-like obedience to their leaders' and their capacity to forget it.[38] Illiterate and probably with nothing to read, they had no independent access to information and were thus easily swayed by rumour, gossip, prophecy, etc. There was thus scope to influence them: hence the

35. Coward, p. 99.
36. C. Hill, *Change and Continuity in 17th-Century England* (London 1974), ch. 8.
37. P. Hammond and A. Sutton, *Richard III: The Road to Bosworth Field* (London 1985), p. 148; J.S.A. Adamson, 'The Baronial Context of the English Civil War', *TRHS* 5th ser. xl (1990), 102.
38. Bernard, *Power*, p. 40.

Tudor homilies and proclamations that pumped out the concept of order, which Drs Walter and Wrightson have argued was effectively internalised and limited the scope, objectives, and operation of riots and rebellions.[39] The manifestoes during the Wars of Roses were designed for an Anglophone popular audience of townsmen that could read – unless they were proclaimed as well as posted – but for most rustics there was surely only information from the lord, if he thought it worth supplying. For them, remember, he also represented royal authority. *Pace* David Carpenter, therefore, 1258–67 seems too early for peasants to be deciding as well as acting in politics.

The gentry lie in between. Their interests were consulted by king and lords from the thirteenth century – though their active role has recently been doubted! – and whole groups can be shown both to have acted in accordance with and against their allegiance. But how well were even they informed? Would the turnout of Lancastrian retainers in 1399 for the future Henry IV or of Yorkshiremen in 1471 for Edward IV have been achieved had they not been persuaded that both kings were claiming merely their ancestral duchies? To maintain and mobilise his retainers' support in 1470 Warwick the Kingmaker felt it necessary both to inform *and* to misinform.[40] Inertia probably brought even gentry into their lord's armies unless they were aware it was treasonable. Even then the dynastic revolutions that occurred six times between 1326 and 1485 shows that many followed their rebellious lords. Much more difficult in 1642, it still proved possible for lords to carry the gentry with them.

39. *Rebellion, Popular Protest and the Social Order*, ed. P. Slack (Cambridge 1984), ch. 6.
40. *The Arrival of Edward IV*, ed. J. Bruce (Camden Soc. i, 1836), p. 4; *Chronicles of the Revolution 1397–1400*, ed. C. Given-Wilson (Manchester 1992), pp. 252–3; A.B. Steel, *Richard II* (Cambridge 1941), p. 264; Hicks, *Clarence*, pp. 66–70.

Chapter 7

BASTARD FEUDALISM IN WARTIME

. . .

ROYAL WAR

Though common, war was never continuous. There were
long periods without war. Campaigns were short and were
separated by frequent and often lengthy truces. There are
few early parallels to the attrition of Henry V's conquest of
Normandy or the Eighty Years War in The Netherlands
that were characteristic later. Lords and retainers were
seldom campaigning and most of the varieties of Bastard Feudalism had other than military objectives. Of
course, the potential was always there. The aristocracy
were a military caste, received a military upbringing, were
expected both to fight and take command, and some
always pursued military careers. The *servitium debitum* and
indentures of war were primarily instruments of recruitment and household-men were taken on with one eye on
their military potential. England maintained permanent
garrisons at Calais from 1347 and Berwick from 1482
and at Cherbourg, Roxburgh and Tournai at other times,
and aristocratic wardens were paid to maintain private
armies against the Scots. There were always wars for
those who sought them against continental foes, along the
Celtic Fringe, on crusade, or as routiers or mercenaries
in fourteenth-century Spain and Italy, for Charles the
Bold of Burgundy (d. 1477), or for Count Mansfeld at
the beginning of the Thirty Years War. Bastard Feudalism
played a crucial role in the recruitment and organisation
of these forces.

185

All the armies used by English kings in warfare contained three different elements in varying proportions. First of all, there were the monarch's own forces discussed in chapter 1. Apart from the garrisons and such permanent additional staffs of the Ordnance and Navy Offices that accrued, the monarch's own forces were members of the household and paid through it, whether from the wardrobe under Edward I or from the chamber during Edward IV's Picquigny expedition of 1475. The military household was predominantly aristocratic, increasingly drawn from leading county families and paid annuities, but included the contingents of the retainers themselves, by 1225–26 at least. Secondly, there were the contingents of the aristocracy themselves, the bastard feudal retinues, which are the principal focus of this chapter. And thirdly there were the county levies, responding to the universal obligation to defend against external threats or alternatively impressed, whose personnel and operation overlapped and interacted with the retinues of the aristocracy and thus demand prior attention here. Thus the retinues raised by aristocrats through Bastard Feudalism were never more than part of a larger whole. The precise proportion varied – one-third, for example, in 1523 – according to where and why the war was fought. It made a big difference whether it was a foreign expedition or resisting a foreign threat or a civil or private war. Such considerations also determined the composition of bastard feudal retinues themselves.

There was an obligation of defence against external threats that rested on all Englishmen throughout the period with which we are concerned. It motivated the county levies in their unsuccessful resistance to the Vikings at Maldon (991) and at Fulford (1066) and the fyrd that performed so disastrously at Hastings itself. Levies from the northern counties regularly turned out to confront Scottish invaders and their southern counterparts stood by against invasion threats under both Richard II and Elizabeth I. From the reign of Henry III they were all required to arm themselves, train themselves in archery, and turn out as necessary. The impressment of ships and shipmoney, the erection and watching of beacons, the equipment and billeting of troops were other facets of their compulsory obligations. Edward I enlisted as many as 30,000 footsoldiers for his Scottish campaigns. Though certainly not picked men or highly trained – desertion was at a high level in Edward I's Scottish levies – they were sufficiently effective for medieval kings to issue commissions of array at every foreign and domestic threat and for Sir John Fortescue to regard their personal equipment as an important resource. From the 1520s, however, this nebulous obligation was reorganised into the Tudor militia, which was actually mustered on occasion and armed with more modern weapons. A series of further reforms initiated and enforced by central government progressively increased the frequency of musters, created structures of command headed by the newly created Lords Lieutenant, drilled and re-equipped the forces from regularly levied rates, and even impressed and despatched them abroad. If not up to the best continental standards or even apparently of the bastard feudal retinues which were exempted from the militia and still constituted an élite, the Elizabethan and Early Stuart militia was militarily far more formidable than the medieval levies and saved parliament from early defeat in the English Civil War. Always, however, the medieval commissioners of array and the later Lords Lieutenants, deputy lieutenants and officers of the militia were drawn from the local nobility and gentry. Such men, in short, found themselves in command of other men's tenants and, indeed, increasingly of their own, for from 1612 the retinues of mere gentry were no longer exempted from the militia. If the military authority was no longer strictly private, it was they nevertheless who exercised it, now perhaps with the additional status bestowed as legitimate royal officers.[1]

. . .

FOREIGN WAR

Between 1150 and 1650 English kings fought many wars on continental soil and against their neighbours in the British Isles. Bastard Feudalism had a role in all such conflicts. Defence against external attack, whether on the

---

1. M.R. Powicke, *Military Obligation in Medieval England* (Oxford 1962); L. Boynton, *The Elizabethan Militia* (Newton Abbot 1970).

Scottish borders or from the sea, involved maximising military resources in the relevant region and sometimes nationally. When the king was present, such armies contained his own men; always they included aristocratic retinues and county levies. Some of the principal victories, such as the Standard (1138) and Neville's Cross (1346), were won by armies of strongly regional complexion. Besides many abortive threats, there were successful invasions in 1326, 1399, 1460, 1470, 1471 and 1485. These last were generally undertaken by dynastic rivals with local support and foreign backing. In such cases defence could be organised in advance, so that Edward IV in 1471[2] and the Earl of Oxford in 1473 were repelled from East Anglia,[3] but defenders were hampered because they knew neither the precise date nor point of disembarkation of the invasion. Once a landing had been effected, it was imperative for defenders to mobilise rapidly to prevent further recruitment. Hence defending armies tended to be large and miscellaneous, to lack coherent organisation or command structure, and to mingle companies of assorted size, standards of equipment and training that had been recruited in different ways. Battles were fought before all available forces were assembled. On such occasions aristocrats deployed everybody they could raise from their households, tenantry, extraordinary retainers, administrations, and livery rolls. The relatively small numbers of experienced soldiers, such as the Calais garrison in 1459–61 and the northern borderers, exercised an influence out of proportion to their actual numbers.

At the heart of military service in England were men of aristocratic birth and military training: members of the upper household and extraordinary retainers. During the feudal era such men were mainly household knights and feudal tenants; from the thirteenth century, members of the upper household and feed men. Edward I's wars against Wales and Scotland were a transitional phase between the two. Feudal obligation endured, but already,

2. *The Arrivall of Edward IV*, ed. J. Bruce (Camden Soc. i, 1836), p. 2.
3. C.D. Ross, *Edward IV* (1974), p. 192.

so it appears, it was fulfilled by those paid to undertake it from among the lord's household and extraordinary retainers. It was retinues of this type, not the more miscellaneous assemblies described above, that participated in Edward I's Scottish campaigns.

But not on the continent. Richard I, King John, Henry III, and Edward I all had difficulty in committing feudal levies against France and the latter two encountered 'massive passive resistance' to attempts to extend compulsory service to the £20 landowners. Of 713 listed in 1297, only 76 are known to have served.[4] The next stage, which was to be commonplace from the reign of Edward III, was for the king to contract directly with his captains to serve on his campaign where he chose with a specified force for an agreed reward. Contracted companies were certainly the most important element in the part of the army that was raised by the aristocracy. So useful were such indentures that kings applied them to other contracts, not all of them military: henceforth admirals, wardens of the marches, captains of Calais and other garrisoned towns indented with the king for their office. In Lancastrian Normandy an elaborate system of muster and review was developed to check up on them.[5]

What were the implications of such developments for the aristocracy? The 130 horsemen taken by Edward I's Earl Marshal to Scotland in 1297 could have been raised from the 17 squires, nine knights and five bannerets of his household and their men: one such banneret, Sir John Segrave, contracted to bring 15 knights with him for pay. Since each had his man, he would bring 32 of the 130 himself.[6] Magnates had paid for military service long before Edward I's reign, but it was apparently only then that the classic indentures of retainer and indentures of war were devised. Though they already reserved the retainer's service in both peace and war, the earliest indentures of retainer were primarily military documents. They contain details about slain horses and the like, but

4. Prestwich, p. 104.
5. R.A. Newhall, *Muster and Review* (Cambridge 1940).
6. Prestwich, p. 35.

relatively little specifically about peacetime uses.[7] Such retainers were embarking on long-term contracts that would guarantee their military service whenever required. This was a relatively expensive arrangement that made best sense for those who fought frequently and wanted to secure the requisite manpower: a description that certainly applies to John of Gaunt, who made extensive use of such contracts and for whom the additional cost was perfectly bearable.[8]

Obviously it was more economical only to retain men when specifically required: thus William de Valence re-cruited extra household knights on short contracts in wartime. A cheaper alternative to the indenture of re-tainer, which was also more adaptable to the needs of the moment, was the indenture of war. The earliest such indentures, somewhat primitive in form, were made by the Lord Edward for his crusade in 1270.[9] Like later contracts, these did not create new long-term relationships, but merely ensured the lord of the service of the retainer for a specific military campaign. Often such indentures were subcontracts, whereby the lord sought to fulfil the obliga-tions of his own indenture to the king: thus George Duke of Clarence, who contracted to take 120 men-at-arms and 1,000 archers to France in 1475, indented with the esquires James Hyde and William Floyer for two men-at-arms (themselves) and eight archers. Twenty-four survi-ving subcontracts provided Sir Hugh Hastings with 53 of the 120 troops he had contracted to raise for Thomas of Woodstock's expedition in 1380.[10] An even fuller picture emerges in 1422–23 for the Earl Marshal, who paid wages of war to Lord Berkeley's company of 70, to three knights with companies of seven to 22, to 33 others with companies of one to seven, and to a herald and 63 other individuals, mainly valets and clerks from his household.

7. E.g. N. Denholm-Young, *Seignorial Administration in England* (Oxford 1937), pp. 167–8.
8. Walker, esp. p. 15.
9. S. Lloyd, 'Lord Edward's Crusade 1270–2: Its Setting and Signifi-cance', *War and Government in the Middle Ages*, ed. J. Gillingham and J.C. Holt (Woodbridge 1984), pp. 126–33.
10. Hicks, *Clarence*, p. 169; P.R. Coss, *The Knight in Medieval England 1000–1400* (Stroud 1993), p. 105.

The household was permanently retained; so, too, were many of the captains – most notably John Birminghill, steward of the household;[11] it was their men and those captains without prior ties for whom indentures of war may have been required. Not indentures of retainer, because they were required for one campaign only.

Noble retinues can be arranged in four grades according to the type of campaign.

The largest numbers were produced when they levied all their own men in all categories and those of the surrounding counties, whether under commissions of array or through the militia. Such arrays, which stripped the whole countryside of manpower, could only be brief if the force was to be fed and economic ruin was to be averted, and were probably useful only for defence.

Secondly, lords could muster their own men only, who were so assiduously listed by Tudor lords. Such numbers could be very large: the 4th Earl of Northumberland, for instance, had 6,000 men-at-arms against the Scots in 1482 and 6,700 against rebels in Yorkshire in 1487; his son, as we have seen, had over a hundred household men and over 6,000 Yorkshire tenants. About 1450, Walter Strickland listed 290: 11 from his household and 279 tenants. All were armed with bows or bills. Of the 290, however, only 69 bowmen and 74 billmen had horses, padded jackets or breastplates: 71 bowmen and 74 billmen were unmounted and without protection.[12] The latter were scarcely effective: immobile and vulnerable. It follows that a full turnout was useful only for purposes of defence or against 'naked men' as ill-equipped as themselves, such as the Pilgrimage of Grace in 1536. And only briefly, for the same economic reasons as before.

For a planned campaign within Britain, therefore, a third, more select force was deployed. Only 21 of Howard's household of about 70 served on expeditions to Holt and the North in 1463–64, only 24 of Lord Darcy's 80 and only 64 of Northumberland's household in 1523, and only 13 of the Earl of Rutland's household in 1542. Similarly,

11. BL Add.MS. 17209 mm.2–3.
12. J. Nicolson and R. Burn, *A History of Westmorland* (1777), i.96; Hicks, p. 389.

Howard took only 100 tenants to Holt and from Rutland's Belvoir estate in 1542 there were sent only 77 tenants and six carters drawn in twos and threes from villages with much larger male populations.[13] The Yorkshiremen whom Northumberland actually mustered at Newcastle in 1523 numbered only 762: 64 from his household; 409 from 15 of his own properties – 54 per cent of the total; 172 from his three stewardships of Holderness, Kirkbyshire, and Whitby Strand; and nine gentry contingents totalling 117 and ranging from two to 43 in size.[14] In such cases, men were not only selected but equipped: the Belvoir details come from the countess of Rutland's 'coat and conduct' book.

Fourthly, for service overseas the Earl Marshal drew his own men only from his own household, not from the tenants of his estates, and from extraordinary retainers among the subcontractors. Who were the subcontractors' men? Ralph Moberley's contingent consisted of the kin, friends, and neighbours of the captain: men of gentility rather than the peasantry.[15] Certainly such men were volunteers, who wanted to serve. The great exception, once again, may be Lord Bergavenny, whose 984 men in 1515 and 521 in 1514 were presumably based on his 470 illegal retainers of 1506.[16] Even they, being liveried, were more than mere tenants. Details of total numbers, length of service, proportion of archers to men-at-arms and much else were fixed by the monarch by indenture and checked at musters. Retinues of war for service overseas were thus more selective and of better quality than those for service in Britain and were much better, if much less numerous, than those for home defence. Remember that Gaunt's indentured retainers – the best quality manpower of all! – were primarily for military service abroad.

A further distinction can be made between wars that were continuous or intermittent and isolated campaigns.

13. *Household Books of John Howard, Duke of Norfolk, 1462–71, 1481–3*, ed. A. Crawford (1992), xxvi; Cooper, p. 85; E101/531/34; R.B. Smith, *Land and Politics in the England of Henry VIII* (Oxford 1970), p. 137.
14. E 101/531/34.
15. Coss, *Knight*, p. 106.
16. Cooper, p. 89; Cameron, pp. 31–4.

When Edward III, Henry V and Edward IV declared war on France, they enjoyed widespread support, which was reflected in the particularly high proportion of the nobility in their invading armies. To serve on one such expedition, however, was quite different from protracted campaigning over several years, particularly when it was unspectacular or unsuccessful, as under Richard II, during Edward I's and Edward II's later campaigns in Scotland, or during Henry V's systematic reduction of Normandy. When campaign succeeded campaign, the character of the high command and indeed the rank and file changed, as an essentially amateur force evolved into a professional army. Few noblemen wanted to serve every-where every year: they had estates, families, countries, and interests to consider. So, too, had retainers, who wished to omit particular campaigns; the more militarily minded wished to serve when their lords did not, as the Earl Marshal's Sir John Segrave so often did, or to transfer to other companies. The proportion of nobility and gentry alike fell, as they ceased to serve or served intermittently and were not wholly replaced by firstcomers. Those who remained were the most military-minded, perhaps the best soldiers, such as Henry of Grosmont, Duke of Lancaster (d. 1361), Thomas Earl of Salisbury (d. 1428), and John Earl of Shrewsbury (d. 1453). New commanders with less impressive lineages emerged from the lesser aris-tocracy (Sir John Segrave), from foreign mercenaries (Sir Walter Manny and Sir Andrew Ogard), and even from the ranks (Sir John Hawkwood). So, too, with the rank and file. As lords returned with their retinues and others were depleted by casualties and desertion, outsiders reinforced existing companies, new ones were formed, and the original identity with a particular lord, estate, or locality broke down. We can see this happening under Edward I, where there was little overlap between the ret-inues raised by the same captains in different years. 'This was not a stable system', writes Professor Prestwich. 'It was possible for magnates to buy support on a large scale, but there was no consistency in that support, no solidarity in the ties linking men to lords'.[17] But there never was

17. Prestwich, pp. 35–6.

such stability when wars dragged on. In the fourteenth century unwanted veterans marauded in Italy, France and Spain in the Free Companies. The phenomenon recurred in Lancastrian Normandy, where the musters reveal the emergence of a professional army from many distinct companies, even as early as 1417.[18] And we can see it also in the regrouping of the Roundhead forces into the New Model Army. The over-matured Lancastrian armies were largely destroyed in 1449–53, relatively few veterans participated in the Wars of the Roses, and in 1475, 1492 and 1513 new armies of the old kind were required.

. . .

PRIVATE AND CIVIL WAR

Our evidence of who fought in the various civil wars of our period is frustratingly scanty. Often we know about high-ranking casualties, of those knighted, rewarded or who suffered forfeiture, but these never amount to more than a fraction of the total manpower involved, in 1215 or 1471. Those defeated had good reason to conceal their presence. It is hard to tell whether those we know are representative of the whole – thus whether there were actually many more notables present than are recorded – or whether they were all those of eminence there were. Just as the Stanleys retrospectively upgraded their role at Bosworth, so perhaps the Lancastrians and Cheshiremen celebrated in the ballad of *Bosworth Field* were added after the battle was safely won![19] Whilst our sources make much of the *scale* of the major engagements, they reveal little about most of the personnel. We can be sure that on such occasions household men, feudal tenants or feed men, and tenants were involved, but in what numbers and what proportions? Should we envisage my first category –

18. A.J. Pollard, *John Talbot and the War in France 1427–53* (1983), 83–95. I am indebted to Dr Curry for the information on 1417. For what follows, see C.H. Firth, *Cromwell's Army* (4th edn 1962), pp. 31–3.
19. M.A. Hicks, *Richard III: The Man Behind the Myth* (1991), p. 155; C. Richmond, '1485 and All That, or what was going on at the Battle of Bosworth', *Richard III: Loyalty, Lordship and Law*, ed. P.W. Hammond (1985), pp. 173–210.

the involvement of all able-bodied manpower of whatever type – or my fourth, a select élite?

Some light is cast by material relating to the events of 1399 recently collected by Dr Given-Wilson. Richard II was actually in Ireland when the future Henry IV invaded, which may explain the relatively small numbers involved; another factor, clearly, was that each side drew on a limited geographical area. It is obvious, however, that much less than the maximum potential was raised from those areas that were represented. Both armies were raised the same way: both contained aristocratic retainers; probably both used county levies; what was missing was the royal household, with the king in Ireland. £4,900 was paid to 50 aristocratic captains in the rebel army: 40 per cent to the Percies. There were three other peers. The other captains therefore brought far fewer men, some very few indeed. Rather more informative is the data on the supporters of the absent king, approximately 3,300 in number, to whom Edmund Duke of York paid £2,035. Just over a third, 1,150, had been arrayed by the sheriffs of 10 counties in contingents ranging from 11 to 250 men. The remainder served in bastard feudal retinues. The two largest, those of York himself and the Marquis of Dorset, contained 100 men-at-arms and 200 archers; another 57 made up the balance. Many of these were quite small: 12 Hampshire gentry brought only 129 between them. Moreover, many of these contained only a single man-at-arms: the captain himself. Only 14 of the Hampshire-men were knights and esquires and at least 100 were bowmen.[20]

Several deductions can be drawn. First of all, that by 1399 at least all those involved in civil war expected to be paid: sergeants and archers in castle garrisons were paid in the twelfth century; for foreign wars all but the magnates had been paid by Edward I and even them by Edward III. Those on the losing side did not necessarily secure their money! It would be interesting to know if a payment in advance was called for, which would clearly place a finan-cial limit on the numbers recruited. Secondly, significant numbers of those arrayed were outside noble retinues: a

20. C. Given-Wilson, *Chronicles of the Revolution 1397–1400* (Man-chester 1993), pp. 247–53.

reminder that at all times there were always able-bodied
men available for the fyrd, for array or for the militia,
many or all tenants of those who were not militarily active.
Thirdly, bowmen were commonplace, hardly surprisingly
since archery was required of all able-bodied men from
the mid-thirteenth century, and were predominantly of
humble rank, but men-at-arms were less numerous and
almost confined to aristocratic retinues, perhaps indeed
mainly aristocrats themselves. That suggests that they
were not mere billmen, but had both weapons and the
training to use them. Fourthly, for whatever reason, the
size of retinue increased with rank quite out of proportion
to the captain's wealth: perhaps because they included
many sub-retinues? This was certainly how the earls of
Northumberland and Oxford raised their retinues in
1487, when the former led 6,000 men; 20 gentlemen
raised 168 men for the latter by 18 July and another
nine a further 66 by 20 July. Others were hired with
monetary contributions or raised from the villages.[21] And
it was presumably also true of the 3,000 of those 'toward
the Lord Hastings' and the 4,000 raised by Clarence
in 1471.[22] And fifthly, many of the retinues were very
small – in single figures: just like those of the Earl
of Northumberland in 1523 and the Earl Marshal a
century earlier, both of which – as we have seen – were
selective. Were they all? When lords were asked to bring
as many armed men as possible, did it mean that only
those who were properly equipped were required? Not
only in 1399 but on all such occasions, the contending
armies comprised much less than the total of able-bodied
males in the areas where they recruited and much less,
for example, than the rebel forces of the Peasant's Revolt
(1381) and Pilgrimage of Grace (1536).

Of course, lords used their manpower on many other
occasions: for forcible entries, riots, and private wars.
Again, the forces varied with size of estates and rank:
though indictments claimed much larger numbers, only
between 13 and 26 individuals were actually named as
accomplices in Sir Thomas Malory's crimes in 1450. The

21. *Household Books of John Duke of Norfolk and Thomas Earl of Surrey
    1481–90*, ed. J.P. Collier (Roxburghe Club 1844), p. 389.
22. *The Arrivall*, pp. 8–11.

Pastons, too, never disposed of more than 30 men –
numerically far inferior to the 160 that the Duke of
Suffolk's bailiff of Costesey led against Heylesdon in
1465![23] Similarly at the Bedford election riot of 1437,
rioters supporting the established Lord Grey of Ruthin
were drawn from 37 manors, Lord Fanhope's men from a
mere 16.[24] The logical result usually followed. 'The wealth
of the party involved', observes Bellamy, 'was the deciding
factor'. Contemporary complaints about overwhelming
force and violence need to be treated with scepticism.
The intention was seldom to fight but to overawe without fighting: the threat of violence, ideally timed when
there could be no opposition, was often enough. Bellamy
reports that Elizabeth Brews once asked for a dozen
men; Justice Yelverton once used eight.[25] Two hundred
men were sometimes taken to quarter sessions. The 150
men who won the 1460 Nottinghamshire election by a
landslide haled predominantly from the north of the
county, in particular Bassetlaw, and were predominantly
tenants, neighbours and friends of local landowner John
Stanhope, now MP. In 1451 210 men sufficed for the Earl
of Devon in his conflict with Lord Bonville; in 1455 it
was 351.[26] Similarly, the Duke of Buckingham summoned
tenants during the crises of the 1450s from certain estates:
never from all, because he judged the numbers sufficient.
So, too, in 1450, when he struck in person at Malory, he
took only 60 tenants, plus presumably his household: his
judgement was vindicated by Malory's bloodless arrest.[27]
And in 1461 at 2nd St Albans 'the substance that fought
that field were household and feed men', not tenants.
That was because the ordinary rustics, mere 'naked men',

23. Bellamy, p. 47; P.J.C. Field, *Life and Times of Sir Thomas Malory*
(1993), pp. 96–101n.
24. P. Maddern, *Violence and the Social Order* (Oxford 1992), p. 215.
25. Bellamy, 41–2.
26. Myers, *EHD*, p. 1125; S. Payling, 'The Widening Franchise – Parliamentary Elections in Lancastrian Nottinghamshire', *England in
the 15th Century*, ed. D. Williams (1987), pp. 178–85; M. Cherry,
'The Struggle for Power in Mid-Fifteenth-Century Devonshire',
Patronage, The Crown and the Provinces, ed. R.A. Griffiths (Gloucester
1981), p. 143n. These figures relate to those indicted: total numbers
were allegedly 800 horse and 4,000 foot.
27. Field, *Thomas Malory*, pp. 100–1.

were routed, as they were also at Dunstable (1461) and Losecote Field (1470); they were slaughtered at Blore Heath and were ineffective at Ludford, both in 1459. They were no match against feed aristocrats. Similarly, the Yorkshire rebels of 1489, who out faced the Percy feed men who were only 'privy harnest', fled without striking a blow at the approach of the king's vanguard.[28] During the Barons Wars, large numbers of ill-equipped peasants were killed by well-armed, armoured, mounted and trained aristocrats.[29] It may be, indeed, but it is impossible to tell, that such ineffective troops were county levies, the products of commissions of array rather than bastard feudal tenantry. It was only when the whole countryside was in arms that numbers really told, the rebels could not be attacked, and that it was possible only to wait for them to disperse.

Again, therefore, there was a process of selection. Not everyone was arrayed and many of those who were had a decidedly secondary role commensurate with their ineffectiveness. In later conflicts a minimum standard of equipment was required. Henry VIII was often specific about the composition and equipment of the forces he requisitioned from northern lords. The 800 footmen and 80 mounted on great horses that the Earl of Arundel brought to London against Wyatt's Rebellion in 1554 were more impressive than thousands of poorly equipped peasants. In 1588 the 300 horse and 500 foot offered by the Earl of Pembroke were all to be 'armed at my own cost and with mine own store'.[30] Strickland and Howard are unlikely to have been alone in listing their men or Buckingham and Howard in arranging for them to be paid. Some were household men, some gentry, some tenants, and some liveried: indeed, in times of crisis, for private or civil war, lords such as Northumberland in the 1450s and York in 1460 recruited more retainers with hostilities in mind.

28. Hicks, pp. 399–400; M. Bennett, 'Henry VII and the Northern Rising of 1489', *EHR* cv (1990), 34–59; A. Goodman, *The Wars of the Roses* (1981), p. 147.
29. As suggested by D. Carpenter, 'The English Peasantry in Politics 1258–67', *P&P* 136 (1992), 12.
30. Cooper, pp. 87, 91.

Speed was another advantage. Most campaigns of the Wars of the Roses and other internecine struggles were shortlived: less than a fortnight for the Stoke campaign (1487), a few weeks for the Northampton (1460) and Bosworth (1485) campaigns, three months for the Wakefield and Towton (1460–61) and Barnet and Tewkesbury (1471) campaigns. Whereas in 1537 the Duke of Norfolk could promise 100 household-men within three days, other categories took longer; unmounted, ill-armed and unwilling tenants presumably longest of all. It may be that northern tenants were more accustomed, inclined and equipped for warfare, and hence more fought in the Wars of the Roses, giving – for example – successive lords of Middleham particular clout. Unfortunately, their example of indiscipline and unseemly manners contributed to Queen Margaret's failure to enter London in 1461 and Richard III's inability to appease the southern shires.

Even when tenants were employed, they needed organisation and direction. In 1523 the Percies' Yorkshire contingent had a command structure comprising six head captains and seven petty captains,[31] probably gentry and estate officers. Similarly 19 per cent of Devon's forces in 1451 and 9 per cent in 1455 were gentry. Suffolk's bailiff of Costesey in 1465 and the Percy bailiff of Pocklington in 1454 had crucial roles in mustering and commanding tenants. Popular rebellions, like the Yorkshire uprising in 1489, faltered without gentle leadership. And negligence, desertion or treachery by such gentry, like Henry Vernon in 1471, deprived lords of their own men as well as the retainers' men.

Fear of the consequences and divided loyalties contributed to such defaults and perhaps also to the sparse turnout in 1399. How far gentry or tenants were informed on such matters is uncertain: Charles I memorably believed that 'both officers and soldiers ... who are now in Rebellion against him are ignorant against whom they fight'.[32] They were certainly the targets of propaganda from both sides. That Northumberland in Yorkshire in

---

31. PRO E 101/531/31.
32. J.S.A. Adamson, 'The Baronial Context of the English Civil War', *TRHS* 5th ser. xl (1990), 112.

1471, Bergavenny and Guldeford in 1497, and Shrewsbury in his country in 1536 have been credited with
restraining tenants and neighbours who wished to rebel
shows that their views had to be considered.[33] Could
Lord Hastings have raised 3,000 men *against* Edward IV?
Such issues have been briefly discussed in chapter 6.
Once levied, however, and under military command, they
were more readily controlled and even diverted to other
purposes. This was true of Lord Strange's Shropshire men
in 1403, of the Grey of Ruthin contingent at Northampton
(1460), of Clarence and Warwick in 1470 and Clarence
alone in 1471, to name only a few. The evidence indicates
that it was aristocratic retinues that decided all the civil
wars before the New Model Army, because it was they
that were assembled quickly; they that were effective
combatants (properly equipped and perhaps trained); and
it was they that had appropriate structures of command.
The nostalgic romancing about ploughmen-soldiers of
More and Starkey – like Machiavelli's dream of a citizen
army! – was no substitute for great households staffed by
those selected and trained for war.

33. *The Arrivall*, p. 6; Cameron, 31; Bernard, *Power*, ch. 2.

Chapter 8

BASTARD FEUDALISM: THE END?

· · ·

TERMINAL DECLINE

Although Bastard Feudalism survived into Tudor England, it was already in terminal decline and duly expired by the Civil War. Retaining, legal or not, had largely ceased and bastard feudal corruption of the law was past. Any remaining instances of retaining or abuse of justice, it follows, were primitive survivals most commonly found in the neo-feudal periphery. But why? The older interpretations had the considerable merit that they attributed the change to well-established and well-substantiated historical facts, such the destruction of the old nobility in the Wars of the Roses and the sustained campaign of Henry VII and his successors against Bastard Feudalism and its abuse. If these can no longer do, must we not now substitute a process of gradual attenuation attributable to yet more profound changes in society itself that somehow rendered Bastard Feudalism redundant? What were these changes and how did they operate?

We now have no overarching explanation, but rather a series of explanations of different parts of the decline. These pose problems because there is no agreement about what Bastard Feudalism was and hence no consensus about what was to be explained. This chapter treats the nobility, the evidence that such ties were decisively loosened, the impact on how Bastard Feudalism was used, and ends with the situation at the beginning of the Civil War.

. . .

THE FATE OF THE NOBILITY

It is obvious to many historians that 1500–1650 witnessed major changes in the power of the nobility and decline in aspects of Bastard Feudalism. Indeed they often find it difficult to separate the two. Even if both shared the same fate, it is nevertheless desirable to preserve the distinction. Conceivably Bastard Feudalism survived whilst the power of the nobility was curbed. Moreover, Tudor historians often treat the nobility in isolation, forgetting that the gentry inhabited households and held estates populated by tenants and estate officials that seem small only in comparison with those of the nobility: a distinction that Professor Bellamy appreciates.

If the Tudors did curb the nobility and destroy Bastard Feudalism, they did not do it at once. The old nobility was destroyed neither by the Wars of the Roses nor by the purges of Henry VIII. 'The fall and rise of families', concludes Miss Miller, 'shift the pieces in the mosaic without destroying the underlying structure of power'.[1] Bastard Feudalism adapted to Henry VII's changes in the law and still delivered the committed manpower that the crown required. 'There is no reason to suppose that there was any decline in the fortunes of the nobility as a whole *c.* 1485–1560: there was no early Tudor crisis of the aristocracy'. The same view is implicit in Stone's decision to commence his 'crisis of the aristocracy' in 1558. At no point during the Tudor and Early Stuart period was the crown committed to the destruction of noble power, military or any other kind. Whilst convinced of Bastard Feudalism's vitality before 1560, modern historians almost without exception are agreed that it did not survive much longer, finally succumbing later in the sixteenth century or – at worst – early in the seventeenth. Between them, they offer a variety of causes. Obviously Bastard Feudalism *did* die. There did come a time when, in Stone's unflattering words, 'the unenlightened factious territorial warlords of the fifteenth century' were transformed 'into

1. H. Miller, *Henry VIII and the English Nobility* (Oxford 1986), p. 256; Bernard, *Power*, p. 174.

the cultivated capitalist parliamentary oligarchs of the eighteenth'. Certainly by the eighteenth century, he says,

> the State [had] fully established its authority, that dozens of armed retainers were replaced by a coach, two footmen and a page-boy, ... private castles gave way to private houses, ... then that the north and west were brought within the national orbit and abandoned their age-old habits of personal violence.

But had this occurred by 1640? Stone takes stock:

> There was nothing particularly feudal about the peers in 1641: if they fought for the State, they were paid for their services; their seats in the House of Lords bore no relation to feudal tenure; their client gentry were bound to them by personal not feudal ties; the feudal aspect of their relations with their tenants was confined to the intermittent enforcement of obsolete taxes like fines for wardship; their estate management was as modern as the times and as their paternalist notions of fair treatment of tenants would allow ...[2]

All these observations are true, but they apply equally to the 1450s, when Storey wrote much the same, or of any period back to Edward III or perhaps even to Edward I. Stone did not appreciate how the nobility have already changed or what constituted Bastard Feudalism.

Yet the composition of the aristocracy did change. There were several stages to the process. If the great nobility were not *destroyed* by the Wars of the Roses, the greatest families – and overmightiest of subjects – did disappear. No great families emerged on the scale of the houses of Lancaster and York, Warwick the Kingmaker, or the last Stafford Duke of Buckingham. Potential Tudor royal dukes or Lord Protectors failed to establish themselves. The outstanding Tudor magnates, Percies, Stanleys, Howards or Talbots, commanded less resources than the great magnates of the past. Moreover, rising food prices and the dispersal of monastic estates did enable many more gentry families to establish themselves in control of a significantly higher proportion of land. Elizabeth had to search more widely for the bastard feudal manpower she required. And as the number of aristocrats

---

2. Stone, pp. 1, 11, 15. For what follows, see R.L. Storey, *End of the House of Lancaster* (2nd edn Gloucester 1986), p. 22.

increased, so the capacity of the greatest to forge bonds with them all and to direct their inferiors diminished. The aristocracy still dominated the localities, as they were to do for centuries yet, but authority was more widely spread. If some areas were still lordly spheres of influence, it appears ever more common for power to be shared by a county community of leading families that often included the lesser peerage, like Lord Powlett in Carolean Somerset.

Probably attitudes were changing too. This is a particularly difficult topic, because we have only limited anecdotal evidence both for the degree of loyalty and subservience in the past and how it was changing and little hope of supplementing it statistically. Plenty of people in Tudor and Early Stuart England thought things were changing, for better or worse depending on vantage point: often they can be shown to be wrong, projecting into the past nostalgic beliefs of what ought to be rather than what was and generalising from isolated anecdotes. Scattered evidence suggests that from the late sixteenth century honourable service by one aristocrat to another, especially in the household, was in decay and literary criticism of the idleness of servants in old-style great households was growing. Perhaps calculations of mutual advantage were increasingly replacing 'faithfulness'. Exceptions may well have been concentrated in the highland zone. One beneficiary was the crown, whose service was still honourable and indeed applauded by humanist authors, and whose right to obedience increasingly overrode more 'natural' local rulers. Kings always had intruded their men into the localities, often with corrupting or disrupting effects. That Henry VII's experiment with the Earl of Surrey as warden of the marches was so apparently successful doubtless owed much to the absence of traditional ruling families due to minority (Percy), forfeiture (Neville), and feeble-mindedness (Clifford, Roos), who resumed office in due course. Far more surprising and symptomatic of compliance was the long domination under Elizabeth of the eastern marches of Sir John Forster.[3]

3. M.M. Meikle, 'A Godly Rogue: The Career of Sir John Forster, an Elizabethan Border Warden', *Northern History* xxviii (1992), 126–63.

Another reason why noblemen were increasingly regarded as equals of their gentry neighbours arose from
the growing local influence of the crown. Status, power
and authority derived less from relationship to a lord
than from office held of the crown without intermediaries. As local offices multiplied and as duties became ever
more onerous, responsibility could no longer be confined
to county élites, but stretched to the lower ranks of the
gentry. Very few officers were indispensable and immune
from dismissal. When almost all significant gentry had
direct relations with the crown and leaders of national
factions, noblemen lost their roles as power-brokers and
mediators with the crown. Indeed, officers were dismissed
if they were retained. That they were expected to report
on the defects of fellow officers encouraged them to be
critical of both peers and superiors, to be independent
of them, and to imagine themselves capable of initiat-
ing change themselves. If courtiers and faction leaders
became more influential and ever more worth cultivating,
it was no longer so honourable to serve another local
aristocrat or so beneficial to have his patronage for self-
advancement. The tie between magnate and retainer, lord
and servant, was of diminishing importance in local society. But though that link weakened, all the aristocracy –
nobility and gentry – were nevertheless bastard feudal
lords themselves in command of their own households
and tenants. But they did not see themselves in that way.

Moreover the crown sought to confine the benefits
of what retaining there was to itself. Monarchs were
still retaining gentry themselves: Henry VIII, indeed,
recruited Percy retainers. Moreover they attached additional obligations to existing relationships: thus Henry VII
required his grantees to perform military service subject
to resumption of their rewards in 1495 and declared in
1502 that he had reserved the retainer of all subjects to
himself alone so that they should come when summoned –
regardless of any other commitments. Sir William Bulmer
had not broken any contract with Henry VIII when he
was additionally retained by the Duke of Buckingham,
probably a secondary tie, and yet both incurred royal dis-
pleasure and Bulmer was imprisoned for a time: evidently
the office of a king's knight had been changed and would

henceforth entail exclusive service to the crown. By an act of 1487 royal tenants were to be deprived of their leases if they were retained by anyone else; Henry VIII and his successors sought to prevent retainer of tenants, especially those of the duchy of Lancaster, by even his own councillors of the North! Whereas in 1346 it had been only the judges whose retainer was restricted to the king, the same applied to members of the royal household from the early sixteenth century and by 1595 to justices of the peace, who could not be appointed if they were retained.[4] The privileges of royal service were extended at the price of other ties and retaining fees. In future aristocrats were to be free to use their manpower not as they wished but only as the monarch or the state permitted. If Edward Duke of Buckingham needed permission from Henry VIII for an armed escort to deal with his own recalcitrant Welsh tenants, by 1642 royal commissions to array on behalf of the king were considered of insufficient legality for many local aristocrats. Insofar as Bastard Feudalism provided aristocrats with the manpower for military action or corruption of the law, it had been nationalised and was in danger of being neutralised; insofar as it was a source of political and electoral influence it remained, of course, very much alive.

. . .

CASTING OFF THE BONDS

The crucial ties of Bastard Feudalism were those that secured the service of a lord's household, tenants, and extraordinary retainers, feed or liveried. Professor Stone, Dr Jeremy Goring, and M.E. James have argued for the collapse of all three.[5]

The household, as we have seen, was the central nucleus of any connection: it provided the necessary display, the core personnel for all purposes, and its members were most closely committed to their lord. The strength of the ties did not relax during this period: this was *the* era of the patriarchal nuclear family, when the authority of

4. Cooper, pp. 81–4; Dunham, pp. 72n, 73n.
5. Stone, pp. 149–234; James, p. 297; J. Goring, 'Social Change and Military Decline in Mid-Tudor England', *History* lx (1977), 185–97.

masters and the obedience of servants were allegedly ever more absolute. But what of the size and composition? Was it at this date that households ceased to be opportunities for opulent display, that numbers diminished to conform to actual domestic demands, and that they became less military, staffed by butlers and footmen and females of all kinds? So, certainly, claims Stone. The Price Revolution of 1515–1650 cut back the income of the nobility, forcing some to sell up, others to maximise their incomes or cut expenditure, especially on the household. Noblemen could no longer afford to keep open house to all comers nor to support such large numbers of servants. Already by the mid-sixteenth century, argues Goring, households were less exclusively male. Chambermaids, footmen and pages were replacing 'tall men'. M.E. James points to the decimation of many of the greatest households around 1570 and Stone cites statistics of the declining size of even the greatest households. Whereas Elizabethan noblemen like the Earl of Oxford and Lord Burghley kept 80 to 100 servants, Robert Earl of Salisbury saw no such need and nor indeed did the Restoration dukes of Richmond and Albermarle. In 1572 Mr Segarston MP lamented that gentlemen worth £100 a year now kept only one page.[6] Moreover, even the exceptional cases where large numbers remained, such as the 210 on the checkroll of the Earl of Rutland in 1612, no longer included the client gentry, but were predominantly menial servants. A desire for greater privacy was replacing old-style public life and open-handed hospitality. The subdivision of the great hall of Brancepeth Castle symbolised the withdrawal of the nobility into their private apartments in anticipation of upstairs/downstairs division characteristic of later centuries. It was only the most conservative backwoodsmen who continued with old-style 'medieval' lavish housekeeping.

The tenantry had supplied the numbers but did so no longer. Here the Price Revolution prompted landlords to raise rents and entry fines in line with best capitalistic practice. Some tenants were displaced, causing depopulation, and others were alienated. The Earl of

6. *Proceedings in the Parliaments of Elizabeth I*, i, ed. T.E. Hartley (Leicester 1981), p. 366.

Cumberland alienated his tenants by raising entry fines; Edward Duke of Buckingham was also unpopular. The 'ancient and laudable' but unwritten obligation of military service was everywhere repudiated, as tenants asserted their lands to be held only for rent. In 1542 the tenants in Derbyshire and Shropshire refused to serve and even those on the borders declared themselves obliged only to defend and not to advance into Scotland. Beneficial leases were no longer recognised as such. Yet others, in 1536 and after, refused to serve except for pay; tenants failed to support their lords against rebels in 1536, 1549 and 1569, against Queen Mary in 1553, and for the rebel earls in 1569. 'Neo-feudal loyalties' were no longer enough, notes M.E. James: 'By 1569 therefore the whole structure of seigneurial administration was weakened and crumbling and the earl [of Northumberland]'s authority questioned and flouted'.[7]

Members of the gentry had served in noble households, as estate officers, and as extraordinary retainers. Henceforth few served, Stone claims: they hardly occur in the households of others and fees and liveries diminished. Knight service and baronial courts had dwindled to almost nothing by 1570. Henceforth, we may presume, lords had more difficulty in mustering and directing their connections and could no longer count on the gentry to dominate the localities. Certainly they were in no position to enrol *en masse* the many newcomers who rose into the gentry from the inflated agricultural profits of the Price Revolution.

With the possible exception of the gentry, the cases of Stone, Goring and James are unproven. Annuities and liveries, knight's service and baronial courts were defunct before 1500 and military tenants and households, it can be argued, still had some time to run.

However widespread was the threatened loss of control over the tenantry, it was evidently limited or averted. The difficulties were not insuperable. Probably there was never a time when everybody followed their lord. Those landlords who were unwilling to abandon military service from their tenants enjoyed the backing of crown and parliament in determined efforts to maintain it. They seem to

7.   James, p. 297.

have enjoyed a fair degree of success. Resistance to military service presumably explains why so many landlords in so many counties started to insert military service into their leases, as they could well do at a time of competition for tenancies; though such cases must have been a minority. One landlord successfully enforced military service on his tenant in court and in 1549 an act of Parliament specified that those who failed to serve would lose their lease. Whatever the difficulties, it appears at first sight that the nobility successfully rode out the storm. Many noblemen succeeded in mobilising their tenants during the 1540s and 1550s, some in crises such as Wyatt's Revolt.[8] Moreover, both Goring and James rely unduly on unsubstantiated literary evidence. James relies too much on the Percy estate officer George Clarkson, who was writing nearly thirty years later and suffered from a romantic and impractical nostalgia about one particular estate. Clarkson ignores the 100 per cent turnout of tenants achieved for the earls in certain bailiwicks in 1569 and the role of other factors elsewhere, such as the inadequacy or absence of leadership. That the Earl of Shrewsbury also failed to mobilise his tenants in 1569, retorts Bernard emphatically,

> was not a sign of any long run structural decline in seigneurial authority or of any transformation in ideas of service and honour. What counted were the immediate political circumstances, the efficiency of a nobleman's planning, the quality of his leadership . . . .[9]

The same applies to the Stanley estate: 'Stone's contention that the bonds between landlord and tenant were weakened in the early seventeenth century remains largely untested', observes Coward.[10] What was true of the Percy estates – if true indeed – may not have applied elsewhere. What is clear is that noblemen did succeed in mobilising their tenants on several occasions in the late sixteenth-century and that tenants were still numbered in their retinues. When eventually tested, in 1642, many followed their masters. Possibly less estates remained militarily

8. Cooper, p. 87.
9. Bernard, *Power*, p. 182.
10. Coward, pp. xiii–xiv.

effective. Certainly the tenants and households of the gentry were included in the militia from 1589.

So, too, with the household. When swopping anecdotes, one finds that there were plenty of great households in the old style, like those of the earls of Dorset and Rutland in 1612, of the 9th earl of Northumberland in 1621, and of the Earls of Worcester and Derby up to the Civil War.[11] Professor Bossy has stressed the importance of large seigneurial households kept by peers and gentry as centres of Catholicism.[12] Even if these are concentrated in the highland zone – though Sussex features prominently! – all aristocrats maintained large households by modern standards. Indeed, the apparent growth of the largest households in the early sixteenth century and the rotation of those in attendance, a more economic way of maximising numbers, actually allowed scope for some reduction thereafter without a disastrous change in character or significance. Some of these diminished households look large by late medieval standards. Even the division of Brancepeth Castle hall was foreshadowed by more than two centuries by lords' withdrawal into their great chambers, where they had resided throughout the early sixteenth-century efflorescence of the great household so stressed by James, Robinson, Coward and others. And new men, like Lord Treasurer Burghley (d. 1598), continued to live grandly in the old way.

. . .

MILITARY POTENTIAL

That household, tenantry and gentry still featured in bastard feudal connections is not to say that they were militarily effective or as numerous as in the past. Early Tudor England, argues Goring, suffered from a general military decline that affected the tenants of the aristocracy as much as the rest. Ploughmen, hardened by toil and proficient in arms, gave way to shepherds. Unable to wear armour, to ride horses, or to practise archery, they were timid stay-at-homes, who served only for wages and

11. F. Heal, *Hospitality in Early Modern England* (Oxford 1990), *passim*; Coward, p. 92.
12. J. Bossy, 'The Character of Elizabethan Catholicism', *P&P* 21 (1965), 10–12.

not against rebels. Borderers would no longer equip themselves for self-defence. And even the fine figures of men in the households, whose relative importance should have been enhanced, were now too accustomed to a life of idle ease. George Clarkson for the Percies and John Smyth for the Berkeleys lamented the decline that had occurred. And on the national scene, where once 'there were many earls could bring into the field a thousand barbed horses, many a baron five or six hundred, now', observed Sir Walter Raleigh, 'very few of them can furnish twenty for the king'.

Such testimony is almost wholly anecdotal, nostalgic and ill-founded. The comparisons are with an idealised and probably imaginary past. It is only in the six-teenth century that we are accurately informed about the numbers, equipment and preparedness of the militia and the tenants of the nobility. We have no earlier data for comparison and may legitimately doubt how typical was the rugged ploughman proficient in all martial pursuits. The equipment of the mid-fifteenth-century Bridport citizens and Walter Strickland's borderers fall well short of this standard. Did magnates *ever* deploy the resources attributed to them by Tudor commentators?

Very few feudal tenants had a *servitium debitum* of over a hundred knights and even Gaunt's indentured retainers amounted to a mere fraction of Raleigh's rec-ollection. Is not this another 'optical illusion' like that identified by Coward, by which the resources of the Stanleys and the Percies were unfavourably compared to a mythical past when 'the north knew no king but the Percies'? The Percies never possessed such power,[13] nor did the Stanleys, so the comparison is inappropriate. Stone's declining stockpiles of arms are less impressive once it is recognized that such stores are themselves innovations without earlier parallels.

Yet such material does indicate that the cost of maintain-ing a separate military capability was going up. From the fourteenth century county levies were paid at the expense of local communities and in the mid-fifteenth century

13. M. Reiss, 'A Power in the North? The Percies in the 15th Century', *Historical Journal* xix (1976), 501–9.

the standard of equipment, to judge from the Bridport muster roll of 1457, was no worse than Strickland's bastard feudal retinue. The reorganisation of the militia from the 1520s repeatedly upgraded the militia at public expense. Handguns replaced bows, drilling and instruction in weaponry occurred, and aristocratic officers took over from rustic constables. Probably therefore any gap in effectiveness between the bastard feudal tenantry and militia was reduced or erased; indeed, from 1612 the distinction was no longer made, without apparent public resistance.

There was no significant decline in the military manpower of the nobility before 1607, when official muster returns revealed that lay peers and bishops alone could raise 20,000 armed men and 4,000 horses. There were only 7,513 horsemen from all sources. As J.P. Cooper remarked, 'over half the most expensive part of the available forces were reckoned to come from the personal followings of the magnates'.[14] The rest of the cavalry and the vast bulk of the infantry were provided by the militia, which was numerically much larger. The nobility had never provided a majority of *total* manpower. Like their late medieval counterparts, so too early Stuart aristocrats commanded the county levies as Lords Lieutenants and militia officers. In characteristically bastard feudal manner, they had made the militia into a further instrument and reflection of their private influence that obviated much of the need for their own private armies. Why incur military expenditure yourself when it could be financed from the rates?

To muster, of course, is not to mobilise. The real measure of the continued military significance of Bastard Feudalism must be whether it was still capable of making a crucial or even substantial contribution to the recruitment of armies. The evidence of the English Civil War is that it was. The rest of this section therefore explores what the events of 1642–45 can reveal about the continued effectiveness of Bastard Feudalism as a means of military recruitment.

The king's West Country army, so Mr Edgar reports,

14. Cooper, p. 93.

predominantly were their own relations, tenants, neighbours and retainers. Apart from the voluntary aspect, their recruitment in some cases had certain features of the old feudal levy. Between them and the colonels existed bonds of long association and familiarity. The loyalty of the principal landlords to the King was reflected in the allegiance and attainment of their own dependants.[15]

For Professor Kishlansky 'the armies were formed, on both sides, through the old noble and gentry networks', for Dr Manning 'traditional ties of loyalty and habits of deference were sufficient to account for such success of the royalist nobility and gentry in gathering forces for the king', and for Professor Fletcher 'the royalist army at this stage [1642] was an army of enthusiasts leading their tenantry'.[16] However, the historian of the Royalist Army, Dr Ronald Hutton, is of a different opinion. 'The civilian Clarendon', he writes,

> has left behind a persisting but misleading impression that the Royalist army was, like a feudal host, recruited from the tenants and dependants of the Royalist magnates. It seems in fact to have been raised in a more 'modern' manner.

This more modern manner, he explains, 'was not, ultimately, the Commission of Array. It was a different sort of commission, issued to a single man to raise a number of regular soldiers under him in one of the partisan armies'. Commonly those commissioned became colonels and appointed officers. Thus Lord Paget raised his regiment of foot only in part from his own estates and the rest from south Staffordshire and from those gentry who raised their own companies.[17] Whilst admittedly this is not feudalism, it is Bastard Feudalism, which, understandably, Hutton does not fully understand. The system he outlines has much in common with the indenture system of contractor and subcontractor used by kings from Edward III to Henry VIII to raise armies for foreign war, or the

15. F.T.R. Edgar, *Sir Ralph Hopton* (Oxford 1968), p. 52.
16. M.A. Kishlansky, *Rise of the New Model Army* (Cambridge 1979), p. 6; B. Manning, *The English People and the English Revolution* (London 2nd edn 1991), p. 324; A.J. Fletcher, *Outbreak of the English Civil War* (1981), p. 325.
17. R. Hutton, *The Royalist War Effort 1642–6* (1982), p. 22.

ways in which York in 1399 and Northumberland in 1523 assembled their forces. Those raised, from the household, tenantry, and estate officers of the lord and from lesser aristocratic associates, represent all the elements of a bastard feudal affinity. It is not the phenomenon that has changed, but the mechanism: as Charles I had perforce to re-invent the wheel after almost a century when the commission of array and the indentured retinue of war had been out of use. Like other such colonels, Paget equipped his men himself and paid them their first month's pay; others supplied horses, armour and uniforms. What was it distinguished that troop of horse decked out in buff coats, scarlet hose, rich scarves and feathers, or Newcastle's Whitecoats, or even Hazelrigg's Lobsters from the liveried retainers we have just been discussing? Little reliance needs to be placed on the 'civilian Clarendon'. Dr Richard Baxter reported that 'a very great part of the gentlemen adhered to the king and most of the tenants of these gentlemen . . . did follow the gentry and were for the king'.[18] The earls of Worcester, Newcastle, Lindsey, and Warwick, Sir Henry Hastings and Sir Francis Widdrington are examples of those who raised regiments of foot or troops of horse in the same way. 'To enforce his will', Hutton continues,

> each possessed a body of regular soldiers, which he led in person and maintained like a private army. They resided in great castles and mansions, to which the local population brought tribute. They had become warlords, masters of chunks of territory which they ruled by the skill of their swords. They were English gentry turned feral, spiritual descendants of the robber barons of the middle ages.[19]

So the results were bastard feudal too.

Bastard feudalism was of course only one element even at the beginning of the English Civil War, just as it had been in earlier conflicts. There were other sources of manpower, such as the trained bands, the Irish and the Scots, and many seem to have made their own choice. Not for the first time, bastard feudal armies proved ill-suited for a protracted war and it was the army that became most

18. D.R. Guttery, *Great Civil War in Midland Parishes* (n.d.), p. 11.
19. Hutton, *Royalist War Effort*, p. 104.

professional that won the war. Uniquely, the standing army thereby created outlived the conflict and thus greatly reduced the value of bastard feudal retinues in future. Nevertheless, there is a striking parallel here with the transformation in the Lancastrian army of occupation in fifteenth-century France, which became increasingly professional and detached from its geographical and seigneurial roots the longer the Hundred Years War lasted. Dr Adamson concludes:

> The ancient military power base of the nobility, personal command of armies in the field – a power base upon which Essex had effectively built in the early years of the war – was effectively disbanded in England after 1645.[20]

But surely only temporarily. The society that made such a military role possible and the actual mechanisms surely remained, even if not to be exercised. On the one hand, the Jacobite rebellions and the Volunteer Regiments of the Napoleonic War demonstrate that the potential remained, though ever more marginal, attenuated, and overawed by the professional standing army. On the other hand, was not the monopoly to be achieved by the English aristocracy of commissions within England's standing army just another form of bastard feudal penetration of national institutions?

. . .

LEGAL POTENTIAL

If lords still possessed the manpower to pervert the administration of justice and the judicial system was essentially unchanged, it is hardly surprising that such cases continued to occur. Far from being suppressed by the early Tudors, Bellamy finds such activities very much alive a century later.

> If we judge by the number of times the offences which were part of bastard feudalism appear in court records, it seems incontestable that that type of society continued to flourish well into the Stuart period. . . . Only in the 1620s and 1630s may this high proportion of bastard feudalism cases have shown a marked decline.

20. J.S.A. Adamson, 'The Baronial Context of the English Civil War', *TRHS* 5th ser. xl (1990), 119.

No less than a quarter of the cases in Star Chamber under James I involved conspiracy, maintenance, embracery and suborning and a further 37 per cent riot, unlawful assembly, and forcible entry. Contemporaries were well aware of it, but were not apparently very concerned: the fines that were imposed were trivial and there were no further statutes of livery after 1546.[21]

What has to be explained is why attitudes to abuse had relaxed. Bellamy makes suggestions ranging from a relaxation of tension to removal of the incentive to misbehave and a marked increase in deterrents. Felonies had diminished in number and bastard feudal *causes célèbres* were far less serious than what was supposed to have been the case in the past. Whilst land disputes continued unabated, for land titles were no more secure, changes in legal procedure had reduced the benefits of violence, there were less juries to influence, and there was much more scope to harrass one's opponents in the course of litigation. Convictions were much more likely and the penalties in serious cases were more drastic. Peers were far more chary about misconduct when detection and conviction was almost automatic. Masters were executed for murders accidently committed by their men. It may be that worship was more appropriately protected man to man, in the duel. But duels were still rare. It was more important that, after a century of Tudor propaganda, legal corruption was no longer a respectable way to behave.

Unfortunately Bellamy has confused the issues and has therefore to explain more than was needed. His definition of bastard feudal cases is problematic in three ways: he has included the root causes of much corruption in the past, the land disputes, whether or not they led to corruption at this time; he has treated all cases of corruption as bastard feudal, whether or not they involve the lords or retainers of the litigants; and he has, perfectly correctly, made no distinction between the nobility and the gentry. As he himself observes, most of these cases involve people below the ranks of the aristocracy, whose offences posed no threat to public order. Hence the lack of concern by the authorities. Where corruption occurred,

21. Bellamy, ch. 6, esp. p. 123.

216

it may as well have been through maintenance by kinsfolk or neighbours as by lords or retainers. Bastard feudal corruption, in fact, had almost disappeared. That was why contemporaries were unconcerned and why further legislation was deemed unnecessary. The aristocracy now pursued their cases through the courts and bled from the purse rather than from wounds: with Professor Stone's approval.[22]

. . .

REVIEW

The aristocracy were still the ruling class, both nationally and locally. No longer willing to subordinate themselves to others, they were still lords and masters, who continued to employ and command their households, tenants and social inferiors. They could still mobilise manpower and dominate the localities as they were to do for military and electoral purposes for centuries yet to come. But they no longer wished to do so: private armies, rebellions, and maintenance were no longer respectable or acceptable. The crown had succeeded in monopolising all the military benefits of their control of men. It was because they were redundant that in 1628 the statutes of livery could be repealed. But were the ways that great Hanoverian nobility with their Palladian houses dominated the localities so very different from their late medieval or Tudor predecessors? Were the votes they bought and the sinecures they secured so different from the payments and offices with which their predecessors secured services? They would not be legal today. Admittedly they thought them different. For every George Clarkson and John Smyth who regretted the passing of the glories of the Percies and the Berkeleys, there were many Lord Chancellor Bacons and Sir John Harringtons to rejoice. Bastard Feudalism is not a term used by eighteenth-century historians. The label was obsolete; the phenomenon remained.

22. Stone, pp. 241–2.

Chapter 9

IMPACT ON POLITICS AND SOCIETY

Bastard Feudalism supplied the manpower that the aristocracy used to dominate society, both in peace and war. It has consequently been blamed for much that went wrong in the later middle ages. Bastard Feudalism knit together criminal conspiracies and corrupted justice. It made possible all kinds of aristocratic violence – from brawls and riots to private and civil war. Bastard Feudalism enabled the aristocracy to thwart kings and parliament and to obstruct progress and reform. It was ultimately responsible for lawlessness and civil war. Without Bastard Feudalism, it follows, there would have been no civil wars, a higher standard of order, and a more equitable, democratic and progressive society.

Behind such charges lies much wishful-thinking emanating from both the Whig and the Marxist 'determinist' interpretations of history.[1] But the age of Bastard Feudalism was merely a middle phase in a thousand years of aristocratic domination of politics, not just in England but throughout Europe. Rulers controlled the localities through local notables or aristocrats – perhaps could only control them in this way and certainly considered this the only option – and ordinary people lacked the education, the organisation, or the sustained interest to manage their own affairs. Even such radical reformers as the Lollards envisaged changing and adding to the aristocracy, not abolishing it. That society eventually changed and ceased

218

to be aristocratic needs to be seen in its chronological context: it is anachronistic to accelerate a gradual process, to read the result back in time, or to suggest another type of society was possible then. History is about what happened, not might-have-beens. Whilst individuals are faced with distinct choices and sometimes make recognisable errors, it is hard indeed to accept the same for society or to envisage any alternatives viable for this chosen period.

By abandoning its hold on local government and justice in the thirteenth century, argues Coss, the crown lost its opportunity to secure the impartial rule of law. Both he and Storey back the gentry against the nobility under Richard II. They consider, as have so many others, that the chance was missed to abolish retaining and hence for quelling aristocratic lawlessness and faction. Hidden behind such preferences are a series of debatable assumptions: that the crown was less partial and oppressive and its administrators and judges, less prone to abuse of power than the aristocracy, and anyway preferable; that the gentry differed in outlook and conduct from the nobility and were less prone to abuse; and that retaining was wholly illegitimate. Such assumptions themselves depend on an irrationally hostility towards the nobility: the belief that noble rule and the command of others are both inherently wrong. In reality it was protests from below that swept away the government's direct rule of the localities both in the thirteenth and seventeenth centuries, that permitted the rule of the aristocracy, and that restricted retaining by the gentry more than by the nobility: Parliament had more confidence in the management of their men by the nobility than by the gentry. Much retaining was accepted as legitimate by everyone at all times. Where noble hegemonies succeeded county communities run by the gentry, it was because they offered advantages to the gentry: force alone never sufficed. The gentry as lords relied on Bastard Feudalism just as much as the peerage and used their men in the same way. It is not clear that the larger number of small scale connections in the English Civil War were more conducive to order and peace. There is a built-in assumption that all uses were illegitimate and that civil war for example was the fault of Bastard Feudalism, whereas the civil wars of late medieval England are more commonly interpreted as the regrettable but necessary result of bad rule. Bastard Feudalism here was on the side of the angels.

Bastard Feudalism was used by all parties for all purposes – by the crown as well as the aristocracy, for defence as well as offence, for peace-making and rebellion, for the restoration of order besides the fomentation of disorder. Given that law and order depended ultimately on force, some means of deploying that force was necessary. During our period, it was Bastard Feudalism: for the not dissimilar situations before and afterwards, the dynastic revolutions of 1066 and 1688, other means were employed. Bastard Feudalism was the means, not the cause. Had it not existed, aristocrats would have found other ways to exercise their power and the armies that fought in civil war – for good reasons – would have been raised in other ways. 'Men use and develop whatever instruments lie to hand', observes Coss.[2]

If Bastard Feudalism is to be blamed for lawlessness and civil war, it must be recognized that levels of lawlessness fluctuated and that civil war was not continuous. If Bastard Feudalism was the cause, presumably it fluctuated in strength and virulence according to period and was sometimes strong enough to provoke disorder and sometimes not. The 1450s, brilliantly examined by Storey, are a case in point. It was then that violent *causes célèbres* proliferated, that a whole series of feuds escalated into private war, and that private wars merged into civil war. Similar underlying disputes occurred at other times, however, both before and after, which did not escalate out of hand; indeed certain longlasting feuds were acute during this period and not in others. Given the same stimulus, Bastard Feudalism was not the same. What made the difference, so McFarlane argued and most others have found irresistible, was the weakness of the crown, represented in the 1450s by the feeble-minded Henry VI, who could not impose order on his magnates or resolve their disputes. Henry V, immediately beforehand, and Edward IV and Henry VII thereafter, as Professor Ross

2. 'Debate', 194.

220

observed in an unpublished paper, had encountered similar problems, which they effectively quelled: not perhaps permanently, but for the time being. The main periods of disorder featured weak or incompetent kings – such as Henry III, Edward II, Richard II and Charles I – and witnessed magnates eliminating royal ministers and favourites (1311, 1386, 1388, 1450, 1455, 1460, 1469, 1628, 1640), seeking to impose their own alternatives, constitutional checks, reform, or all three. It was only kings who failed to adapt and repeated their mistakes who were eventually, reluctantly, deposed. Those who could bend with the wind, like Edward III and Henry IV, even *reculer pour mieux sauter*, like Edward I, survived, to die in their beds still kings. It was because so many English kings, regrettably, failed to learn the harsh lessons offered them that so many fell: not because of the unconscious determinism with which Dr Gross has recently charged the McFarlane school. Nor indeed because of the social tensions, social instability and disequilibrium, or social crises of the thirteenth – seventeenth centuries identified at specific points by such different historians as David Carpenter, Michael Prestwich, Peter Coss, and Lawrence Stone. Indeed, given the limited and gradual evolution that befell the aristocracy, that scarcely altered over time, how could they be? England was never ungovernable. Its problems could be managed by effective kings. Unfortunately only half the Plantagenets proved effective.

Bastard Feudalism, in short, was the means of pursuing interests and prosecuting quarrels, not the cause. Lawsuits did not arise because the means existed to subvert the law, but because there were legal issues to subvert. Bastard Feudalism itself was morally neutral. So, too, is an aristocratic or any other ruling class. Times change: though we live in a parliamentary democracy, we no longer suppose, as Whig historians did, that our system is perfect. For the period 1150–1650, five centuries of growing law and order, Bastard Feudalism and aristocratic rule alike were indispensable.

GLOSSARY

Affinity	Connection of a magnate based on his personal standing rather than tenure of land.
Aid	Feudal incident; payment due to lord on special occasions, e.g. knighting of eldest son and marriage of eldest daughter.
Allegiance	Over-riding loyalty to king taking priority over loyalty to lesser lords.
Annuity	Annual payment, usual for unspecified service, from a lord to his retainer.
Arbitration	Settlement of disputes out of court involving mediation and decision (award) by an arbiter or arbiters chosen by both parties. Arbitration awards were commonly enforced by penalties in the common law courts.
Aristocracy	Noble or gentle élite based on inheritance of large estates. Nobility and gentry constituted a single class, the aristocracy.
Array	See Commission.
Attainder	Corruption of blood suffered by traitors and their heirs from the fifteenth century, commonly by parliamentary act of attainder, which confiscated possessions of the traitor and prevented heirs from inheriting.

Bachelors	Thirteenth and fourteenth century knights resident in lord's household; often bound by indenture of retainer.
Banneret	Senior knight entitled to display banner and command other knights.
Baron	Originally a companion, whether of the king or some other great lord (honorial baron); lord of a feudal barony and over-lord of other knights; from the fourteenth century the bottom rank of the parliamentary peerage.
Barony	A feudal estate, held in chief or of another great lord, which included subinfeudated knights fees and a baronial court.
Bastard Feudalism	The set of relationships with their social inferiors that provided the English aristocracy (1150–1650) with the manpower they required.
Connection	Complete following of a lord including all categories of retainers.
Champerty	Support of false claim for share of profit.
Chancery	The principal royal writing office that issued formal letters, grants, commissions, pardons, writs, etc, under the great seal.
Commission	Written authority from the king to named individuals (commissioners) to perform specific tasks in a specified county or counties. Most commissioners were aristocrats. There were many different types of commission: the most important are defined below. Commissions of the peace were continuous; others were short-term.
Commission of array	Commission to collect able-bodied men for military service, usually in defence against rebellion or invasion.

Commission of peace	Commission to judge minor crimes, mainly in quarter sessions, but also out of court and from 1631 in petty sessions. In the Tudor period commissioners (justices of the peace or JPs) acquired many administrative responsibilities.
Commission of oyer and terminer	Commission to hear and try certain specific offences, often by specified individuals; the usual response to major rebellions or riots in the fifteenth century.
Common law	The law based on custom and precedent administered in the king's common law courts of Common Pleas and King's Bench, most of which was initiated by writ.
Common Pleas	Royal court of common law sitting at Westminster concerned with civil suits between parties, mainly about land and debt.
Coroner	From 1194 the royal official responsible in each county for inquests into homicide, treasure trove, etc.
Crime	A breach of the law.
Demesne	Land of lord that was not subinfeudated to knights or rented out to tenants from the twelfth to the fourteenth centuries; from the late fourteenth century most demesnes were leased out.
Distraint of knighthood	From the thirteenth to the seventeenth centuries, payment by gentry who qualified for knighthood to avoid taking up knighthood.
Dower	Right of widow of landholder to one-third of his land for life.
Earl	Highest rank of nobility until 1337, when the higher rank of duke was created.
Embracery	Bribery of jurors.

Enfeoff	To settle land on an individual or group of individuals (feoffees). This kind of settlement was an enfeoffment.
Entail	Title to land that restricted who could inherit, usually male heirs. Created by enfeoffment on specific terms.
Entourage	Those in attendance on a lord.
Escheator	Royal official responsible for administering feudal revenues of the crown, usually in one or two countries.
Esquire	Gentleman entitled to bear arms who had not been knighted.
Extraordinary retainers	Retainers who were not members of the household or officials who either held knights fees or received annuities from their lord.
Eyre	Judicial progress by the king's judges in the localities between 1194 and 1336.
Fealty	Personal oath of loyalty from a feudal vassal to his lord.
Fee	Reward for service: either in land (knights fee) or in money (an annuity).
Feoffees	Trustees.
Feudalism	Set of relationships based on tenure of land by which lords secured services from their tenants.
Feudal incidents	Occasional aspects of Feudalism that were financially valuable to lords, e.g. aid, wardship.
Feudal tenure	System of land-holding by which all properties were held of a lord, were subject to services and incidents, and accordingly to specified inheritance customs (especially primogeniture).
Fief	Feudal estate held in return for service.

Franchises	Royal privileges or liberties attached to a lord's estate, e.g. right to summary execution of criminals; hence privileged estates were often called liberties or franchises.
Gentry	Lesser aristocrats who were not members of the parliamentary peerage.
Good lordship	Obligation of a bastard feudal lord to support his just cause.
Homage	Ceremonial acceptance of inferiority to a lord as condition for taking possession of land as his feudal tenant.
Honour	Large geographically dispersed fief held by a great lord including many knights fees and honorial court.
Household	Family and servants of lord who lived, slept and dined in same house. Aristocratic households were commonly much larger than the lord's immediate family.
Hundred	Major sub-division of a county with its own court and bailiff; originally royal but often granted as private franchise.
Indictment	Formal accusation of a crime made by a jury (of presentment); a second, trial, jury tried the offence.
Indenture	Duplicate copy of a document (usually a contract) indented along join with another indenture to prevent forgery.
Indenture of retainer	Indenture binding a bastard feudal retainer to service for life in peace and war; service was not always military.
Indenture of war	Indenture binding a bastard feudal retainer to military service on a specific campaign.
Indentured retainer	Bastard feudal retainer bound to service for life in peace and war by an indenture of retainer.

Justice of the peace	Royal commissioner (JP) to try minor crimes in a specific county (see Commission of peace). Usually an aristocrat; some were lawyers, including most of the quorum without whom quarter sessions could not be held.
King's Bench	Royal court of common law at Westminster handling civil and criminal cases; senior criminal court.
Knight	Soldier who had been knighted; trained and equipped to fight on horseback. From the twelfth century, knights were senior gentry and knighthood was a mark of social distinction, wealth, and local government responsibility.
Knights fee	Estate, usually a manor, granted to a feudal vassal for military service of one knight.
Law	Standard of right and wrong agreed by crown, magnates, parliament, etc; new law was made by agreement, e.g. acts of parliament; breaches of law were crimes.
Livery	Distinctive clothing, badge or hat that identified membership of a particular connection.
Livery and Maintenance	Pejorative description of Bastard Feudalism as source of corruption of justice.
Magnate	Great man; term applied to the wealthiest and most powerful of the late medieval nobility.
Maintenance	Support of own or another's legal case in lieu of allowing the law to take its course.
Manor	Small estate, usually compact, with desmesne, tenants, and manorial court.
Mark	Unit of currency worth two-thirds of a pound sterling (13s. 4d. or 66p.).

Mesne tenant	Intermediate tenant between tenant-in-chief and knights fees.
Militia	Home-guard made up of all able-bodied men organised more efficiently by Tudors under Lord Lieutenant in each county.
Muster	Assembly of armed force, e.g. army, garrison, militia, for inspection or payment; commonly recorded in muster rolls.
Nobility	Parliamentary peerage; high-ranking lords, e.g. viscount, earl, marquis, duke, and barons from mid-fourteenth century. Only eldest sons of English noblemen were themselves noble.
Oyer and terminer	See Commissions.
Peerage	Members of House of Lords defined and restricted in the fourteenth century.
Relief	Payment by feudal tenant on entry to tenancy.
Retinue	Following of lord for a specific purpose, e.g. retinue of war.
Scutage	Payment by feudal tenants in lieu of military service in time of war.
Servitium debitum	Service of knights due from feudal lord in time of war.
Sheriff	Principal royal official in each county with important financial and judicial duties. From the thirteenth century chosen annually from a leading member of the gentry.
Sub-infeudation	Feudal process of granting land to lesser men in return for service.
Sumptuary	Sumptuary laws sought from 1363 to regulate dress according to social class and to restrict more elaborate/expensive attire to those of high rank.

Tenants-in-chief	Feudal tenants who held land directly of the king.
Trailbaston	A commission introduced in 1304 to inquire into breaches of peace and maintenance.
Treason	Betrayal of lord, especially the king; breach of Statutes of Treasons; most heinous offence punishable in the most horrible way.
Wardship	Guardianship by feudal lord of person of under-age vassal and custody of his estates.

BIBLIOGRAPHY

This is a brief guide to works of use on the general topics covered by each of the chapters. All books were published in London unless otherwise stated.

. . .

CHAPTER 1: WHAT IS BASTARD FEUDALISM?

The starting point for all studies of Bastard Feudalism are two books by K.B. McFarlane, *England in the Fifteenth Century* (1981) and *Nobility of Later Medieval England* (Oxford 1973). For the aristocracy, see also D. Crouch, *Image of the Aristocracy in Britain* (1992), P.R. Coss, *The Knight in Medieval England 1000–1400* (Stroud 1993), N. Saul, *Knights and Esquires* (Oxford 1981), and M.C. Carpenter, *Locality and Polity* (Cambridge 1992). For the early period F.M. Stenton, *First Century of English Feudalism* (2nd edn Oxford 1961) remains fundamental; several key articles are reprinted in M. Strickland ed., *Anglo-Norman Warfare* (Woodbridge 1992); and D. Crouch, *William Marshal* (Harlow 1990), P.R. Coss, 'Bastard Feudalism Revised', *Past and Present* 125 (1989), and Crouch, Coss, and Carpenter 'Debate: Bastard Feudalism Revised', *Past and Present* 131 (1991) are essential. For the late medieval period, see M.A. Hicks, 'Bastard Feudalism: Society and Politics in the 15th Century', *Richard III and his Rivals* (1991). For the post-medieval period, M.E. James, *Society, Politics and Culture* (Cambridge 1986) and G. Bernard, *The Tudor Nobility* (Manchester 1992) are crucial. A mass of relevant material is collected in J.P. Cooper, *Land, Men and Beliefs* (1983)

230

and in G. Bernard, *The Power of the Early Tudor Nobility* (Brighton 1985).

. . .

CHAPTER 2: VARIETIES OF BASTARD FEUDALISM

There are no satisfactory studies of the household, tenantry, estate officials, or of livery. K. Mertes, *The English Noble Household 1250–1600* (Oxford 1988) is pioneering but highly inaccurate. J.M.W. Bean, *From Lord to Patron* (Manchester 1989) is best on indentured retaining and breaks much new ground in a limited timespan, and M.E. James, *Society, Politics and Culture* (1986) has much on Tudor households. Tenants are treated by Bernard, Cooper, James and in B. Coward, *The Stanleys, Lords Stanley and Earls of Derby 1385–1672* (Chetham Soc. 3rd ser. xxx, 1983). For extraordinary retainers, see also K.B. McFarlane *England in the Fifteenth Century* (1981), G.A. Holmes, *Estates of the Higher Nobility in 14th Century England* (Cambridge 1957), and S.K. Walker, *Lancastrian Affinity 1361–99* (Oxford 1990). M.C. Carpenter, *Locality and Polity* (Cambridge 1992) makes most of witnesses.

. . .

CHAPTER 3: QUANTITY AND QUALITY

This chapter draws on material that is particularly widely scattered. T.B. Pugh, 'The Magnates, Knights and Gentry', *Fifteenth-century England 1399–1509*, ed. S.B. Chrimes, C.D. Ross and R.A. Griffiths (Manchester 1972) and S.K. Walker, *Lancastrian Affinity 1361–99* (Oxford 1990) are best on numbers. Chronologies have been proposed by W.H. Dunham, *Lord Hastings' Indentured Retainers 1461–83* (Transactions of the Connecticut Academy of Arts and Sciences xxxix, New Haven, Conn. 1955), and the works of Crouch, Coss, Waugh, Bean, Stone and James. James, Dunham, and C. Richmond, 'After McFarlane', *History* lxviii (1983) diverge sharply on loyalty. For stability, see M.A. Hicks, *Richard III and his Rivals* (Cambridge 1991), ch. 1. For affinity see D. Crouch, *William Marshal* (Harlow 1990) and P.R. Coss and D.A. Crouch, 'Debate: Bastard Feudalism Revised', *Past and Present* 131 (1991).

CHAPTER 4: THE LEGALITY OF BASTARD FEUDALISM

The most far-reaching critique is now P.R. Coss, 'Bastard Feudalism Revised', *Past and Present* 125 (1989). J.G. Bellamy, *Bastard Feudalism and the Law* (1989) is a pioneering and up-to-date survey; his *Crime and Public Order in the Later Middle Ages* (1973) treats the worst cases and his *Criminal Justice and Society in Later Medieval England* (1984) the procedural countermeasures. There are excellent studies of particular aspects in J.R. Maddicott, *Law and Lordship: Royal Justices as Retainers in 13th- and 14th-Century England* (*Past and Present* Supplement 4, 1978) and P. Maddern, *Violence and the Social Order* (Oxford 1992). On the statutes of livery, see also J.M.W. Bean, *From Lord to Patron* (Manchester 1989), W.H. Dunham, *Lord Hastings' Indentured Retainers 1461–83* (Transactions of the Connecticut Academy of Arts and Science xxxix, New Haven, Conn. 1955); M.A. Hicks, *Richard III and his Rivals* (1991), ch. 12; R.L. Storey, 'Liveries and Commissions of the Peace 1388–90', *The Reign of Richard II*, ed. C. Barron and F.R.H. Du Boulay (1971); N. Saul, 'The Commons and the Abolition of Badges', *Parliamentary History* ix.ii (1990); and M.A. Hicks, 'The 1468 Statute of Livery', *Historical Research* lxi (1991). For competition see C. Given-Wilson, 'The King and the Gentry in 14th-century England', *TRHS* 5th ser. xxxvii (1987) and M.E. James, *Society, Politics and Culture* (1986), though both see developments in unduly short chronological perspective.

CHAPTER 5: BASTARD FEUDALISM IN PEACETIME

Two good contrasting discussions are in F. Heal, *Hospitality in Early Modern England* (Oxford 1990) and R.E. Horrox, *Richard III: A Study of Service* (Cambridge 1989). Most of the books cited contain relevant material. On good lordship, see especially M.A. Hicks, *Richard III and his Rivals* (1991), ch. 7, and on practice, C.E. Moreton, *Townshends and their World* (Oxford 1992). Arbitration

by lords is best treated through C. Rawcliffe, 'Great Lord as Peacekeeper: Arbitration by English Noblemen and their Councils in the Later Middle Ages', *Law and Social Change in British History*, ed. J. Guy and H. Beale (1984).

. . .

CHAPTER 6: POWER AND POLITICS

For local government see H.M. Jewell, *English Local Administration in the Middle Ages* (Newton Abbot 1972). For stimulating overviews, see P.R. Coss, 'Bastard Feudalism Revised', *Past and Present* 125 (1989) and G.L. Harriss 'Political Society and the Growth of Government in Late Medieval England', *Past and Present* 138 (1993). Local politics is best approached through M.A. Hicks, *Richard III and his Rivals* (1991), esp. ch. 1 and works there cited, to which should be added M.C. Carpenter, *Locality and Polity* (Cambridge 1992), M.E. James, *Society, Politics and Culture* (1986), and G. Bernard ed., *The Tudor Nobility* (Manchester 1992). Although often updated in detail, R.L. Storey, *End of the House of Lancaster* (2nd edn Gloucester 1986) remains the best treatment of aristocratic feuds in the 1450s. On parliament see now *History of Parliament 1386–1421*, ed. J.S. Roskell, L. Clark and C. Rawcliffe (4 vols Stroud 1993).

. . .

CHAPTER 7: BASTARD FEUDALISM IN WARTIME

McFarlane's work remains fundamental. For military obligation, see M.R. Powicke's rather dated *Military Obligation in Medieval England* (Oxford 1962) and L. Boynton, *Elizabethan Militia 1558–1638* (1968). On foreign war, see additionally M. Prestwich, *English Politics in the Thirteenth Century* (Basingstoke 1990) and M. Prestwich, *War, Politics and Finance under Edward I* (Oxford 1972), and A.J. Pollard, *John Talbot and the War in France 1427–53* (1983). For private and civil war, see now especially A. Goodman, *The Wars of the Roses* (1981); P.R. Coss, *The Knight in Medieval England 1000–1400* (Stroud 1993), and C. Richmond, '1485 and All That, or what was going on at the Battle of Bosworth', *Richard III: Loyalty, Lordship and Law*, ed. P.W. Hammond (1985).

233

. . .

CHAPTER 8: BASTARD FEUDALISM: THE END

There is no satisfactory discussion of the decline of Bastard Feudalism. The fullest surveys are L. Stone, *The Crisis of the Aristocracy 1558–1642* (Oxford 1965) on the political aspects and J.G. Bellamy, *Bastard Feudalism and the Law* (1989) on legal developments. Though unduly reliant on literary material, M.E. James, *Society, Politics and Culture* (1986) and *Family, Lineage and Civil Society* (Oxford 1974) treats the decline from a regional perspective. There is much relevant material in J.P. Cooper, *Land, Men and Beliefs* (1983) and in B. Coward, *The Stanleys, Lords Stanley and Earls of Derby 1385–1672* (Chetham Soc. 3rd ser. xxx, 1983). G. Bernard, *The Power of the Early Tudor Nobility* (Brighton 1985) and *The Tudor Nobility* (Manchester 1992) argues for continued vitality. For the early civil war armies, see B. Manning, *The English People and the English Revolution* (2nd edn 1991) and R. Hutton, *The Royalist War Effort 1642–46* (1982).

INDEX

The following abbreviations have been employed: bp = bishop; c = count and countess; d = duke; e = earl; fam = family; k = king; ld = lord; m = marquis; s = son; v = viscount; w = wife. Personal names have been abbreviated thus: Edm = Edmund; Edw = Edward; Geo = George; Hen = Henry; Ric = Richard; Rob = Robert; Thos = Thomas; Wm = William

INDEX

Swillington, Sir Adam, 59
Swinburne, Wm de, of
　Capheaton, 58

Talbot fam, 10, 18, 133, 157,
　160, 162, 165, 178, 203
Talbot,
　Geo, 4th e of Shrewsbury
　　(d 1538), 37–8, 63, 142, 200
　Francis, 5th e (d 1560), 143
　Geo, 6th e (d 1590), 209
　Gilbert, 7th e (d 1616), 37
　tenants, 5, 12–14, 21–4, 30,
　　36–40, 42, 48–52, 90–3,
　　207–10
　Thomas, d of Gloucester
　　(d 1397), 98
　Thomas, e of Lancaster
　　(d 1322), 59, 62, 96, 102, 144,
　　159, 163, 183
Throckmorton, John, 140
Townshend, Sir Roger (d 1551),
　57
Tresham, Sir Thos, 85
Tuchet, John, ld Audley, 180
Tudor, Jasper, e of Pembroke,
　99
Twynho, Ankarette, 159

Usher, John, 60

Valence,
　Aymer de, e of Pembroke, 70,
　　101
　Wm de, 50, 59, 101, 106
Villiers, Geo, d of Buckingham,
　10, 106–7
Vere fam, 21
Vere,
　Elizabeth de, c of Oxford, 66,
　　97
　Edw de, e of Oxford (d 1604),
　　143, 207
　John de, e of Oxford (d 1513),
　　48, 50, 64, 98, 143, 161, 188,
　　196

Verney,
　Edm, 95
　Sir Ric, 148
Vernon fam, 38, 74, 158–9, 183,
　199

Walter, Dr John, 184
Warenne,
　John, e of (d 1347), 142, 151
　Wm, e of (d 1240), 75
Wars of Roses, 50, 64, 72, 84,
　112, 176, 184, 194, 199, 201–2
Warwick, 148, 159, 164, 176
Warwick, earls and d of, 96–8,
　and see Beauchamp; Dudley;
　Neville; Rich
Waterton fam, 44
Waugh, Prof Scott, 11, 20, 24
Westby, Gregory, 66
Wharton, Thos ld, 37, 107–8
Whig Interpretation of History,
　15, 112, 221
Widdrington,
　Sir Francis, 214
　John, 80
Willoughby fam, 44
　Sir Hen, 39
William I, 10, 12, 21, 114, 125
Williams, Dr Penry, 11, 34
Wolsey, Thos, cardinal, 62
Worcester, earls of, see Somerset
Wrangwish, Thos, 81
Wright,
　Dr Franklin, 49
　Dr Susan M., 159
Wrightson, Dr Keith, 184
Wyatt's Rebellion, 198, 209
Wydeville fam, 40, 145
　Anthony, 1d Scales and e
　　Rivers, 141, 175

York,
　city of, 81, 135, 144, 165, 179
　dukes of, 18, 96 and see
　　Edmund; Richard

243